The Supervisory Encounter

The Supervisory Encounter

A Guide for Teachers of Psychodynamic
Psychotherapy and Psychoanalysis

Daniel Jacobs, M.D.
Paul David, M.D.
Donald Jay Meyer, M.D.

Yale University Press   New Haven and London

Published with assistance from the Mary Cady Tew
Memorial Fund.

Designed by Sonia L. Scanlon.
Set in Minion type by Keystone Typesetting, Inc.,
Orwigsburg, Pennsylvania.
Printed in the United States of America by Vail-Ballou
Press, Binghamton, New York.

Library of Congress Cataloging-in-Publication Data
Jacobs, Daniel, 1937–
    The supervisory encounter : a guide for teachers of
psychodynamic psychotherapy and psychoanalysis /
Daniel Jacobs, Paul David, Donald Jay Meyer.
    p.   cm.
    Includes bibliographical references and index.
    ISBN 0–300–06200–1 (alk. paper)
    1. Psychoanalysis—Study and teaching—Super-
vision.   2. Psychodynamic psychotherapy—Study and
teaching—Supervision.   3. Psychotherapists—Supervision of.   I. David, Paul, 1948–   .   II. Meyer, Donald
Jay, 1949–   .   III. Title.
[DNLM: 1. Psychoanalysis—education.   2. Psychoanalytic Therapy.   WM   18   J16s   1995]
RC502.J33   1995
362.2'1—dc20
DNLM/DLC
for Library of Congress   94-47180
                                    CIP

A catalogue record for this book is available from the
British Library.
The paper in this book meets the guidelines for perma-
nence and durability of the Committee on Production
Guidelines for Book Longevity of the Council on
Library Resources.

10   9   8   7   6   5   4   3   2   1

For
Susan, Tom, and Anna
Preston and Zelda; Deena, Jenny, Avi, and Jonah
Gail, Jessica, and Andrea

Contents

Acknowledgments

Many people have contributed to our thinking about supervision and to the writing of this book. Janet Pine, M.D., Judith Herman, M.D., and Dorothy Austin, Th.D., were early members of a supervision study group at the Cambridge Hospital (Massachusetts), where lively discussions of supervisory process and problems began to shape our thinking. The late Norman Zinberg, M.D., was an occasional participant in this group, and his keen insights challenged us to define more clearly the issues we were exploring.

Steven Bernstein, M.D., Renee Gelman, M.D., Judith Kantrowitz, Ph.D., Charles Magraw, M.D., S. Joseph Nemetz, M.D., Malkah Notman, M.D., Anna Wolff, M.D., Judith Yanof, M.D., and Joan Zilbach, M.D., participated in a supervisors' study group at the Boston Psychoanalytic Society and Institute. Their monthly discussions of the challenges in teaching were always caring, thoughtful, and stimulating.

Michael C. Miller, M.D., Allen J. Palmer, M.D., and Randall H. Paulsen, M.D., read early drafts of several chapters as part of a clinical writing group at the Beth Israel Hospital (Boston) and gave us perceptive advice on the content and presentation of the material.

Dan H. Buie, M.D., Rohn S. Friedman, M.D., Lewis A. Kirshner, M.D., Margaret Vasington, MASP, and Patricia Wright, M.D., read sections of the manuscript and provided careful criticism.

Paul Dewald, M.D., and Robert Glick, M.D., discussed ideas that eventually became part of this book. Their experience and kindly criticisms were helpful. George Fishman, M.D., and Ted Jacobs, M.D., Joyce Lerner, LICSW, and Ellen Rowntree, M.D., each in his or her own way, offered encouragement and support.

Gladys Topkis, senior editor at Yale, provided invaluable assistance from framing conceptual issues to line editing. Her mastery of style along with Noreen O'Connor's attention to detail improved the presentation of our ideas in countless ways.

Our wives and children have given us love, support, and encouragement and have allowed us the time to complete this study.

Most of all, we would like to thank all our supervisors and supervisees, who taught us about teaching and, in the process, about ourselves.

The Supervisory Encounter

Introduction

Ultimately you cannot learn how to do
psychotherapy by reading a book,
working on a computer, watching a video,
or participating in a bureaucracy; you
must learn it intimately from other
people. . . . Supervision is . . . an
anachronism in our contemporary world
because it partakes in a tradition of oral
and intimate one-on-one passing on of
knowledge. (Smith, 1990)

In the process of becoming a psychotherapist or psychoanalyst,
the supervisory encounter is second in importance only to the
clinical encounter itself. No other aspect of psychotherapy education provides the student with the opportunity to speak intimately, individually, and over time with an experienced teacher.
Because supervision is so central to the personal and professional
growth of a therapist, it is important to understand what it involves. What helps deepen the supervisory dialogue? What limits
the ability of teacher and student to talk openly with one another?

Supervisors are often left to answer important questions like
these for themselves. There is still little if any formal preparation
for becoming a supervisor. There are relatively few courses or

workshops on the subject offered by the teaching institutions in which the supervisor is likely to work. The number of study groups available on a national or local level has been meager. As a result, most supervisors have developed competence in treating patients, but have often given less thought to how to teach others about treating patients. Although a student's performance as a therapist comes under scrutiny, the supervisor's pedagogical abilities are rarely evaluated. This leaves supervisors in a less favorable educational situation than their students. Students' problems in learning and in mastering a field are pointed out to them. Supervisors' difficulties in learning how to teach are often not discussed. Because of this omission, supervisors' ability to learn how to become better teachers is unnecessarily compromised.

Supervisors can always learn by reading or talking with colleagues. A number of books on supervision are already available, but many draw upon the experience of a particular discipline—psychoanalysis for Wallerstein (1981) and Dewald (1987) and social work for Kadushin (1976). Furthermore, a good deal of the earlier literature (Fleming and Benedek, 1966; Robinson, 1936, 1949), while helpful, stresses a master-apprentice model of teaching and learning, which often seems stilted and authoritarian. The literature rarely deals with the inner experience of the supervisor or supervisee and its influence on the development of the supervisory relationship.

In reading the literature and talking with colleagues one quickly learns how little agreement among supervisors there is, even among those in the same institution, about the goals, expectations, and techniques of supervision. Some supervisors feel that the focus should be almost exclusively on the patient, whereas others prefer to focus on the therapist and his or her countertransference reactions. Some supervisors favor the use of audio or videotaped sessions over the presentation of process notes, or the even more informal use of a therapist's recall and associations. Some are agreeable to writing detailed evaluations of their students, others are not. On the one hand, this lack of unity in supervising allows a rich diversity of opinions and practice. On the other hand, it fosters confusion and misunderstanding about what the goals of supervision are and how they are to be achieved. Supervisors may try to deal with these varied and conflicting approaches by modeling themselves after their own supervisors, teaching the way they were taught. Although identification with one's own teachers can be helpful at times, it does not encourage supervisors to think in new or creative ways about the educational process. Furthermore, it runs the risk of inadvertently repeating unpleasant or unhelpful aspects of supervision (Nason, 1994).

One aspect of an older way of supervising that may be passed along is the failure to distinguish clearly between training and treating the supervisee. This lack of clear purpose is reflected in the tendency to transplant therapeutic concepts such as defense, resistance, and problems of narcissism from the therapeutic realm directly into the educational one. The use of these psychodynamic concepts and the language that accompanies them helps illuminate the intricacies of the supervisory process and helps supervisors talk to one another about supervisees and the supervisory dialogue in familiar ways. But, too strictly applied, it can lead to the supervisor analyzing the student's personality rather than analyzing the educational situation. Significant limitations in the supervision can then occur. The tendency to think of supervisory difficulties in terms of neurotic conflict (more often construed as the student's than the supervisor's) can rob supervisors of the opportunity to see these complications as problems in learning and teaching. This approach often limits a teacher's capacity to develop a deeper understanding of the educational encounter and prevents her, at times, from finding a didactic approach tailored to the particular learning situation.*

Supervision occurs within a social context that can have profound effects on the evolving discourse. Zinberg (1986) noted:

> The aim of being able to provide therapy which is reasonably reliable and consistent is certainly humanistic, but has political and institutional implications as well. Once we begin to look at therapy and supervision from that point of view, it has as Georg Simmel pointed out long ago "an inherent tendency toward conservatism, institutionalization, and . . . stress." The formation of every social organization has its own costs and benefits, creating possibilities while foreshadowing others. . . . As he [the student] learns more, he begins to understand both historically and currently that . . . theoretical constructs reflect conflicts in the field and have political and institutional impacts as well as educational potential. (p. 3)

The changing nature of training in psychiatry, psychology, and social work is bound to affect the methods and goals of supervision. The decreasing emphasis in most training programs on psychodynamic psychotherapy puts strains on those still trying to learn and teach it. In *The Supervisory Encounter,* we try to provide a theoretical and technical framework for thinking about teaching psychotherapy and psychoanalysis. Our emphasis is on the supervisor's *choice* of educational interventions. We describe some of the modes of thinking that therapists and analysts employ and explore how they can be fostered. Of course, a student's ability to learn will be influenced by his feelings about himself, his patient, his teacher, and the educational process in which he is

---

*To avoid the generic pronoun *he* in general discussions, the feminine pronoun will be used to refer to the supervisor and the masculine pronoun will be used to refer to the therapist-in-training.

engaged. The supervisor needs to be aware of these feelings in order to know how best to proceed in teaching. We explore issues of emotional closeness and distance in the supervisory interaction and the challenges to self-esteem that supervision may raise for both teacher and student.

Discussions of supervision tend, at times, to focus on the psychodynamic and psychoanalytic theories being taught. Although the didactic content of supervision is important, exclusive focus on it detracts from the examination of how content is taught. Theories of treatment and the content of the supervision may vary with each mental health discipline and with each supervisor. Given the evolving state of our knowledge, they will continue to vary, but the psychological processes involved in learning and teaching seem to us to apply across multiple theoretical frameworks. We are interested less in what theory is taught than in *how* it is taught. We focus on the modes of thinking and attitudes that need to be fostered in a therapist regardless of the specific theoretical approach he is being exposed to or may already espouse.

The process of supervision involves the supervisee's experiences of self and other (the patient) in the presence of a teacher. What aspects of the patient-therapist relationship are recalled, the manner in which they are remembered, the meaning given them and how these meanings are arrived at all may be explored in supervision. For the student, a deepening supervisory process requires his developing an ever-increasing ability to describe what he observes about his patient, himself, and even his supervisor that may shed light on the patient's conflicts and his responses to them. The supervisor helps the therapist expand this ability. She tries to enlarge the student's ability to observe others (primarily his patient but also at times his teacher) as well as himself. She encourages him to examine and reflect on the meaning and value he gives to those observations. There are many obstacles to learning or teaching—for both student and supervisor. Sometimes lack of experience or knowledge as to how to proceed may be the impediment. At other times it is restrictions in the capacity to think or feel that prevent learning. Sometimes the impediment is due to feelings one is ashamed of and does not know how to discuss. Feeling safe is central to the supervisory endeavor, yet learning often disturbs the sense of self. Approaches that may help the trainee feel safer and therefore freer to express himself in supervision are examined.

Supervision is a process during which supervisor and supervisee are learning together—about the patient, about one another, and about themselves. Of course, there are differences in status and experience that make the learning experience in supervision different for a teacher and a student. Such differences cannot be denied and should at times be openly acknowledged and discussed. We try to elaborate on when and how such discussion should take place.

This book is designed for supervisors of psychotherapy and psychoanalysis. Because we emphasize educational processes and supervisory approaches rather than the content of what is being taught, we hope that this book will be useful to readers from diverse disciplines and theoretical orientations. Although our discussion is directed toward the supervisory task, we feel that supervisees, as well, will find guidance for their educational journey.

We begin with a brief history of supervision that emphasizes the conflicting ideas that arose among supervisors about how to best teach—conflicting notions with which we still struggle today. We then discuss the opening phase of supervision, which often sets the tone and establishes the method of communication favored. Different approaches to the opening phase are explored. Chapters 3 and 4 concern modes of thinking that we feel are essential for a supervisee to develop. We discuss why these modes are important and illustrate how they can best be fostered. Learning, of course, occurs within an interpersonal context, but how personal should that context be? What are the potential risks and benefits of self-disclosure for both supervisor and supervisee? These questions are explored in chapter 5. The ability to recognize and tolerate the affects involved as well as discuss them when appropriate is essential to being a good therapist. How these issues are addressed in supervision is the subject of chapter 6. Based on an assessment of the student's stage and modes of learning, the kind of interpersonal relationship he is forming, and his ability to deal with affects, the supervisor makes a choice of supervisory interventions. The types of intervention are defined and the ways of choosing among them are discussed in chapter 7. Learning often involves a disruption in the established sense of self. In the course of treatment, a therapist often learns more than he expected about his patient and himself. He is confronted with ways of thinking and feeling (his patients', his supervisors') that are different from his own. These experiences may be felt as challenges to his self-esteem. The supervisor needs to titrate her interventions, if they are to be most effective, in a way that maintains the student's sense of professional and personal well-being while asking him to expand his ways of knowing and feeling. This task of titration and the influence of the supervisor's own self-esteem on it is the subject of chapters 8 and 9. Although much has been written about the termination phase of treatment, the ending of supervision has been rarely discussed. The supervisor's role in helping to shape the termination phase can have a profound impact on the entire supervisory experience. Problems in ending supervision and experiences of termination, both good and bad, are discussed in chapter 10. *The Supervisory Encounter* is filled with vignettes drawn from our own teaching and learning experiences. We have also included the supervisory experiences of others whom we have met in local study groups and at national and international meetings and workshops on the subject.

The complexity of the supervisory encounter precludes absolute answers to many questions that are raised in this book. By sharing our own thoughts and experiences, we hope to encourage our readers to better formulate their *own* ideas on the subject. Whether readers' ideas correspond to our own is less important than their having been stimulated to think through and articulate their own reasoned approach to supervision.

Many areas remain to be explored and understood about the supervisory process. We need, for instance, to learn more about supervision from the vantage point of the supervisee. We favor the creation of study groups and fora on supervision in which supervisees can participate and share their experiences about learning, good and bad. Moreover, continued study and ongoing discussions about the goals and techniques of supervision need to be a part of our professional lives and part of the lives of the institutions where we teach. This book is part of the process of our becoming better teachers. We hope it will stimulate others to think, read, talk, and write about their supervisory encounters and will lead to spirited discussions about how supervision can be made most meaningful for teacher and student.

1

A Brief History of Supervision

When a first-year psychiatric resident asked his supervisor, Dr. Elvin Semrad, how often he should see his patients, Dr. Semrad replied, "As often as you can stand each other" (Smith, 1993). However impractical such advice might seem now in an age concerned with rising medical costs and managed care, it conveys an important message. If a student wants to learn about another's life, it takes time. He needs to immerse himself in his patient's most personal thoughts, fantasies, and feelings. And there are moments when such immersion is hard for both therapist and patient to tolerate. The student, new at his profession, obviously needs guidance in this process of immersion. He turns to a supervisor for help in making sense of his numerous observations, impressions, and emotional reactions. Often he wants to learn but is fearful of learning as well.

Supervisees and supervisors these days are involved in discussing many kinds of treatment. They learn not only about insight-oriented psychotherapy but about crisis intervention, brief treatment, the management of disturbed behavior, psychopharmacology, and family and group treatments. Any of these treatments should be built on a psychodynamic foundation. Understanding a patient's conflicts and defenses, his values and ambitions, and his ways of relating helps the clinician in developing a treatment plan that is both acceptable and meaningful to the patient. An approach to learning psychotherapy (of any kind) that emphasizes the student's immersion for a time in both his patient's experiences and his own responses to them furthers the therapist's ability to understand his patient and to know how best to communicate with him and help him.

The supervisor's responses to her student's clinical involvement are rooted in her own experience as a therapist, her feelings about both the student and the patient he presents, her personal ambitions and conflicts, and her views about what students need to learn in order to be good therapists. Through her interactions with the student, the supervisor helps him construct meaning from data gleaned from his treatment hours. The data will vary from "objective" observations of the patient to subjective experiences of him, from facts about the patient's life to fantasies about him. The supervisor, in turn, will have her own cognitive and emotional reactions both to her supervisee and to the image of the patient that, with the student's help, is being built up in her mind. The patient supervisor and supervisee speak about is not the real and complicated person existing somewhere beyond the supervisor's consulting room, but rather the person constructed through the sensibilities (observations, emotions, and conflicts) of the therapist. The supervisor's grasp of the patient depends in part on the supervisee's ability to portray enough about the patient to allow her to picture him. Where the supervisor's ability to picture the patient or to understand the patient-therapist interaction fails her, her questions for the supervisee often begin. It is in the fluid "potential space" between supervisor and supervisee—that space of contained imagination and observation, understanding and confusion, objectivity and subjectivity—that meaning is forged through the act of creating and discovering the patient.

For such a creative educational encounter to take place certain preconditions must be met. The supervisee must be able (or must learn) to tolerate the disruption of the sense of self that learning requires and to live with the feeling of vulnerability that often accompanies new knowledge. He must be able to marshal his ego's capacities for confronting new information about both his patient and himself, while evaluating these capacities so as to hone or reshape them. The supervisor is there to help in this complex process. But she should do so within the context of a pedagogic approach that respects the differences between supervision and therapy, between imposing an approach to treatment and allowing the supervisee to develop his own, between helping to "manage" a case and making it meaningful in ways that neither she nor the supervisee could have imagined.

The supervisor and supervisee try to develop a language that fits their needs and those of the patient under discussion. This is no easy task. It requires time and patience and a faith that they can find the language for what they most need to understand and communicate. If they are lucky, the supervisory dialogue can gradually enlarge and allow for unusual and profound communication that enriches and enlivens their perspective on patients, themselves, and the processes that lead to change and growth. It is this process and the teacher's participation in this dialogue that we describe as we examine the supervision of psychodynamically oriented psychotherapy and psychoanalysis.

Both teachers and students are bound to ask themselves about the nature of supervision—how as a learning process it is similar to or different from psychotherapy, how "deep" or personal should it be, how painful or pleasant the process of growth and change will be. For Felman (1991), a teacher and a student of psychoanalysis, real learning involves self-transformation that is never easily attained.

Teaching in itself, teaching as such, takes place precisely only through a crisis: if teaching does not hit upon some sort of crisis, if it does not encounter either the vulnerability or the

explosiveness of an (explicit or implicit) critical and unpredict-
able dimension, it has perhaps not truly taught: it has perhaps
passed on some facts, passed on some information and some
documents. . . . Teaching and psychoanalysis have precisely to
live through a crisis. Both are called upon to be performative,
and not just cognitive, insofar as they both strive to produce,
and to enable, change. Both this kind of teaching and psychoanalysis are interested not merely in new information, but,
primarily, in the capacity of their recipients to transform themselves in function of the newness of that information. (p. 68)

To Felman the teacher is the midwife attending the ongoing birth
of the self. We do not fully agree: we feel that this portrayal of
teaching and learning does not take into sufficient account the
pick-and-shovel work that makes change possible—the laborious
and hard-won mastery of the facts, vocabulary, and grammar of a
discipline that the teacher helps provide. Of course, both portraits of learning are true. Discoveries come only after the way
is prepared for them. Creative impulses come to naught if not
matched with well-honed skills that can fashion and realize them.

For a psychotherapist, one of the skills most needed in helping
others is knowledge of oneself. So it is no wonder that ever since
inception of psychoanalytic psychotherapy, learning how to help
others has been linked with learning about oneself. A major influence on the development of supervision came from the psychoanalytic movement, where the link between helping others and
the need for self-knowledge was clearly recognized. As early as
1910, Freud emphasized the need for self-examination on the
part of the would-be analyst. "We have become aware," he wrote,
"of the 'countertransference' which arises in him [the analyst] as a
result of the patient's influence on his conscious feelings and we
are almost inclined to insist that he recognize the countertrans-

ference and overcome it. Since analysts have begun to exchange observations with one another, we have noticed that no psychoanalyst goes further than his own complexes and internal resistances permit and we consequently require that he shall begin his activity with a self analysis and carry it deep while he is making observations on his patients" (pp. 144–145). Although Freud emphasized self-analysis, his phrase "almost inclined to insist" suggests an uncertainty about how best to handle the analyst's resistance and countertransference in educational terms. It was not until a decade later that the therapist's own personal analysis would be required and a clearer division between it and supervision would be made. But from its inception, supervision of psychoanalytic psychotherapy and analysis required the teacher to teach the student not only about others but also about himself and his responses to patients. For the supervisor to do this well requires the utmost tact, sensitivity, and knowledge in her own mind of the boundaries between the essentially educational function of supervision and the therapeutic function of treatment. The history of supervision is full of interesting debate about just where these boundaries should be drawn.

In the beginning, learning to be a dynamically oriented psychotherapist was much more informal than it is today. The first model for becoming a psychodynamic psychotherapist was the one Freud himself provided. He had no supervisors, no training analyst other than himself, and no training courses other than the ones he himself gave. In the early 1900s, the only clinical and theoretical seminars on psychoanalysis he attended were the meetings of the Wednesday Psychological Society, which convened weekly in Freud's waiting room. The members of the group changed over the years, but the number always remained small. Max Graf, a musicologist who was an early participant, described the meetings: "The gatherings followed a definite ritual. First, one of the members would present a paper. Then black coffee and cakes would be served; cigars and cigarettes were on the table and were consumed in great quantities. After a social quarter of an hour, the discussion would begin. The last and decisive word was always spoken by Freud himself" (Gay, 1988, p. 174).

In those days, one became an analyst primarily through individual initiative and interest. As Freud recalled, "a number of younger physicians gathered around me with the declared intention of learning, practicing and disseminating psychoanalysis" (Jones, 1953–57, p. 173). Freud and his followers believed that putting his theory in the hands of these would-be analysts would provide them with the key to the understanding of their own unconscious. They vastly underestimated the personal resistance an individual could have to applying those theories to his own psyche (Kovacs, 1936).

Over time, the necessity for a student of analysis to undergo treatment became increasingly clear. A training analysis might, as Kovacs suggested, "loosen his cramped humanity, grown stiff through habit and automatic behaviour, and . . . show him the many potentialities which lie dormant within him. This alone can give him a greater elasticity, enabling him to have insight into the difficulties of those patients whose character is wholly opposed to his own." By 1924, in Berlin, at least, the requirements of psychoanalytic education included a training analysis of at least six months' duration.

At first, Freud was the only teacher, but almost nothing has been written describing his supervisory activity, which, for the most part, was informal and without the boundaries now established. Because so little was known about the subtleties, intensity, and enduring aspects of transferences in treatment and in learning, the lives of patients and analysts, teachers and students were intertwined in a way that no longer seems advisable. The early experimental nature of analysis allowed for greater liberties, including Freud's freedom to supervise the husband of a former patient on the treatment of their son. The "Little Hans" case can be read profitably as a description of early supervision.

Herbert Graf (called "Little Hans" in Freud's [1909] case report *Analysis of a Phobia in a Five-Year-Old Boy*) had developed a fear of horses that caused him great anxiety. He was afraid that a horse might bite him and that one of the large dray horses he saw pulling wagons and coaches might fall down. These irrational fears made him afraid to see or be near horses and prevented him from going out into the street, where in Vienna at that time he was sure to encounter them. The boy's mother had been a patient of Freud, who knew Herbert and took him a present on his third birthday (Gay, 1988). In 1908, when this bright and lively child began to suffer from a progressively debilitating phobia, Freud worked almost exclusively through the child's father to cure him.

In an attempt to help his son, Max Graf began to interview him and to report the sessions to Freud in detail. Like many beginning therapists (and fathers), Graf had his own ideas about the etiology of the boy's troubles. He attributed them to the excessive sexual stimulation of an overindulgent mother and to the boy's guilt and fear over masturbation. But as the treatment proceeded, Graf's supervisor developed a more elaborate theory. To Freud, the treatment of Herbert's childhood neurosis demonstrated clinically what he had described theoretically in his *Three Essays on the Theory of Sexuality* (1905) and further confirmed *in statu nascendi* his theories of the oedipal complex. Freud, primarily a psychoanalytic investigator and secondarily a supervisor to a willing therapist, demonstrated that the source of Herbert's phobia lay in his repressed erotic longings for his mother and his competitive and death wishes toward his father, whom he also loved. The little boy was trying to deal with these unacceptable wishes by erecting barriers of disgust, shame, and inhibition and by developing a phobia.

The Little Hans case not only sheds light on infantile sexuality and the oedipus complex, but it is also the first detailed account we have of a psychodynamically oriented supervision. Freud seemed unaware of how tangled and intrusive an educational experience it was for everyone involved. At times, it is not clear who is treating Herbert—Freud or the boy's father. For the most part, Freud relied on suggestion and didactic instruction in his supervision of the treatment. But through this educational process, flawed as it may have been, the patient got better, the therapist developed a deeper understanding of his patient's dynamics, and the supervisor further developed and elaborated his own ideas.

The supervisory situation was not without its difficulties for Freud. In ways not unfamiliar to supervisors, he did not always approve of the elder Graf's technique: "He asks too much and investigates in accord with his own presuppositions instead of letting the little boy express himself." (Perhaps Graf was imitating a style of inquiry he had learned from his supervisor!) But, nevertheless, to continue the treatment along these lines, Freud feared, would make the patient's problems impenetrable. When the treatment stalled, the therapist brought his patient to his supervisor for consultation. This meeting helped further the treatment but probably reinforced in the boy's mind that there was a higher authority involved in the endeavor than his father-therapist. In an exchange in which Herbert disagreed with his therapist, he told him to consult his supervisor. When Herbert reported to his father-therapist that he wished his younger sister would fall into the bathwater and drown, his therapist, hardly neutral on the matter, replied, "And you would be alone with Mummy. And a good boy doesn't wish for that!" Clearly the therapist was trying to show the patient the conflict his wishes create in him while suggesting suppression of such wishes. But Herbert did not pick up on the conflict and seems to have heard a judgment in the remark. He tried to hold on to his wishes and to come to some agreement with his therapist. "But he may think it," he replied. When his father continued to object, the patient, frustrated by not feeling validated by his therapist, summoned the image of a more knowledgeable and understanding supervisor. The boy refused to recant his wishes and subtly called on Freud for help in this argument with his father: "If he thinks it, it's good just the same, so he can write it to the professor." Since then, how many therapists and supervisors have heard patients make similar allusions and appeals to a hoped-for higher authority: "I hope you're discussing this with your supervisor," and "You get it! Have you been talking to your supervisor since we last met?" In the case of Graf, the therapist is the patient's father and, therefore, has a lot at stake beyond understanding alone—the welfare of his infant daughter, for example. But today, even though therapists are no longer relatives of patients they treat, they still may, like Graf, take positions that clearly convey subtle judgments about their patients' thoughts and actions. Such judgments usually inhibit the patient's freedom to communicate, develop, and analyze his own values and the life choices that derive from them.

The model of supervision presented here is a limited one. Freud did not write about Little Hans with the intention of elaborating a theory and technique of teaching. Graf was too much an intermediary between Freud and his son and not enough of an independent therapist. Furthermore, the patient was fully aware that his therapist needed and was getting help from a more knowledgeable teacher. The goal of this supervision, furthermore, was not to teach Graf to be a therapist; he already had a profession. Nevertheless, the case remains an interesting account of a form of supervision, demonstrating how supervision, even today, may focus on the patient in treatment to the exclusion of what the supervisee is learning, often leaving the therapist feeling like a conduit between supervisor and patient.

Max Graf was not the only one to have Freud as a supervisor, although this was not a role Freud emphasized in his writings. Many of Freud's analysands were themselves therapists and sought advice from him about the treatment of their cases during their own analyses. After termination, they frequently turned to him for supervision through letters and in personal meetings. It was through these letters to Freud and to one another, through personal analyses, private meetings, small study groups, and international congresses that analytic knowledge was transmitted in the days before analytic education became formalized and associated with institutes.

Although this type of education had the advantages of both intimacy and zeal, Karen Horney (1930) pointed out that "the concept of personal aptitude was still totally lacking" (p. 48). All one needed was perseverance. In Vienna or Berlin, putative psychoanalytic therapists started their education by reading and discussing what Freud and others had already written. Most of them voluntarily entered an analytic treatment that lasted up to a year in hopes of learning more about themselves and the conduct of an analysis. Their analysts frequently supported their career goals by referring analytic patients and by issuing them invitations to join analytic study groups. Thus, from its inception, for those interested in becoming an analyst, their analyst was mentor and teacher, and often someone the trainee knew socially outside the consulting room.

Until the 1920s, the learning and supervision of analytic theory and technique were uneven and unsystematic (*schlampigkeit* was Grete Bibring's term for it), depending more on the zeal and particular penchants of the individual (and his or her analyst) than on any well-organized method of teaching and assessing learning (Fleming and Benedek, 1966, p. 7). In Zurich, for instance, the first city in which psychoanalysis was officially taught and practiced in a clinic setting, training consisted of reading analytic works, learning the use of Wundt's association tests, and experimenting with associative techniques (Kovacs, 1936, p. 374), while in Berlin or Budapest the emphasis was on a more intense study of Freud's work.

As the number of people interested in becoming psychoanalytic therapists grew, a crisis in education developed. The old system of training through personal apprenticeship no longer seemed adequate. The wide disparity in the aptitude of analysts for psychoanalytic work as well as their informal training made clear the need for structuring the educational experience. Horney, in her report (1930) about the development of the Berlin Institute, wrote, "Those who wanted to be trained as psychoanalytic therapists at the Institute increased so in numbers already in the first three years [1920–23] that it proved pointless to hand over the admission of candidates and the selection of topics for teaching to the initiative of . . . individuals" (p. 48). The increasing amount of work involved in processing applications and in training ever larger numbers of candidates inevitably led to the formation of committees to determine admissions and curricula, to the creation of a stronger central organization, and to the gradual development of systematic education procedures. Furthermore, as important differences in analytic theory and technique developed and led to serious rifts in the analytic community, the need for clearly stated educational objectives became apparent. In addition to the requirement established at the Berlin Congress of 1922 that prospective analysts have a training analysis of at least six month's duration, more serious attention was paid to the best method of helping students in their clinical work. The rules for training which were devised at that congress, published two years later, included the requirement that candidates have at least two years of clinical work with analysands as part of their education.

The requirement that such training cases be seen under supervision was begun at the Berlin Institute by Karl Abraham, Max Eitingon, and Georg Simmel. It is said that the idea of supervision arose when Hans Sachs complained to Eitingon that he was tired of hearing his patients talk so much about their own patients in their analyses with him. In the beginning, Eitingon interviewed prospective patients, matched each with an available candidate, and provided some supervision. Although Horney, Franz Alexander, Jeanne Lampl, and others joined the staff of the Berlin Clinic to teach and to supervise, there seems to be no accurate record of who else in Berlin might have been a supervising analyst at that time. How one was appointed to that position and how often supervisor and supervisee were expected to meet are not recorded. It seems clear, however, that trainees often undertook clinical psychoanalytic work after the completion of their own analyses and found supervisors other than their own analysts to help them with their cases.

In Budapest, Sandor Ferenczi and Otto Rank (1924) were emphasizing a different educational approach than the Berlin model. They recommended that a *Kontrollanalyse* serve as a continuation of the training analysis. In their plan, the therapist would begin the treatment of an analytic patient while the therapist himself was still in analysis, using his own treatment to explore his relation with his patient and thus to obtain a deeper understanding of his own resistances and difficulties in conducting analytic work. In this way, the therapist's analyst would become his first supervisor. This suggestion formalized what many would-be analysts had already been doing: namely, turning to their analysts during analytic hours for help in treating their own cases. They often received in their analyses direct instruction and advice on how to proceed. Helene Deutsch, for instance, was advised to terminate her analysis of Tausk by her own analyst, Freud (Roazen, 1969). This method of supervision, which the Hungarian School tried to systematize, had certain advantages. The candidate's analyst in many ways knew the therapist best and could address in the greatest depth and with the greatest certainty any factors in his makeup that might affect his ability to conduct an analysis. It was with his analyst that the candidate could have the most open and far-reaching discussion of his reactions to his patient and their origins. Furthermore, free association could be used in supervision to encourage the deepest exploration of the candidate's own analytic work. The Hungarian method emphasized what Freud had already noted: that an analysis cannot go further than the unresolved complexes of the analyst.

The Hungarian proposal was debated at both Four Countries Conferences in 1935 and 1937, where it was generally agreed that the student's reaction to the transferences of his patients needed much more attention and that teaching analytic technique through supervision was an important aspect of training. To emphasize the difference between the two tasks, supervision with its analysis of the student's countertransferences to and treatment of his patient was called Kontrollanalyse, whereas his own analysis was referred to as the *Analysenkontrolle*. It was clear to many outside of Hungary that the training analyst would conduct Analysenkontrolle, but that another analyst would be responsible for the Kontrollanalyse (Balint, 1948). Some objected that the Hungarian method of analytic education gave the training analyst too much control over the candidate's learning experience and too much power over his professional development. Eitingon (1936) argued that candidates should be exposed to a number of supervisors so that they could see more than one individual analyst at work. But according to the Hungarians, what was gained by such breadth was not worth the superficiality of the supervision that accompanied it. For when the supervisor was not the therapist's analyst, her ability to understand the origins of the therapist's reactions to his patient was severely limited. Information could be passed along, but the crises and confrontations with oneself (for both supervisee and supervisor) necessary for true learning might not occur. Kovacs wrote:

> It is true that during his analysis I have an idea about the limit to which a particular candidate can adapt to his environment, but the situation becomes entirely different once he begins to work with patients. Naturally, this is even more difficult when he has been analyzed by someone else. When in such cases I undertook the supervision of such control cases, I was always obliged to confess my great embarrassment: I could not orient myself to the pathology, however well presented, because I did not know the character of the candidate and his modes of reacting, also I could not tell from what point of view he assessed the different situations recounted. The difficulties of this work are much greater than the results obtained. It was satisfying for neither me nor the candidate. (cited in Moreau, 1970, p. 83)

Her words for the most part went unheeded. In 1990, Istvan wrote:

> At present, I am the only one who uses this way of training analysis. The newly formed Hungarian Society works as prescribed by the IPA TC [International Psychoanalytical Association Training Committee] in order to be accepted by the IPA. . . . Only through a thoroughly deep exploration of the uncon-

scious backgrounds of the interpretive activity and of the control of countertransference, to be attained only in the psychoanalytical situation, renders the trainee capable to interpret [as] extensively and deeply as necessary. . . . In supervision, which is a sort of tutoring, this cannot be achieved.

These ideas find an echo in Harris and Ragen's (1993) report on "mutual supervision" in which the authors describe "consulting with a colleague over a case, presenting personal material, and allowing the consultant to do, almost simultaneously, analytic work and supervisory work" (p. 199).

Although by the late 1930s most institutes had rejected the Hungarian model, supervisors kept exploring, in ways less daring than that of Harris and Ragen, how introspection and the exploration of countertransference could best be fostered in the supervisory situation. Grotjahn (1955) and Keiser (1956) thought there might be value in having a later case being supervised by one's analyst. Blitzsten and Fleming (1953) stated that supervision of analysis included therapeutic work with the supervisee: "Good supervision [helps] the student recognize his still unresolved conflicts which interfere with his becoming an effective analyst and [helps] him to work these through" (p. 119). In 1963, DeBell pointed out that there had, in fact, been no extensive refutation of Kovacs's position in the literature. That same year, Arlow tried to clarify the limits of the supervisory situation: "The supervisor's interventions and observations are limited in scope. They apply only to the surface phenomena. They can reach only approximately toward the unconscious motivation of the candidate, and . . . cannot be considered the equivalent of a therapist's interpretation. . . . One can never escape the reality . . . that supervision is essentially and fundamentally a teaching experience" (p. 587).

This concise description of the limitations of the supervisory process grew out of the earlier decision, made at a crossroad in the history of psychoanalytic supervision by every institute but the Hungarian, that the function of the supervisor be separated from that of the training analyst. There are still some individuals whose ways of analyzing and supervising are influenced by the Hungarian method, for the move away from the Hungarian approach sacrificed to some extent the supervisor's access to the supervisee's inner life and deeper understanding of his countertransferences. Yet most supervisors embraced this development, for what is gained—namely, the supervisee's sense of privacy and protection from the potentially transference-laden and intrusive elements of supervision—allows for the development of an educational dialogue that is truly more interactive and collaborative. As Gray (1993) states, "Our manner of requiring a series of supervisions, from different supervisors, typically places an inordinate task on the candidate. But I know of no better alternative. To be subject, in an overlapping way, to a variety of supervisors' predilections, to contain a growing body of knowledge, and yet maintain an ability for independent openness to personal appraisal, is having to experience the task of an 'impossible profession' at an early time. But that is precisely what supervisees need to learn" (p. 8). Bakanowski (1989) has pointed out that the introduction of a supervisor gives the analytic candidate a view of analysis different from that of his own analyst. The introduction of a third person into the candidate-analyst dyad helps the candidate to ameliorate any fantasies he may have about his analyst's omniscience and to evaluate more carefully his own treatment. The advantages are clear, yet each supervisor's knowledge of the supervisee is limited and the scope of the supervisory dialogue is circumscribed.

While psychoanalysts pondered the nature of psychoanalytic

supervision, social workers were exploring the psychodynamics of supervision in casework. What had started before the turn of the century as the administrative supervision of volunteers who hoped to uplift the underclasses by providing social services had become by the 1930s a much more complex endeavor. Schools of social work started in the 1920s were graduating professionals who, influenced by the ideas of psychoanalysis, became increasingly interested in individual casework. For many social workers, the client's individual psychodynamics, which were considered both the result of and a contributing factor to his or her current social situation, became the focus of attention. This interest went hand in hand with the development in social work of an articulate and sophisticated theory of supervision. Robinson (1936), for instance, pointed out that the supervisee might well bring ways of relating from his own interpersonal history into his work with the client or with the supervisor. The supervisor's task, she stated, was not to explore the student's past but to pay attention to his ways of relating that were relevant to the current work and to "shut off the escape into attitudes that belong to an older situation" (p. 6). But how this was to be achieved through an educational process was not always clear.

Limited access to the supervisee's unconscious, his personal history, and the value system he brings to his therapeutic work taxes the supervisor's understanding and makes her task more difficult. It demands that supervisors develop new ways of understanding, assessing, and responding to the needs of their supervisees that differ significantly from those they have used with clients or patients. Limited knowledge of their supervisees requires that supervisors be able to assess how a student best thinks and learns, what may get in the way of that learning, and how these obstacles can be surmounted. Supervisors also need to be able to measure progress in learning. In addition to their responsibility to educate their trainees, supervisors also feel responsible for the adequate care of the patient being seen. This dual responsibility can become particularly difficult if the trainee is having problems learning while his patient is urgently in need of help. In such cases, the supervisor may have to be directive, telling the supervisee what to do while explaining why the therapeutic interventions are necessary. At times, the supervisor may choose to interview the patient herself, as Freud did with Little Hans, so as to better help the student assess a critical situation.

Freud's lack of interest in articulating a theory of teaching and supervision influenced his followers, who then also paid relatively little attention to the subject. Social workers such as Robinson (1936) and Kadushin (1976) articulated theories of supervision, but their contributions, while often valuable, tended not to be read by those outside of their own field. Supervisors often undertook teaching without much training in or discussion of a theory or technique of supervision. Psychologists like Styczynski (1980) pointed out that beginning supervisors should utilize their experiences as a supervisee, teacher, therapist, researcher, colleague, and consultant to help orient them to their new task: "These experiences are provided by most traditional clinical training programs, but are seldom taught for the purpose of developing supervisory skills" (p. 29). Hess (1987) stated that competence as a therapist is essential but not sufficient for the practice of psychotherapy supervision, and that the training necessary for the two endeavors are different. Yet in the field of supervision, there is still no agreed-upon theory of learning, no recognized technique, and often no clearly stated goals by which to measure failure or success. Each supervisor has been left to her own resources, forced to piece together a patchwork of ideas and theories regarding supervision from reading when she has time and from informal discussions with colleagues. Despite a sizable literature and

the contributions of skilled clinicians like Wallerstein and Dewald, the theory, practice, and goals of supervision remain for a
good many supervisors and teaching institutions poorly defined.
Although clinicians are trained to think about theory and technique in psychotherapy, they are not expected to do the same for
supervision. Supervisors often apply what they know of the psychodynamics of psychotherapy to the supervisory situation. Thus
they may tend to use the vocabulary developed to describe patients and their pathology in their descriptions of the learning
situation in supervision.

This book offers a model of supervision and a vocabulary that
are not based on the student's intrapsychic conflicts and an associated vocabulary of clinical pathology to describe an educational
process. Instead, we emphasize a careful, ongoing evaluation and
description of the student's capacity to expand his thinking and
enlarge his ability to use his feelings in forging a better understanding of himself and his patients. In the past, teaching psychotherapy has too often depended on the authority of the supervisor who tells the supervisee how to treat his patient and who
determines what in the supervisee's report is most relevant. We
develop a contrasting model that calls for mutual collaboration
and joint discovery by supervisor and student and that seems less
hierarchical and more collegial.

Quiet debates about power and authority in supervision have
gone on for a long time. Early in the history of analytic supervision, Helene Deutsch warned against the tendency of the supervisor to impose his own theory and technique upon his student.
"Within the framework of the technique given by Freud," she
wrote in 1935, "every individual has his own methods and variants which correspond to his own personality. In the same manner, the candidate would be permitted to fight his way through
any difficulties and thus retain the personal note in his analytic

activity. Introducing the . . . candidate into the arcana of one's own incomplete views and initiating him into often unstable technical variants of a purely personal nature, must be considered one of the greatest mistakes [a supervisor] can make" (p. 62).

Despite this warning, Freud's (1914) commanding words echoed in the mind of many supervisors: "I know only too well the pitfalls lying in wait for anyone who undertakes analysis and hoped that many might be avoided if someone prepared to instruct and admonish could be established in a position of authority" (p. 329). In the past, an authoritarian and hierarchical system in which received wisdom is passed from one generation to the next through supervision substituted for more collaborative exploration of the therapeutic endeavor. Many felt that because supervision was seen primarily as a pedagogic endeavor, clear methods of teaching and associated lesson plans could be developed. This task was performed with much more seriousness by supervisors in social work than by psychoanalysts, who often carried over from analytic technique a less structured view of the supervisory task. Deutsch (1935), for instance, felt that a candidate's taking notes for supervision while conducting an analysis "disturbs the young analyst's intuitive attitude and makes him concentrate too much on . . . the intellectual working up of the material." She advised that the candidate be allowed to "reproduce the material in free association" (p. 65).

In spite of marked differences in their approaches, many early supervisors gave the vivid impression of knowing how clinical teaching (and treatment) should be conducted. For better or worse, they provided a clear plan for how to proceed in the supervisory task. A sense of open and mutual exploration that may have been lost in the supervisors' certainty about how to proceed was, for many students, more than compensated for by the structure and direction their supervisors gave to the educational endeavor.

Kadushin's *Supervision in Social Work* (1976), for instance, contains specific lists of principles, techniques, and instructions that the supervisor is to follow. Robinson (1936) offered clear advice to the young supervisor that is not unlike the advice that might be given to a beginning schoolteacher. "The young caseworker supervising for the first time, and therefore as much a student in relation to this new practice as her student is in relation to casework, has much to do to establish her difference from the student in her attitudes. . . . She will of necessity have to assert her difference arbitrarily at first and support it by every formality. The limits of the conference hour have to be rigidly held to, the content of the case discussion planned carefully in advance" (p. 281). Such advance planning was aided by the request that the supervisee submit written process material to the supervisor before each meeting. This approach allowed the supervisor to review the student's work at leisure and to focus on what she felt the student most needed to learn about theory and technique from the therapy hours submitted. Although the pros and cons of such an approach to supervision may be debated, its objective was to help both student and supervisor focus on those aspects of the case most salient to the student's development as a clinician.

This same didactic and somewhat authoritarian approach is described and illustrated more subtly in Fleming and Benedek's pioneering *Psychoanalytic Supervision* (1966). In many of the supervisory encounters they report, the supervisor is telling the candidate something he needs to know. And one feels that the candidate, in turn, will tell his patients something they need to know. This leaves out of the supervisory process a needed emphasis on mutual exploration, mutual wonder, a dialogue in which neither participant always knows which is the best tack to take, but in which the two make discoveries together that ultimately help both the patient and therapist find their own voices. For example, in a vignette described by Fleming and Benedek (p. 109), a supervisee starts an hour by asking "Could we start with the learning problem that came up last time, or would you rather talk about the patient?" A learning difficulty seems evident in his query: he cannot decide for himself, and his judgment is compromised by his wish to please his supervisor. The supervisor's response, "Well, suppose you tell me what you think about your learning problem," encourages the student to express his own thoughts, but in a manner that at the same time reinforces the supervisor's authority to choose the direction of their dialogue. What is given with one hand is, in a sense, taken away with the other; the supervisor remains the arbiter of what it is best to talk about. Thus a subtle hierarchy is maintained. This style of teaching reflects Fleming and Benedek's view that "The supervisor is usually the one to select the event to be focused on for immediate examination. He also selects the mode of viewing. By this we mean the supervisor determines how the analyst proceeds to study the event selected" (p. 72). But in proceeding in this manner it is not always clear what the student "sees" and whether the event the supervisor focuses on is the one of most interest to the student and from which he can learn most at that moment.

To be fair, the supervisor in Fleming and Benedek's example focuses on her interaction with the student later in the hour, but she classifies it, not inappropriately, as "a transference reaction to the supervisor," and begins to apply a model of intrapsychic conflict to the learning situation. In talking about the candidate's tendency to bring highly abstract summaries of his work to supervision, his attitudes toward the supervisor (the transference reaction) are revealed as is the supervisor's response to them.

Candidate: I had an insight while you were talking, and it's this: that I think my need to prove myself to you, what I can do plays a role in my isolating in just this kind of way, in making this kind of fractionation . . . that is, to talk about the process and then emphasize, look at me. Look what I'm doing to hasten, to facilitate this analysis. I expect all this comes in and works against just that goal in the need to show it to you, an important authority to me. (p. 111)

The supervisor chooses not to explore with the student in what way she has become an important authority for him or to ask further about his experience of the supervision so far. Instead, she replies in a way that reinforces the student's observations about himself while subtly reprimanding him for his wish to impress her.

Supervisor: Yes, but you see what you're eager to show me is not the analysis but your interpretation of it, and that's not the same thing; that's more like the student trying to demonstrate to the teacher how much he knows, how much he knows about the things that the teachers are supposed to know. (p. 111)

There seems an implicit assumption, furthermore, that this wish of the candidate developed apart from the supervisor's teaching style or supervisory interventions. The analysis of the situation lacks any reference to what, if anything, the supervisor might be contributing to the candidate's attitude toward her. What is left out is a self-reflective attitude on the supervisor's part. Casement (1993) notes:

When I hear too much of my own thinking turning up in a student's work with a patient, I know I should not just question the student's lack of independence: I must also examine my own way of supervising. Am I being too active in the supervision, too directive, or too dogmatic? Am I being too quickly critical of the student's way of interpreting? Am I leaving enough room for the student to develop his/her own thinking, in supervision and in the clinical work with the patient? In other words, I need to bear in mind what my own contribution might be to the difficulties being experienced by the student. (pp. 390–391)

Casement's remarks reflect an ongoing change in attitudes. Greater attention given to modes of listening (Schwaber, 1983, 1992) and to theories of intersubjectivity (Hoffman, 1992) has influenced our approach to supervision as well as to therapy. Interest has shifted toward an even closer examination of supervisory process and the exchanges within a supervisory hour than Benedek and Fleming initially provided. Wallerstein's *Becoming a Psychoanalyst* (1981) and Dewald's *Learning Process in Psychoanalytic Supervision* (1987) are among the first to focus on how the supervisor listens and understands his interactions with his supervisee. As the pendulum continues to swing, we will see an even greater focus on the supervisor's experience in the emerging literature on supervision, just as we are beginning to see in the psychoanalytic literature a more self-revelatory exploration of the analyst's feelings and responses (Jacobs, 1991; Mclaughlin, 1981). The examination of such responses, once confined to self-analysis or supervisory sessions, is now finding its way into the public forum. This focus more often takes the form of open and honest descriptions of the experience of being supervised than of supervising (Dick, 1987; Crick, 1991).

Kohut's contributions (1971, 1977) have also greatly influenced the conduct of supervision by heightening our awareness of the development of the sense of self and the vagaries of injuries to self-esteem, not only in the patients reported upon but in the supervisees themselves. His work, along with the more recent work of Nathanson (1987) and Morrison (1989), has made us more attuned to the possibilities for shame and humiliation in supervision, an educational process that calls for an ongoing revision of the sense of self. Robinson pointed out that the student social worker's established sense of identity would oppose the pressures and expectations of training. The necessary change in her sense of herself could not be realized without considerable disruption and disorganization in her existing ways of thinking and behaving. From this would proceed reorganization and a new professional self.

In the following chapters we will explore how this reorganization in the sense of self can take place; how it can best be measured and described educationally in terms of changes in the student's thinking and use of feelings. We will look at the effects on self-esteem of attempts at learning. We will discuss, in the light of the rejection of the Hungarian model and the subsequent limitations on the supervisor's knowledge of her student, how and for what educational purposes a supervisor might focus attention on the student's personal feelings. We will describe the supervisor's role in helping to bring about change, first through careful evaluation of the student's ways of thinking, imagining, and feeling, and then through well-timed interventions, designed to make supervision as much as possible a collaborative learning experience.

We will begin with the opening phase of the supervisory dialogue, for the tone and method it establishes largely determine whether and at what rate the supervisory experience can foster growth and change.

2

The Opening Phase

The opening phase of supervision involves a complex set of evaluations and preliminary explorations on the part of both supervisor and supervisee. As they try to begin a meaningful dialogue, each is listening to the language of the other: its tone, its organization, and its aim. Each is aware of what the other chooses to focus on and when. They take note of one another's body language, as well: the way the other sits, what she does with her hands and eyes, how he dresses, how she says hello and good-bye. Each is trying to understand how flexible and open to influence the other is and how issues of power and gender may influence the developing relationship. All these data are gathered and collated not only in relation to the setting in which the supervision is taking place (whether a training program, an agency, or a private consultation), but also in relation to the age, gender, education, history, life situation, and affects of each participant. It is also influenced by the goals, conscious and unconscious, that both supervisor and supervisee bring to the encounter. In our experience, it is the unexplored and unstated goals of each participant that, when in conflict, can seriously limit the effectiveness of the supervisory process.

The supervisor tries to begin supervision in a way that limits misunderstandings and impediments to free and open learning. She may start by obtaining, in a friendly and interested manner, an educational history from the new supervisee. Where is he in his training? What are his thoughts about his training so far? What have been its strengths and weaknesses? How much supervision has he had and how has it helped or disappointed him?

What does he feel, at this point, are his strengths and weaknesses as a therapist, and what would he like to derive from a supervisory experience? All this, of course, is tied to his professional goals for himself. Does he want to be primarily a therapist, researcher, or administrator? Is he or has he been in therapy himself? Obtaining this information at the beginning of supervision helps orient the supervisor. In turn, the supervisor may invite the supervisee to ask her questions if he wishes—about her training, her current work, her theoretical leanings.

In our opinion, a supervisor should not begin by asking questions about the student's personal life or expect him to ask about hers. When a student asks a personal question, the supervisor may or may not answer. She may also wonder aloud what relevance the student feels his question has to supervision and the learning situation. If the supervisee asks her about her marital status, for instance, she might ask if it would make a difference to him whether or not she were married, or had children. If the trainee asks about the supervisor's age, gentle questioning may reveal a student's wish for an older, more experienced teacher—or a younger one whom he imagines will better sympathize with his struggles.

If the student volunteers information about his personal life, the supervisor should express interest and, perhaps, think about how and when the information was offered and what light this may shed on the student's capacity to learn. A student who tells her new supervisor that she has just had a baby, for instance, may be especially sensitive to developmental issues or issues of parenting as they come up in relation to her patient. Thus, while being a new parent can present certain difficulties in learning in that the student may be tired or preoccupied, it also presents new opportunities of which the supervisor needs to be aware. It is helpful if the supervisor is also alert to recent changes in her own life of which the supervisee may be aware (e.g., a promotion or new position, a serious illness, a publication or talk, a change in marital status). She can then gauge how these may subtly change her approach to supervision as well as watch for how they may affect the supervisee. Dick (1987), for example, describes how a serious illness of her supervisor early in supervision—one that they do not seem to have discussed much—played a part in her fantasies about him and in her early responses to supervision. One wonders what the advantages and disadvantages to learning might have been if the supervisor had openly addressed the illness with his supervisee and explored its real or imagined effect on the supervisory process.

If a supervisor is expected to write a formal evaluation, how, when, and in what form that evaluation will be done is usually best discussed early in supervision, so that the power differential between student and teacher can be acknowledged and its impact discussed, if necessary. Whenever possible, the evaluation should be a joint effort. When a report is due, the student may be asked to evaluate his own work as a therapist, with the supervisor adding her own perceptions. The student may also be asked to comment on the supervision: what have been its most helpful features and what aspects have not furthered the student's learning? The supervisor may then add her thoughts and submit a final report on the student's work and the work of supervision to the appropriate training committee. Even where supervision is being conducted on a private basis and is open-ended, the supervisor may suggest a time when such a mutual evaluation may be undertaken in order to help supervisor and supervisee understand how the other feels about the process in which they are engaged. These periodic evaluations often reveal previously unexpressed ideas and feelings about how the supervision might be more fruitful. If a satisfactory way of proceeding can be worked out at the beginning of supervision, both supervisee and supervisor are more likely to experience the supervisory work as a collaborative process in which statements made about the patient, the student, or the supervisor are arrived at through a mutual process of discovery and dialogue. This is not to say that the supervisor does not have knowledge to impart or that the relationship between supervisor and supervisee is one of full equality. Clearly the difference in age, knowledge, and experience as well as the fact that the supervisor may have to evaluate the trainee's performance belies any overly egalitarian approach to supervision. But within the context of acknowledged differences, an open process of discovery through dialogue may be encouraged through the manner in which an evaluation of his work is conducted.

Despite its merits, this collaborative method of evaluation often meets deep-seated resistance. The student may feel anxious at the thought of being evaluated. Some may be more than willing to have the supervisor submit a report without their knowing about it or having to discuss it. For others, self-reflection and evaluation, in particular in the presence of another, may be difficult. Still others may not want to judge the supervision, especially in the supervisor's presence.

Although these very real concerns of the student need to be addressed, as much resistance comes from supervisors, in our experience. Fleming and Benedek (1983, p. 232) claim that supervisors are often reluctant to pass judgment on or grade a supervisee lest this inhibit the student's freedom and limit "the courage of his own stupidity," so necessary for true learning. These supervisors express the confusion that can arise from the clinician's conflicting identities as a therapist, whose professional work requires that he not pass judgment on his patients, and as a teacher, for whom an openly discussed evaluation is an important part of the educational process. Isakower (1957) describes this confusion as an "occupational ailment" that besets the supervisor: "In his main capacity, he is a therapist and not an educator. I maintain that this can constitute a disturbing interference. . . . Analysts when engaged in the capacity of educators should be particularly alert to a potential liability of slipping from a didactic into a therapeutic attitude toward the student, especially so in supervision" (p. 186). This therapeutic attitude can take the form of a reluctance to evaluate and report on the student's progress. An open and honest evaluation succeeds only when both student and teacher are able to experience it as an educational opportunity from which both can learn. Such an evaluative process develops naturally in supervision that from the outset has fostered a frank and, as much as possible, nonhierarchical dialogue. Where the evaluative function and context of supervision is uppermost in the mind of either the student or the supervisor but is not addressed early, the results can be unfortunate, as in the case described below.

In one mental health clinic, a staff member who was deemed to be doing poorly was placed on probation by the director. In addition, unlike other junior staff, who could ask for any supervisor they wanted in the clinic, the social worker was given a list of supervisors from which he could choose. The list contained the names of supervisors whom the director both respected and knew well—colleagues he felt he would feel comfortable contacting about the trainee's progress. The supervisors on the list had been apprised of the difficulties the staff member seemed to be having and knew that if they were chosen by him, they would be asked to monitor his work carefully and to report to the clinic director.

The therapist chose a female supervisor who was generally thought to be kindly and a good teacher. The meetings began on a cordial but slightly strained note. The supervisee arrived looking anxious but ready for work, process notes in hand, and almost immediately launched into his work with a particular patient. The supervisor felt uncomfortable in her evaluative role—keenly aware that her report might be pivotal in determining whether the staff member would be able to keep his job. After a few meetings, it became clear to her why others had been concerned about the quality of this staff member's work. The therapist, while well meaning, seemed unable to convey in an organized way what he was doing with the patient and why. Despite or perhaps because of his voluminous process notes, the therapist's presentation seemed to the supervisor scattered, tangential, and unfocused. The basis for his comments to the patient were hard for the supervisor to understand and difficult for the supervisee to elaborate upon. The supervisor began to interrupt the almost constant flow of reporting by the therapist to ask for clarification of certain facts about the patient.

The supervisor's apparent discomfort and subsequent attempts to structure the interactions, in turn, worried the supervisee. He began to look uncomfortable during the supervisory sessions, took to watching the clock, and then began smoking during the sessions. Furthermore, the supervisee set the alarm clock in his office, where the supervision took place, so that it went off some time before the end of the supervisory session. He explained that he needed time to get to another appointment in the clinic, an explanation that seemed to the supervisor only further evidence of the therapist's somewhat idiosyncratic approach to problem solving. The supervision limped along, with the supervisor trying to clarify what was happening in the therapy hours while the staff member both figuratively and literally set up a smoke screen of obfuscation. What the supervisor, intent on doing a good job of evaluating for the clinic director, failed to understand from the outset was just how alarmed the staff member was and how concretely he expressed it. She herself was focusing on assessing the supervisee's capabilities before she had examined the situation with him. What needed to be discussed was how they were going to reconcile the supervisor's need to report with the supervisee's need to feel safe enough to discuss his work honestly, both of them knowing that his job was on the line and that he was being closely watched. How did the supervisee understand being placed on probationary status? What had it been like for him to be given a special list of supervisors? Why had he chosen to work with this supervisor? What did he understand the goal of supervision at this point to be? How could it best be accomplished? These questions needed to be discussed openly and honestly before any meaningful supervision of cases could begin. The fact that the supervisee, anxious and ashamed, preferred to avoid such a discussion by immediately jumping to case material could have been gently pointed out to him. As this situation illustrates, the atmosphere in which supervision takes place can foster learning or detract from it, in which case feelings of lack of safety should be addressed first.

In the initial phases of supervision, the supervisor tries to create an atmosphere in which a meaningful dialogue can take place. Schafer (1992) has pointed out the centrality of an ongoing dialogue not only to learning, but also to progress in the fields of psychotherapy and psychoanalysis. He notes:

> Progress in any discipline has always depended on continuing dialogue. Continuing dialogue over conflicting aspirations and truth claims helps refine one's notions of importance, one's methods, samples, arrangements of data, one's logical tools, one's conclusions and always the rhetoric one relies on to make a case persuasively. Through dialogue one learns better how the opposition makes its case. Learning that, one tries to find

common ground, and, failing that, one begins to develop more persuasive arguments for one's own point of view. In the process, once the questions asked are modified, the answers are framed differently, and even the subject of inquiry may be changed to whatever now seems to be more urgent or more fruitful than its predecessors. Goals are never set with finality. (p. 4)

It is this spirit of inquiry and view of dialogue that should pervade the developing supervisory discourse.

In the example above, where there is an initial impediment to the creation of such a dialogue, the supervisor should help the student address it. There is a big difference between a dialogue and an interview. Many supervisory hours inadvertently turn into interviews, with the supervisor playing the part of the interviewer. The interviewer has been characterized as someone who asks questions of interest to herself; someone who, when given responses, uses them only to suit herself; and who translates these responses into her own vocabulary and her own manner of thought. In a supervision subtly modeled on the interview format, the supervisee provides the raw material to which the supervisor gives form and meaning that the student is expected to accept. The trainee may ultimately use the supervisory interview as the model for psychotherapy, thereby limiting the kind of discourse that can develop in his treatment of patients. By contrast, in a dialogue, meaning is co-constructed and neither party is expected to accept what she or he does not believe or understand.

One of the main impediments to the establishment of such a dialogue may be the supervisor's failure to appreciate the extent of the trainee's anxiety and feelings of vulnerability in the new supervisory situation. One beginning candidate described how she coped with these feelings by forcing herself to record honestly and directly what transpired between herself and her patient: "I had to take process notes during sessions because I knew I would not write down the details of my ignorance and ineptitude if I waited until later. I was embarrassed by my blind spots and my lack of knowledge, information, and skill. I felt anything I had to say regarding how I understood a particular interchange would be far too elementary and not complete enough" (Dick, 1987, p. 452). Such initial feelings of helplessness and confusion, which often accompany new learning, must be tolerated by the trainee and the teacher in order for personal and professional growth to occur (see chapters 8 and 9). In our experience, underestimation of the student's narcissistic vulnerability and failure to address it in a kindly and understanding way can lead to difficulties in teaching and in learning. Baudry (1993) has pointed out:

> The supervisory relationship requires on the part of the supervisee a considerable amount of personal involvement and degree of revelation of the workings of his or her mind and sharing of emotions. This process creates intimacy and is also quite threatening. In contrast to the analytic relationship in which patients are assured of an impartial, non-judgmental reception, supervisees know all the time that they will be judged and evaluated by their supervisor and that to a greater or lesser degree advancement in their careers is dependent on the type of evaluation they receive. . . . Thus the process of supervision is, by its very nature, fraught with potential paradoxes and built-in conflicts which must be faced by both participants. (p. 597)

In the following example, the vulnerability of the student was not appreciated, nor was the appropriate educational history elicited. A crisis arose immediately but was not dealt with adequately by the supervisor or the supervisee. As a consequence, an opportunity for further professional and personal growth for both was lost.

At their first meeting, a third-year resident informed his supervisor in an angry and dismissive tone that he had fired two supervisors the previous year. The supervisor, who enjoyed taking time from a busy practice to supervise and, thereby, retained her hospital affiliation and medical school appointment, was surprised by the hostility of this resident, about whom she knew nothing but who seemed to spell trouble. She responded without thinking: "I didn't realize you had hired me." It was downhill from there. The supervisee grew more defensive and the supervisor became more annoyed. She failed to ask the resident what unsatisfactory educational experiences led to his dismissal of previous supervisors. She did not initially recognize that the resident might be extremely anxious about being evaluated and that he might be doing to the supervisor what he feared would be done to him. In his opening remarks, he clearly informed the supervisor that he did not always see supervision and the learning process inherent in it as a collaborative effort. The supervisor's personal goal in this instance was not to deal with a particularly sensitive or difficult learning situation but to have a break from her usual practice, to spend some interesting and enjoyable hours in another setting, and to keep her medical school affiliation. She resented the supervisee, who interfered with her pleasurable goals and sense of self-worth as a teacher, just as the supervisee resented her for her potential to interfere with his progress as a resident and undermine his feelings of self-esteem as a therapist. The supervisor's response indicated that she had not fully recognized and reexamined her own limited goals as a supervisor in order to further the educational process at hand. This defense against self-reflection took the form of being irked by a training program that seemed to allow the resident to dismiss previous supervisors without much inquiry into the matter. She, like the resident she was hoping to teach, began to feel vulnerable and unprotected by the department in which she was working. The resident, in turn, was annoyed by a program that he felt, rightly or wrongly, saddled him with more supervision than he could use and did not allow him enough time to complete the clinical and administrative work expected of him.

Gender also played a role. The fact that the supervisor was a woman only infuriated him further, as most of his immediate superiors in the department who expected so much of him were also women. The supervisor, in turn, was having difficulties with an adolescent son and had not expected another encounter with what seemed to her a rebellious and unappreciative male. Before they had a chance to get to know each other, they were locked in a struggle, each to maintain his or her self-esteem, to gratify immediate and long-term goals that seemed threatened by the other, to avoid further painful experiences.

Not all supervisions start in so difficult and dramatic a way. But the issues raised by the vignette confront every supervisor and supervisee as they begin to work together. Many of the difficulties described might have been avoided had the supervisor, instead of acting defensively, tried to form an educational alliance with her student, perhaps by showing genuine concern about his previous educational experiences and by trying to understand what had led to the rupture of supervision in the past. She could have found out more about her supervisee's professional goals and the experiences in training that had been most helpful and most frustrating. She could have asked him what he hoped to gain from the supervision. If he did not want to be supervised at all, the reasons would need to be carefully listened to and addressed. All this would be a way of trying to assess what learning could take place in this setting given this particular resident's temperament, ability, experience, and learning style, the supervisor's particular skills and interests, and the demands of the institution on the resident and the supervisor. In addition, the supervisor could have further explored her own motives for supervising and the extent to which they limited her capacity as a teacher and learner in supervision.

This student seemed burdened with certain impediments to learning that most supervisors will recognize. Dewald (1987), in describing the struggle of analytic candidates, points to the experience of students from every discipline who are engaged in learning to be therapists:

> The new supervisor inevitably activates conflicting loyalties and identifications, not only with the candidate's training analyst, but also with previous supervisors as well as other meaningful faculty members. The candidate may experience the new relationship angrily, as a challenge to identification with previous role models; or the new supervisory relationship may offer hopes of fulfillment of regressively reactivated infantile and childhood fantasies. Given the activation of significant personal and professional conflicts, the candidate may resort to preexisting patterns of adaptation and defense. (p. 15)

At the beginning of supervision, some trainees appear unwilling to surrender themselves to any identification with the supervisor (except as aggressor) and so have marked difficulty in learning. What Fleming and Benedek (1966) have called imitative and corrective learning are not open to them. Their sense of their professional or personal identities is so threatened that they do not feel safe with a new supervisor and the possibility of differing ideas or deeper explorations. In these instances, a precarious professional identity and feeling of autonomy is paradoxically maintained through a dislike and distrust of the supervisor. Such supervisees feel the need to tightly regulate the supervisory dialogue. They react to the supervisor initially as a potentially threatening and humiliating authority figure; in her presence they often retreat to a defensive struggle for power. They consciously or unconsciously view supervision and often therapy as a potentially sado-masochistic or suffocating encounter from which they must protect themselves.

Such a difficulty usually requires a long opening phase. The supervisor often must exercise a great deal of patience, self-control, and continual self-analysis so as not to slip into the overt or covert power struggle the trainee most fears and yet invites. In our experience, such learning problems, when they present themselves in the opening phase of supervision, are rarely addressed well by confronting the student about the observed obstacles to learning. To the supervisee, such a discussion often feels like a criticism and often either furthers the power struggle or forces a pseudo-compliance. Instead, a deep appreciation of the trainee's fears and a longer period of allowing the trainee to feel in control of the focus and content of the supervisory dialogue are called for. Allowing the trainee, where possible, to use the supervision in the way that makes him feel safe is the first step. The supervisor can then, as Gardner (1993) suggests, slowly try to identify the student's "hidden questions, questions already being posed, questions [of] which 'the student' is almost, but not quite aware" (p. 7). In such an anxious and vulnerable learner, the first hidden questions that must be answered by the supervisor's sympathetic attitude are will she be on my side and not judge me harshly, as perhaps I already judge myself? Will she let me be my own person and allow me my own aptitudes and deficiencies without trying to control what I do as a therapist? The primary focus of the supervision should be on what the student feels he needs to show his teacher of his work. (This educational focus can be maintained only if the supervisor feels the treatment is going well enough and that the patient, for whom she is also responsible, is not in any danger.) Only after the student understands that what he shows is being seriously considered and that his therapeutic attempts are appreciated will he be able to tolerate his supervisor's comments and questions. If the student, even after gentle questioning, shows too little for the supervisor to get a clear picture of his treatment methods, a fuller discussion of the supervisee's goals in supervision may be necessary. For such a trainee a frequent change of supervisors is not helpful, as he may never get beyond the opening phase with any one supervisor. Ideally he needs to work with one supervisor over several years.

At the opposite end of the spectrum, identification with and idealization of the supervisor at the beginning of supervision are common. Modell (1993) points out: "In asymmetrical relationships in which the other is idealized, individuality is threatened also by the fact that the idealization of the other is accompanied by depletion of the self. What is valued is not in the self but in the other. The other is the person who knows and who has" (p. 116). Despite its drawbacks, idealization early in supervision should usually not be commented on directly by the supervisor. It is often a necessary stage of learning—an attitude that helps the student maintain a sense of professional identity. The creation of an idealized teacher may initially not be an impediment to learning but rather a necessary step in developing and maintaining an educational process. Dewald (1987) points out that although the supervisor may be aware of the idealization manifest in a candidate's behavior, she should adhere "to the pedagogical principle that it is best to acknowledge and accept the existence of transference reactions in candidates as a part of the expected evolution in supervision" (p. 476). A more experienced student may no longer idealize supervisors, but may transfer a needed idealization to a particular theory or school of thought. When idealization of a person or theory persists into the later phases of supervision and training, it needs to be addressed by the supervisor as a limitation in learning, in particular to creative learning and independent thinking. It may be addressed directly through clarifying the student's attitude, asking questions designed to encourage individual conclusions, or offering alternative hypotheses and modeling a point of view that emphasizes healthy skepticism and a more balanced attitude.

Sometimes the affects presented to the supervisor are not a result of the new learning situation alone but are instead feelings about the institution or program in which the student is working. Often the student needs help in sorting out these feelings so that the supervisory hours are cleared for learning and not used for displacement. Picture a trainee who always looks exhausted when he comes for supervision. He slumps in a chair, trying to fish from his briefcase process notes that he clearly has not had time to review before the meeting. On the desk beside him, he has placed a sandwich and a cup of coffee, which he will consume during the hour because this is the only time he has for lunch. Between bites he tells his supervisor of problems he is having with a difficult and demanding "borderline" who is driving him crazy. For this supervisee, the patient hardly seems someone he wants to learn from or even help, but is one more hurdle to be overcome in an unmanageable schedule.

The first thing the supervisor can do is assess the student's state of exhaustion and what, if anything, can be done to provide relief—either through changes in his schedule or changes in his attitude toward his work so that there is room for true curiosity and learning. While the student's state of mind may be primarily the consequence of a hectic schedule, it may also be an elaborate defense against feeling vulnerable in a new learning situation or some statement about his feelings toward the supervisor. His own expectations or those of the agency—and not his patient—may be driving him crazy. Any supervisory dialogue about the patient that does not address why the student is feeling overwhelmed seems absurd. Supervisors find themselves representing the institution, but at the same time becoming keenly aware of the contradiction between the pragmatic needs of the institution and the goals of supervision. How these contradictions are resolved will affect the supervisory dialogue, and if they are not resolved sufficiently, there may be ongoing difficulties in communication.

In this example, the first goal of the agency was to deliver effective care to the largest number of patients in the briefest possible time. But its second goal of providing top-notch education to the mental health professionals who came to it for training was incompatible with the first. The trainee, in order to learn more than mere management skills, may need to spend more time with the patient than is compatible with the institutional pressure for short hospitalizations and quick diagnostic assessments. If the supervisor disregards the needs of the institution for the sake of the supervisee, suggesting that he needs to see this person more intensively, that puts the supervisee in a bind. Going along with the institutional needs for efficient management may sacrifice educational principles by adapting the supervisor's and the supervisee's needs to bureaucratic imperatives. These unspoken pressures on supervisee and supervisor may burden the dialogue if they are not openly explored and an agreement reached on how to proceed.

After such initial impediments to learning begin to be understood and addressed, Alonso (1985) suggests establishing a contract that includes agreement on which patient will be presented and how the case material (process notes, tapes, and so on) will be organized for the purposes of supervision. Our approach is somewhat different. We assume that if the supervisor, after obtaining an educational history, allows the supervisee to speak freely about a patient in any way he chooses without instruction about how to proceed, he will tell the supervisor in both conscious and unconscious ways what he needs to learn and what he may be wary of learning—about himself and others. This approach also gives the supervisor an opportunity to observe and assess how the student organizes information, what ways of thinking he uses (see chapters 3 and 4), and what limitations in learning may present themselves in a relatively unstructured opening phase. She may, therefore, begin by asking an open-ended question: "How would you like to spend this supervisory time?" Often the answer is "I thought of presenting this patient. Do you want me to bring in process notes?"

This is, of course, a reasonable question designed to facilitate communication, but it may also be an important statement about how the student views supervision: as an endeavor to learn by giving the supervisor what she wants in a way she approves and finds most useful. There is not yet enough information to know the full meaning of the question posed by the student, but his approach is worth noting and the supervisor may try to discern further what the student's ideas about the supervisory process are.

One response to the student's question about process notes is "Whatever you feel would be most helpful for you," letting the student decide. This again gives the supervisor the opportunity to see what choices the student makes and what light this sheds on how he organizes himself in relation to a learning experience. This approach differs considerably from that of Gray (1993), for instance, who states: "I differed from the often traditional position of 'helping the supervisee develop his own style.' With my supervisees I assume, and I make it explicit, that they will have many years after graduation to develop their own 'style.' . . . I consider it my supervisory obligation to be the best supervisory teacher of my own views that I can be" (p. 8).

If a trainee begins by bringing in tape recordings of his therapy hours, the supervisor may try in the opening phase to understand whether this is something he has been asked to do in the past. If not, she might wonder to herself whether it is this individual's cognitive perceptual apparatus that makes tape recordings and auditory replay particularly important to learning. Does he spend his free time listening to music, for instance, or in other ways favor auditory functioning? Is there something he specifically wants to know that he feels tapes will best reveal? Or does the use of the tape recorder reflect a distrust of his own cognitive and unconscious abilities to organize the material without the help of something outside himself? By allowing him to take the lead in how to learn, the supervisor may discover something important about his theories and methods of learning that she can discuss with him when appropriate. This method also may help promote in the student a growing awareness of how he learns—how he listens, organizes, and digests what he hears.

In situations where a student cannot organize a meaningful presentation, the supervisor should not let him flounder for very long. Some trainees, especially those just starting out, clearly need structure in order to organize their thinking. Dewald (1987) points out that in the early stages of supervision the supervisor serves as an "active model," making suggestions, revealing her own thought processes, and being, at times, more directive. As the supervision progresses and the student develops greater mastery over theoretical and technical aspects of the treatment situation, the supervisor can become less active and less directive, more a sounding board and facilitator for the student's own thoughts and interventions. When the supervisor allows the student to take the lead in learning for as long as he profitably can, allows him to make mistakes and see the difficulties in his way of proceeding, and then helps him to learn from these difficulties, she makes learning experiential and not just a matter of applying a technique and theory passed on by a teacher.

Fleming and Benedek (1966) describe three types of learning: (1) learning by *imitation*, based on identification with the supervisor without an awareness of the rationale; (2) *corrective* learning, in which different possible approaches to understanding and talking with the patient can be discussed in relation to the theory and technique the therapist has chosen, and (3) *creative* learning, in which the application of accumulated knowledge of the dynamics of intrapsychic conflict and interpersonal relationships and of therapy and technique adds a new and deeper awareness to the therapeutic experience and is integrated into the clinical approach, resulting in original ways of dealing with therapeutic issues.

These classifications of types of learning are also progressive stages in the development of learning. It is helpful if the supervisor is aware of the type of learning in which the student is most heavily engaged. Those students who, at the beginning of supervision, tend to measure supervision in terms of the potential for being shamed, for instance, may find corrective learning particularly difficult and may avoid it, perhaps filling up the hour with so much process material that there is barely time for the supervisor to comment, or taking on a self-critical function in the hope of avoiding the supervisor's imagined criticisms. In such situations, the supervisor can share her own mistakes and difficulties in learning in an attempt to put the student more at ease. Or the supervisor may choose to talk about the patient's potential for feeling shame in the therapeutic situation, thus addressing an issue in supervision by giving attention to a similar issue in the therapy.

The task in the opening phase of supervision, then, is to create an atmosphere in which learning can take place. This can be done only if the supervisee feels that his teacher is sympathetic to and in tune with the obstacles to learning he is encountering. The trainee must feel that the supervisor will help him identify and overcome those obstacles without judging him. The supervisor listens in a concerned but nonjudgmental manner that contains the trainee's anxieties and makes it possible to explore them, not in terms of the student's personal history of conflicts, but only in terms of the impediments they present to new learning. By addressing these impediments, the supervisor helps the student slowly to expand his options for viewing new data and for thinking about what the acquisition of knowledge means. Through the use of a relatively unstructured opening phase, the supervisor has a chance to observe how and along what lines the student organizes or fails to organize his material. It also permits a glimpse into what affects the unstructured situation—not unlike the therapy situation in which the student may be engaged—stimulates in the supervisee and how he handles them (see chapter 6).

Some students will immediately dive into presenting one case while others seem to drift around for a while with one and then another case presentation. If the supervisee cannot organize case material in a meaningful manner, the supervisor must help to provide a structure for learning. If a number of didactic suggestions about how supervision might be organized to best meet the supervisee's interests and goals fail to produce a workable situation, a comment that draws the student's attention to possible obstacles to learning can be made: "Have you noticed your difficulty in organizing the material so that we can look at it together in a meaningful manner?" Depending on the student's reply, one can go further and ask, "Are you aware of any feelings about working with this patient or with me that might get in the way?"

In psychotherapy and psychoanalysis one advances from the surface toward unconscious determinants; in supervision one advances from observing and accepting how the student learns to addressing more directly any limitations to further learning. What are referred to as impediments to learning in the student are often unrecognized differences in the cognitive styles of supervisor and supervisee. Therefore, in considering possible obstacles to learning, the supervisor should try to identify early in supervision the supervisee's cognitive style and to understand the theory of knowledge that is guiding him. She then needs to compare that with her own ways of thinking and knowing, for each person has his or her own system of determining how we know what we know. This epistemological system may be conscious or unconscious, well organized or inconsistent, predictable or ad hoc, apparent or unarticulated. The supervisor needs to try to understand how the trainee critiques, assesses, and integrates new experiences and new knowledge. Does he organize knowledge around empirical data and a wish for objectivity, around explanatory power, around elegance and aesthetic power, around logic, around his own affects and what he *feels* to be right? Furthermore, the supervisor needs to assess how the supervisee uses any increase in clinical or theoretical knowledge. Does he use it primarily as a pragmatic device for getting through a tough schedule and managing difficult patients? Is it a way to get closer to the "truth"? Does it remind him of how much reading in the field he has yet to do? Is its acquisition burdensome or liberating? Is it mainly defensive, a form of insurance against making mistakes, or is it the gateway to greater freedom to take some risks, make some errors?

As the way a student thinks is central to the way he learns, the way a supervisor thinks is equally important to the way she teaches. The supervisor's recognition and assessment of how she and her student are similar or different in their cognitive styles are important aspects of supervision. A supervisor needs to have in mind the ways of thinking she feels are central to becoming a good therapist. In chapters 3 and 4 we will discuss certain types of thinking and their relation to therapy and to supervision.

3

Inductive and Associative Modes of Thought

Both supervisor and trainee come to the supervisory dialogue with an established cognitive style—a stabilized way of perceiving and processing information that is part of his or her personality. Jacob (1981) pointed out that an individual's dominant cognitive style has a formative influence on every stage of his education and "casts a shadow on how he learns any new task" (p. 194). Jacob himself admits, "I happen to have mechanical hobbies and I often 'think' in spatial-physical dynamic images, and use mechanical metaphors. Sometimes this is an asset, sometimes it is, rather, a liability" (p. 197). Every therapist, whether he or she is aware of it, has personal criteria for the kinds of information that deserve serious consideration and the kinds of evidence required for its acceptance and integration. One therapist may be skeptical of psychodynamic concepts because they seem unverifiable when held up to the standards of empirical research in the natural sciences. Another may find these concepts at variance with his own intuition—the main filter he uses for the selection and evaluation of new information. A third may not see the value or relevance of psychodynamic concepts unless he can relate them specifically to experiences of his own. The supervisor should have some idea of the cognitive methods by which she and her supervisee make order of the flood of stimuli and new information, verbal and nonverbal, that is directed toward them. Much attention in supervision has been paid to the clinical material under discussion, to transference, countertransference, the parallel process, and, at times, the supervisee's unconscious process. Less attention has been paid to the cognitive style and methods of thinking employed by trainees (and supervisors) in the work of learning and teaching. Gardner (1985) has helped us to understand the concept of multiple intelligences and varied frames of mind. He reasons that an early assessment of the individual's kind of intelligence may allow that individual "to proceed as rapidly as seems warranted in those intellectual channels where he is talented, even as it affords an opportunity to bolster those intellectual endowments that seem relatively modest" (p. 386). Yet in supervision the intermediate steps that go on silently and almost simultaneously—from new perceptions to the assessment of their relevance to their integration within a specific kind of intelligence—often do not receive specific attention.

The reasons for this lack of attention are many. First, there is no coherent theory of learning to apply to the teaching of psychotherapy or psychoanalysis. As a result, supervisors often do not have available a method of systematically understanding and making use of the different ways of perceiving and knowing they encounter in their students. Second, much of the time the complex interactions between cognitive style and the affective, interpersonal, and narcissistic aspects of personality function silently and relatively smoothly and do not become a specific focus of the supervisor's attention or comments. Modes of learning and knowing are intricately interwoven with personality. Third, supervisors tend to rely on clinical explanations (for example, resistances to affects or ideas, limitations related to character traits or neurosis) to describe issues in learning. The exclusive use of clinical models to explain learning modes, however, can be misleading and incomplete. At times, in particular when there are problems in learning, the trainee's style of learning and thinking become central. In some circumstances it may be most appropriate to conceptualize the learning difficulty in terms of the kind of thinking the trainee uses rather than to relate it immediately to inhibitions or other manifestations of intrapsychic conflict.

If the supervisor looks more closely at the supervisory task in relation to a student's ways of thinking, she is bound to wonder whether certain types of thinking are important to being a therapist and, if so, whether they can be taught. Fleming and Benedek (1966) described different ways of learning—imitative, corrective, and creative—and the supervisor's role in such learning. Our focus in this chapter and the next is on ways of thinking and their relation to learning psychotherapy. Johnson-Laird (1988) has described a typology of thought, from which we have selected four as most relevant to the work of therapy and supervision: (1) inductive thinking, (2) associative thinking, (3) creative thinking, and (4) self-reflective thinking.

Why only four? And why these four? When we consider forms of thought and ways of knowing that seem integral to the ability to be a good therapist, other categories come to mind: intuitive, empathic, imaginative, intersubjective, affective modes of thinking and knowing, to name just a few. We have chosen these four because we believe that they are the most essential forms of thinking necessary to becoming a dynamically oriented psychotherapist; other, secondary forms of thought may be related and may rely upon them. Empathy, for instance, is a complex psychological experience that includes elements of self-reflective, inferential, creative, and associative thought. Intuition, in our view, is a complex and ill-defined concept that involves aspects of induction (inference) based on subliminal, preconscious, or unconscious perceptions. Imaginative and intersubjective ways of gaining and processing information involve combinations of these basic forms of thinking as well. Therapists vary widely in their modes of thought and in the emphasis they give one mode over another. All therapists, however, need to be able to reason, associate, be creative, and be self-reflective to do their work well. Restrictions on the ability to use any of these ways of thinking will limit therapeutic competence.

As we look more carefully at the four principal modes of thought, certain questions may come to mind. Do supervisors assume that trainees inherently possess these modes of thought? If not, can they be taught in supervision? When a supervisor sees evidence of different types of thinking in her student, how do her observations influence the course of learning and the focus of the supervisory dialogue? For example, how might a supervisor approach a student who can gather data and relate them to diagnostic categories but shows little ability to think associatively or to use such thinking to deepen his understanding of his patient? How may a supervisor approach a student who is comfortable using metaphors and analogies to describe the process of therapy but does not use other aspects of inductive reasoning, such as testing of inferences and comparison with data? Stalemates in supervision may arise from a failure to recognize and address the different emphases in modes of thought employed by the teacher and the student. The supervisee's and supervisor's capacity to make use of these four modes of thought in a flexible, productive, and responsive way during therapy and in supervision is an important component of developing competence as a clinician and as a teacher. A supervisor needs to assay the presence or absence and the strength or weakness of these particular modes of thought in her student and in herself. Having done this, she is in a position to try to help the student, when necessary, develop a better balance and increased depth and flexibility in his therapeutic thinking.

Inductive Thought

In supervision, supervisor and supervisee work together to discover and construct meaning and understanding. Both participants use cognitive, affective, and experiential capacities to do this. Intuition, empathy, individual associations, leaps of imagination, and reasoning processes all blend together in the effort to meet, make contact with, and understand the patient. An important aspect of this is the process of induction or inductive reasoning.

Induction can be defined as an inferential process that expands knowledge in the face of uncertainty. Inductive thinking is best explained in relation to deductive reasoning, a process in which a conclusion follows logically from the premises presented, so that the conclusion cannot be false if the premises are true. "If wood comes from trees, and mahogany is wood, then mahogany comes from trees" is an example of simple deductive reasoning. The conclusion drawn is a logical consequence of the propositions put forth.

Induction, by contrast, is a process by which inferences are drawn and new ideas are "built up" prototypically by generalizing from instances. A proposition about a class of phenomena may be established on the basis of observing part of that class. The conclusion arrived at does not necessarily derive from the assumed premises, and there is some degree of probability relative to the premises. "There are cows and goats on the farm. There are many more cows than goats. Therefore, most of the milk the farm produces comes from cows rather than goats" is an example of inferential reasoning. The conclusion has a high probability of being true but is not necessarily so. Inductive thinking, then, draws inferences in order to generate hypotheses that extend one's knowledge. Inferences deal with uncertainty, and good inductive reasoning tries to generate hypotheses that *may be* useful and must be tested in order to select those that *are* useful. Inferences that are useful in a particular domain are guided, in part, by the established knowledge or beliefs in that domain. In the mental health field, part of the knowledge base is that there are conscious mental and emotional states that are, at times, influenced by unconscious psychological forces, by the emergence of medical illness, and by the biochemical status of the body. In reasoning about a particular state of mind, the therapist's ideas and hypotheses are guided by the data base and premises in the domain. He does not, for instance, relate a state of mind to the position of the planets, as an astrologer might.

The use of analogy is a centerpiece in inductive reasoning. Using analogies involves comparing similar relations among objects that also have differences, enabling one to apply knowledge acquired in one domain (the source) to another domain (the target). Thus, in inductive reasoning, if a therapist is at an impasse with a problem (target) and a solution to a different problem (source) occurs to her, she should see if the solution can be applied to the situation with which she is now having trouble. This allows knowledge acquired in one domain (her understanding of psychic conflict as revealed in her own psychotherapy, for instance) to be applied to understanding such conflicts in others.

Induction is, of course, risky. In making inferences, one must take into account the variability that exists in the world and that might render conclusions invalid. If one notices that one's clothes are tight, and the bathroom scale shows a higher number than last week the conclusion "I have therefore gained weight" relies on inductive thinking. But that conclusion is not the only logical one. The clothes, for instance, may have shrunk, or the scale may be broken. The inductive reasoner must try to make inferences that will be meaningful for the discipline in which he operates, must be willing to test new conclusions, and must select those that over time remain useful.

Inductive reasoning in psychotherapy and supervision often operates silently and out of the therapist's awareness. Consider a second-year resident who offered formulations of her patient's dynamics to her supervisor in a tone of confidence and certainty, but left out sufficient details of the therapeutic dialogue so that her supervisor wondered how she arrived at her conclusions and needed to find out whether she would arrive at similar impressions. The supervisor considered whether the trainee's confidence in her formulations came from a thoughtful review of the material, and whether she merely left out some of the steps in her thinking when she described this patient. Alternatively, could she be grasping at some unfounded conclusion based on her own projections or misunderstanding of the patient? At this point, the supervisor's questions have to do with clarifying how and to what degree the therapist uses inductive thinking. She might ask the therapist to support her conclusions with further data from the therapy hour with a remark like, "That is very interesting. How did you arrive at that conclusion?" In so doing, the supervisor attempts to assess the therapist's conclusions while learning about her use of inductive thinking.

We can examine a therapist's faulty use of inductive thinking in the following vignette, in which misleading analogies were drawn. A psychiatric resident was seeing a narcissistically impaired man in twice-weekly psychotherapy, after having treated the patient during several hospitalizations for depression and suicidal wishes. The resident was explicit with his supervisor about some of the similarities he saw between himself and the patient. The patient had demanding parents, with whom he felt constantly inadequate, and strained to win their approval through his performance. The patient, furthermore, devoted much of his attention to the needs of his emotionally distant mother, who did not seem to understand his feelings. He was obsessed with notions of grandiose accomplishments and, unable to fulfill them, had fallen into a life-threatening depression. The resident clearly felt an identification with this patient, especially regarding parental expectations, his high goals for himself, and his experience of fluctuations of mood and self-esteem. On the basis of the similarities between himself and his patient, the resident made some assumptions about what the patient needed and could tolerate in psychotherapy. Specifically, he looked at his own ability to grow and to modify his neurotic conflicts in his personal therapy and inferred by analogy that the patient was ready to confront his deepest conflicts and make a rapid adjustment. This led to the resident's making a series of deep interpretations followed by expectations that his patient would be able to use them and, as a result, perform more maturely in the future. Ironically, this reproduced for the patient the same kind of pressure he was experiencing from his family.

The supervisor helped the resident see that while there may have been some similarities between the patient's difficulties and his own, the patient was a severely impaired young man who had suffered several major depressions, transient psychotic episodes, and serious suicidal wishes. These disturbances were quite far from the experience of the resident, who had a good deal more ego strength and whose problems were essentially of a neurotic nature. The supervisor, over the course of several meetings, helped the resident to readjust his expectations of the patient and to back off from recapitulating in treatment the patient's conflicts with his family. In so doing, he helped the resident gain some relief from the anxiety and expectations engendered by a misleading analogy between himself and his disturbed and struggling patient.

In this situation the supervisory intervention helped the therapist recognize and modify his identification with the patient. It could also be seen as an opportunity for the resident to look at issues of enactment and how they come about in therapy. It could open a discussion with the resident about his own expectations of himself and the demands he felt were being made on him in his training or in the supervision. From the vantage point of cognitive processes and inductive reasoning, however, this can be seen as a problem with analogic thinking. In essence, the resident drew an analogy: "This patient is like me in such and such ways. . . . If he is like me in ways A and B, then perhaps he is like me in ways C and D." He then went on to develop some conviction about his analogy, neglecting its obvious limitations. The result was inaccurate conclusions about the patient and the treatment he required.

One might ask what advantage there is to thinking about this situation from the more abstract vantage point of induction, inference, and analogy rather than in terms of identification, countertransference, enactment, and mastery of technique. These ways of viewing the situation overlap, and we emphasize the use of analogy in this example because such cognitive processes are often overlooked by supervisors, who are more familiar with clinical ways of helping the therapist to understand the treatment and his part in it. The analysis of the therapist's cognitive style and his misuse of analogy can supplement and enlarge his understanding of how his mind works. He may discover, for instance, that he relies heavily on analogies between himself and others as a source of understanding, regardless of the clinical situation. In the process, he may learn to supplement his tendency toward analogic thinking with other methods of observation. In some instances, it may be preferable for the supervisor to address cognitive style first, particularly in situations where the student may experience direct and immediate attention to identification and countertransference as critical, embarrassing, or intrusive. The supervisor's choice of educational intervention will depend on what the supervisee needs to know as well as what he can tolerate.

To address this therapy material as an issue of inference, the supervisor may say: "You inferred that because you and the patient were alike in some ways, he should be like you in other ways. That is not necessarily so." With a more self-revealing, process-oriented resident, the supervisor might opt instead for a more succinct, affective comment on the identification: "You expect the patient to be able to handle things as you would. . . . But you're different."

While the presence or absence of inductive thinking may be noted by the supervisor, the question remains as to how this way of thinking can be fostered in the student. Is it merely part of the natural gifts of any good therapist, or can it be learned? Let us look at a sequence of inferential thinking in order to begin to answer this question. The therapist, in listening to the patient, receives impressions, data, and nonverbal communications. From these, he extracts some meaning: manageable and finite ideas and affects, around which he organizes his thinking and responses to the patient. The therapist seeks patterns in the raw material of the patient's communications and then may attempt to match this to known categories of meaning and experience. If there is a good match, he may form the hypothesis that the present material represents an example of the more general category. This may, in turn, generate new hypotheses and insights, based on what is known about the larger category. These insights are applied back to the clinical situation with, one hopes, a deepening of meaning, understanding, and affect. Finally there is an attempt to assess the validity and value of the new inferences.

The supervisor should look for and make the most of the many opportunities to note the nature and quality of the supervisee's inferential thinking and interferences to its full development. A simple clinical example follows in which we note where the supervisor might intervene in helping the student develop this kind of inductive thinking.

Observation of new data: The supervisee reports that his patient began a therapy session looking distressed and commenting upon how badly her husband had been treating her: he ignored her feelings and played his guitar instead of noticing how depressed she was. Listening to a patient and reporting what one has heard to a supervisor are synthesizing acts. The supervisor has the opportunity to observe how the trainee organizes and synthesizes new data and what cognitive and affective lenses the student is most likely to utilize in making sense of the material presented by his patient. In this example, the supervisor may assess which descriptive categories and contexts (physical appearance, affect, ideational content, sound) are emphasized in the trainee's observing and reporting on the patient's complaint about her husband. What data the therapist collects and what he omits will be influenced by style as well as by inexperience, anxiety, countertransference, distraction, and other elements. What is observed will, in turn, influence the inferences he draws later.

An important educational task for the supervisor that is often overlooked is making the therapist more aware of his own style of listening—the ways in which it is helpful and the ways in which it may limit full observation. Some people have a better ear for the language the patient uses, others a better eye for movement, dress, or facial expression. Some may focus on the life events the patient reports without considering the accompanying affect. Others may be quite attentive to the affect in the patient and themselves but relatively unmindful of other descriptive data about the patient. As an example, a trainee, in describing a patient seen in the emergency room, quite vividly captured the emotional expressiveness, animation, intensity, and lability of the patient but failed to observe aspects of thought disorganization, loose associations, and irrational flow of thinking, which indicated a psychotic (manic) process. There is a clear role for the supervisor in bringing to the student's attention the manner in which he has observed and presented new data.

By making the trainee aware of his style of listening, the supervisor inevitably models basic modes of listening and observing. Once the trainee understands that the supervisor is listening for affect and intrapsychic conflict and not only for the events in a patient's narrative, for example, the therapist's own way of listening may change, influencing what data he observes and regards as relevant.

Abstraction of patterns: The therapist begins to organize the data he has collected into larger, more generalized patterns. In the example of the patient with the guitar-playing husband, these patterns may include this patient's proclivity to experience herself as a victim and present numerous examples of mistreatment, the possibility that her husband is typically insensitive to her emotional needs, or the possibility that the story is an implicit request for the therapist's sympathy or direct help in her outside life. Furthermore, her complaint about not being understood may be a reference to her feelings not only about her husband but about her therapist as well. Therapist and supervisor step back from the immediacy of the patient's story to consider what is familiar, repetitive, or thematic in it: how it is related to other material, and the reason for its communication by the patient at this time. The therapist may need help in recognizing such patterns or in seeing how he fails to identify them. Limitations in pattern recognition may stem from inexperience, overinvolvement with the patient's immediate experience, or an inhibition based on the feeling that such analysis is judgmental or disloyal to the patient. Some supervisees tend to see larger patterns too quickly (or too personally) as a way of dealing with anxiety and uncertainty. The supervisor may help the therapist to see when he could or ought to ask the patient to make some larger sense of what has been said. The supervision (shaped by the theoretical orientation of each participant) can help to develop forms of pattern recognition that are relevant and useful to the therapy.

Match to known categories: After the therapist has found larger descriptive classifications for the data, he tries to match them to known categories of human behavior. The therapist may have in mind an established formulation of the dynamics of masochism that corresponds to the data of the example. The data may also match the therapist's observations that many husbands are, in fact, oblivious to their wives' feelings. The therapist also has a concept that a patient's explicit communications often convey implicit or unconscious feelings about her treatment, such as a request for help or covert hostility. The current data seems well matched to all of these categories. It does not match other categories, such as the fact that people are capable of hallucinations.

Relating the material the patient presents to known or newly created categories in order to discover or construct meaning is the bread and butter of supervision. The supervisor has a series of categories in mind, including clinical models, hypotheses, theories, groupings of character types, groupings of defenses, models of intrapsychic and interpersonal functioning, to name a few. In the language of inductive reasoning, applying known categories to the clinical material represents the use of *domain-specific* knowledge. For example, a patient's behavior within the structure of psychotherapy (actions regarding time, money, cancellations, and so on) is viewed as revealing important information about the patient's feelings toward the therapy and the therapist. This idea, once adopted, attunes one's listening and organizes further listening.

The development of meaningful associations is a dialectic between supervisor and supervisee. The latter may think of patterns and categories that have not occurred to the supervisor, and vice versa. The supervisor brings to this process experience, a fund of information, familiarity with theory, and a distance from the immediate clinical situation that allows for a different perspective on the material. In the above example, the supervisor may feel that the patient's frequent stories about being mistreated involve (along with some likely reality) an attempt to evoke a certain response in the therapist (sympathy, rescue, validation of anger, restitution). If the therapist is identified with the patient in a way that makes this view of the material seem unsympathetic to the patient, there may be an obstacle to his understanding the material more deeply.

Inference and hypothesis formation: All construction of meaning and interpretation in psychotherapy involves the formation of hypotheses about the material the patient presents. In our example, the therapist infers that the patient is experiencing herself in some internally important way as a victim and speculates about the intrapsychic dynamics and external circumstances that give this position prominence in the patient's mind. The therapist's belief that the patient's husband treats her as she describes leads him to hypotheses about why the patient may have selected such a partner. The therapist may infer from past experience with her that if he does not respond sympathetically to the patient, she is likely to feel further hurt and misunderstood. He concludes that the patient is feeling most in need of sympathy, support, and validation of her pain.

Therapists' and supervisors' views vary widely on such issues as how much material one needs to support a hypothesis, how bold or cautious to be in making tentative inferences, and how much certainty to feel about one's own formulations. Schwaber (1992) has pointed out the dangers of the therapist being the formulator of hypotheses for the patient and the arbiter of reality. She points out how the analyst often does not pay careful enough attention to the vantage point and experience of the patient, replacing inquiry into the patient's way of knowing and feeling with his own inferences and hypotheses. A supervisor may also impose her own formulations upon the supervisee rather than inquire about his experience of his patient.

Because there is no clear agreement in the field as to the nature of evidence and the criteria for verification of hypotheses, each supervisory pair negotiates these issues, as the trainee constructs a psychological picture of the patient. Some problems the supervisee may present at this step in the thinking process include excessive literalness (a relative inability or unwillingness to draw inferences from the data), lack of imagination, and a rigid adherence to a particular way of hearing the material. The therapist may be reluctant to formulate or interpret at all, as if doing so were a betrayal of the relationship with the patient. Or, having made inferences, the therapist may be reluctant to expose them to the supervisor or patient. The supervisor's input at this juncture can be valuable in several ways that permit the student not to have to know for certain but to be able to wonder freely. With the literal-minded trainee, the supervisor may allow that the manifest data is important, but demonstrate how imaginative, flexible, and appropriately tentative inferences may also be made. In the case of the trainee whose rigid adherence to established hypotheses seems to limit what he can hear, the supervisor may inquire further about how the trainee arrived at a hypothesis and what data have been used. By emphasizing further exploration of the therapist's thinking and experiences without coming to any conclusion, the supervisor models curiosity and shows the trainee how he can explore different perspectives with a patient while suspending closure on "meaning." Where therapist and supervisee reach different inferences (that the husband really is mean or that the patient is intent on being a victim), they have an opportunity to suspend judgment and to ask one another what constitutes evidence and on what data each builds his or her hypothesis. They may, for a while, agree to disagree.

After clinical observations and hypotheses are formed about the patient, they will generate further inferences. For example, if the trainee formulates that the patient tends to view herself primarily as victim and organizes self and object representations to reflect this view, he may have a hunch that she chooses partners who will confirm her view of herself, or that she selectively sees aspects of her partner that validate her view. Perhaps she behaves in such a way with her partner so as to bring about her suffering (a form of repetition compulsion). This is an elaboration of the hypothesis based on the patient's material and on what has been learned from other patients with similar difficulties. The supervisor's experience and fund of theory and clinical skill may help in predicting which direction may prove most fruitful and how the hypotheses may best be extended. One way a supervisor may help extend observations and hypotheses derived from them is to teach domain-specific *inferential rules,* such as: "If you hear a central conflict in the patient's life and history, you may expect it to appear in the transference and should be ready to listen for it." This inferential rule is a general hypothesis designed to guide listening and inference formation.

Ideally, hypotheses are formed and extended not only *about* the patient but also *with* the patient. The supervisor and therapist should be aware of how much "ahead" of the patient their hypotheses may be, and how these may preclude, as Schwaber (1992) suggests, staying close to the patient's experience or inquiring into the patient's own hypotheses about her own dynamics and those of others, including her therapist.

Application to the clinical situation: The therapist decides how to respond to the patient on the basis of his experiences with and hypotheses about the patient. In the case discussed here, he may choose among offering an empathic remark about the patient's experience of feeling rejected by her husband, asking further about her experience with her husband, or interpreting to the patient that it may be easier for her to complain about her husband than to state her feelings about her therapist. The therapist's assessment of what the patient is ready to hear and bear will influence timing.

The trainee may often feel there is a right response that he can learn from his supervisor. This notion can be reinforced by the supervisor's too frequent reference to what she would have said to the patient—the implication being that she would have made a better choice than the supervisee. The supervisor can be more helpful if she inquires about the thinking and feeling behind the trainee's decision to intervene as he did. She can also help the therapist understand that in order to determine the effect of his intervention, he must listen carefully and try to understand his patient's response to it. This can help the trainee understand that clinical hypotheses and interpretations arise not from theoretical knowledge of human psychology alone, but from the developing dialogue between patient and therapist.

Assessing the hypotheses: In the vignette described, the therapist looks for further evidence of his hypotheses about his patient. The final step in inductive reasoning is the testing of hypotheses: validating, refuting, or modifying them in the light of additional data. A supervisor, upon being told of a dream reported by this patient, may point out, for instance, how the dream refers to aspects of the transference in which the patient feels mistreated by the therapist. Whether the supervisor's statement is taken (by the supervisor or the trainee) as the truth about the situation, as the supervisor's association to the dream (which may or may not prove useful), or as a hypothesis to be tested depends on how the two have decided, consciously or unconsciously, to construct meaning together.

Potential problems are many. At one end of the spectrum is the supervisee who finds no meaning in any formulation offered by the supervisor that goes beyond the concrete manifest content. Such a student, concerned with a stringent test of empirical evidence, may remain skeptical and require of the supervisor, as Freud (1915) described, "the logic of soup, with dumplings for arguments" (p. 167). At the other end of the spectrum is the supervisee whose anxiety about the learning situation puts him in awe of the wisdom of the supervisor; any word from her is taken as gospel, written down, memorized, and dutifully applied and reapplied well beyond its usefulness. In supervision, the two participants must work out together, sometimes through explicit discussion, what they consider to be the nature of psychotherapeutic knowledge. The supervisor will be most useful when she is neither stifled by a radical empiricist critique from the trainee nor entranced by her own inductive thinking because of an unquestioning and idealizing adherent. The student can learn best when he feels free to express his own way of gathering evidence and creating hypotheses, openly comparing it with his supervisor's method.

Problems in Inductive Thought

Having sketched but one simple sequence for inductive reasoning and suggested some supervisory interventions, we will indicate several problems that may arise in inductive reasoning. First, there may be obstacles to observing relevant data from which to make inferences. The therapist may be distracted by anxiety, daydreaming, inattention, or other preoccupations that interfere with hearing the patient. Or the therapist may be so uneasy with the patient's affects that he is reluctant to recognize them. A patient may express overt hostility toward the therapist, who eagerly focuses on some other aspect of the patient's communication, overlooking the affect. The supervisor can help clarify the patient's feeling and the therapist's response. She may choose a Socratic approach, asking the trainee what he feels has led to such an interaction. Or she may take the opportunity to explain countertransference feelings and their use in treatment.

Second, some trainees are quite literal in their thinking, show little natural ability to benefit from analogies, and rarely respond to metaphors. Such students are usually constricted in their ability to associate freely to the patient's material. This constriction limits responsivity to the patient and generation of analogies or metaphors. If the therapist's talent and his imagination seem limited, the supervisor may try to expand associative processes and promote inductive reasoning—showing by example how to associate to the patient's material and draw hypotheses from it. By bringing to the material presented associations from her own clinical work, her own life experience, and literature or films, the supervisor indicates how analogy and inductive thinking can enrich understanding. Or the supervisor may discuss more openly the trainee's understanding of how evidence is gathered and hypotheses are made. If these approaches do not lead to a change, and if the therapist's constrictions in associating and making inferences have been noted by other supervisors and teachers, then the supervisor may consider recommending psychotherapy or psychoanalysis for the therapist. At times a supervisee's way of listening to and thinking about patients is severely limited and does not respond to supervision, teaching, and personal treatment. In this case, the trainee may not be suited to do psychotherapy and should be encouraged to pursue other interests.

The supervisee's readiness to think inductively may also be constricted by the supervision itself. When the supervisor comments on her own formulations about the patient without explaining how she arrived at them, she may stifle inferential thinking by the trainee. To avoid taking on the appearance of a visionary, the supervisor can encourage the therapist to think inductively by explaining her own inferences and the reasoning behind them.

A different extreme is the supervisee who rushes into suppositions about the patient that seem without foundation, confusing such assumptions with inductive thinking. Here the supervisor may help him to distinguish between inductive thinking, which grows out of collecting and categorizing data, and intuitive suppositions that may be only loosely connected to the material. At the heart of the trainee's rush to interpretation is often a fear of not knowing. By asking for more information and presenting alternate hypotheses based on a careful review of the clinical data, the supervisor demonstrates that an attitude of curiosity and questioning can be helpful and that ambiguity in the supervision, as well as in the therapeutic situation, can be tolerated.

Another problem can arise when supervisor and supervisee both use inductive thinking well, but start from different premises and thereby reach different conclusions. When there are significant differences, it is important that they be aired and a way of considering one another's arguments reached. Dick (1987), for instance, in her supervision with Dewald wondered if he approved of her wish to learn more about self-psychology. Dewald apparently neither censured her interest nor discussed his own views of self-psychology. Dick's uncertainty implies that she did not know what ideal model of treatment or learning her supervisor was using. While Dewald's neutral pedagogic stance may have been intended to enable the student to develop her own notions without interference, it may, as Skolnikoff (in press) has suggested, have subtly dissuaded the supervisee from further expression of her interest. A more active engagement around the supervisee's attempts to explore her own analytic theories and their relation to the supervisor's way of thinking might have, in this instance, been fruitful.

In most ongoing therapy, inferences operate silently. From talking with supervisors and reviewing the literature, it is our impression that the analysis of inductive thinking is rarely a topic of explicit attention between supervisor and supervisee, yet inferential decisions are constantly being negotiated between the two. Noting how supervisor and supervisee arrive at their inferences and understanding how differences in their methods of induction may influence their dialogue are central to good supervision.

In this section we have described inductive thinking and reviewed some basic inductive processes that are relevant to psychotherapy supervision. This discussion has emphasized a cognitive approach to patient material, yet we do not mean to imply that inductive thinking is the only or the dominant approach to understanding patients. In fact, inductive thinking alone—employed logically, "objectively"—may be used defensively by a therapist to avoid associations, imagination, affect, or fantasies. Such an overly cognitive approach is less likely if the student also employs associative thinking.

Associative Thinking

Associative thinking is the joining of one thought with another without an immediate conscious goal, in contradistinction to, for example, problem solving or story telling. Associations are often fleeting and involuntary, weaving threads of thought, feeling, memory, fantasy, and meaning into the larger fabric of subjective experience. In listening to associations, we can follow the flow of thought (what the mind is doing) but often cannot understand the process (how or why the flow develops as it does). Daydreams, stream-of-consciousness thinking, automatic writing, less organized fantasies, and sleeping dreams are conspicuous versions of associative thought. Many other forms of thinking rely on more subtle and unacknowledged use of this thought process.

The nature of associative thinking received a new and revolutionary reconsideration in Freud's work. One of his greatest contributions was to extend the search for the understanding of associative links beyond conscious awareness and into the realm of the unconscious. This exploration began with *Studies on Hysteria* (1893–95), in which Breuer and Freud felt that following a patient's associations would lead them to the revelations of memories and ideas that, through repression and dissociation from their affective component, had become pathogenic.

> The pathogenic idea which has ostensibly been forgotten is always lying ready "close at hand" and can be reached by associations that are easily accessible. It is merely a question of getting some obstacle out of the way. This obstacle seems once again to be the subject's will, and different people can learn with different degrees of ease to free themselves from their intentional thinking and to adopt an attitude of completely objective observation towards the psychical processes taking place in them. . . . It is much more frequent for an idea to emerge which is an intermediate link in the associations between the ideal from which we start and the pathogenic idea we are in search of. (p. 271)

The concept that meaning extends to what is "forgotten," into the unconscious and back again to conscious thought, behavior, and symptoms was a central tenet of early psychoanalytic theory. Freud proposed that associative thinking, what Breuer's patient Anna O. called "chimney sweeping," is not random but is ordered and dynamic, based on wish, fear, conflict, and the interplay of conscious and unconscious forces. While Freud used "free association" as a technique for the recovery of lost, repressed, and dissociated memories, more recent thinkers such as Kris (1982) have emphasized the ability to free-associate not merely as a technique for the retrieval of repressed affects and ideas but as a therapeutic goal in itself.

Therapists pay close attention to patients' associations, using them as a primary source of data in trying to understand the patients. Therapists' own associations while listening to patients are another source of vital information. The supervisor, therefore, should be sensitive as to how and to what degree her student uses associations, his own and his patient's, in the course of therapy and supervision. The supervisor will also have to decide in any teaching session whether concentration on the associations of the patient or on those of the therapist best serves her pedagogic purpose. Some supervisors believe that the therapist's own associations, reflections, unexpected fantasies, and marginal thoughts are central and revealing pieces of information. Others hold that information about patients should come largely from the clinical material. The therapist's excessive interest in his own reactions and associations can result in sloppy thinking, countertransference distortion, misidentification of the sources of conflict, and projection.

Nevertheless, the capacity to make use of associative thinking—one's own and one's patient's—and to find a proper balance between the two is a critical and central element in psychotherapeutic competence. How does the therapist-in-training learn about and develop his use of associative thinking as one aspect of his overall competence? By asking the supervisee questions that directly or indirectly encourage the use of association, by associating to some material herself as a way of modeling, and by explicitly explaining, when necessary, the concept of associative thinking and why it is important, the supervisor can assess the trainee's flexibility in exercising such thinking and help him expand his capabilities in this area.

Evaluating Associative Thinking

Assessment of the trainee's capacity for and uses of associative thinking goes on silently and continuously in the course of supervision, although it may not always be the supervisor's primary concern. Psychodynamic supervisors are familiar with students who present material from a therapeutic hour accompanied by rich and varied associations: a memory stimulated by what the patient said, some feeling evoked, a comparison made to another patient, and so on. In contrast, some supervisees present material in a more literal, constricted way, offering little beyond the recorded process notes. They appear so bound to literal description that a marginal thought or fantasy would seem anathema. Still another type of therapist begins associating so freely that the patient seems only the increasingly distant stimulus for his outpourings. Such students require guidance and structure in carefully observing the patients, describing what they see, and building diagnostic formulations.

Differences in the use of associative thinking are noted by the supervisor regardless of whether or not she chooses to make them the explicit focus of attention. If associative thinking becomes an area of more conscious and focused attention, then she may begin to organize her assessment by asking herself: Does the therapist attend to and communicate marginal thoughts or fantasies? Does he bring in thoughts about other therapeutic experiences, life experiences, visual images, or jokes? How comfortable is he relating responses of a self-revealing nature? Do they seem to embarrass him? Is the quality of his associative thinking related to whether or not he is in therapy or analysis himself? How safe does the supervisee feel in the supervisory situation? What are his beliefs about how supervision should proceed? Is the supervisor doing something with this particular supervisee that either fosters or inhibits associative thinking? Situations in which the trainee presents material and the supervisor explains "what it means" bypass the trainee's own associative responses and deny him the opportunity to wrestle with the material and find his own meaning in it.

Teaching Associative Thinking

Teaching the value of listening to associations often involves the willingness of the supervisor to demonstrate her own associative capacity and its usefulness. This may be particularly important at a time when the stress on pragmatic, time-limited approaches to patients' problems (brief treatments and psychopharmacology, for instance) makes paying attention to the patient's associations seem a luxury at best or old-fashioned at worst. Nevertheless, as the vignette below suggests, the interplay of shared associations between supervisor and supervisee can add richness, creativity, and depth to the dialogue and demonstrate to the supervisee the usefulness of associative thinking.

Dr. Y., a first-year psychiatry resident working on an acute, unlocked, inpatient unit came to supervision one day weary and discouraged by the conflicting pressures upon him. He was expected, he felt, to try to understand his patients in some depth while, at the same time, arrange for their rapid discharge and disposition. He spoke of a middle-aged, obese patient with a history of physical and sexual abuse and of chronic depression who had become increasingly suicidal prior to admission. The instructions to Dr. Y. upon picking up this patient had been "Let's keep this to a ten-day admission; she'll be impossible to get out of the hospital."

With this mandate in mind, the resident attempted to avoid a "regressive" hospitalization by focusing on concrete goals that would allow for rapid discharge. In immediately narrowing his focus to the logistics of discharge and aftercare, Dr. Y. tried to minimize his attention to the patient's associations and increased feelings of distress. The patient countered by enumerating a large number of somatic complaints and expressing anger at the staff for not providing her with relief from them. The resident, feeling increasingly frustrated, pressured, and annoyed by the patient as well as by the mandate for her rapid discharge, confronted the patient by saying that he could not possibly evaluate all her somatic complaints and asked what was the real problem. He did not, at the time, recognize that part of the problem was his own failure to listen carefully and associatively to her complaints. The patient's outside therapist told the patient that her anger and complaints were related to her feelings about the impending discharge. This contributed to the patient's bellowing at the resident: "Fuck you and fuck the hospital." As the date for discharge approached, the patient reported that she was "not safe," and Dr. Y. arranged to transfer her to a locked unit.

In discussing the case in supervision, the resident's main concern was about the appropriateness of the transfer. Had he done something wrong that allowed so much regression? Had he been overly focused on discharge and insufficiently attentive to what had led to the patient's hospitalization? He appeared frustrated, angry, and self-critical. The supervisor did not answer the resident's questions directly, modeling an approach that did not reach a conclusion right away. Instead, he chose through a less direct question to begin to focus the trainee on his own associations to and feelings about his patient. He asked what the patient looked like. Dr. Y. provided a vivid association: she was like a slug. When she came to his office, she lay back in the chair, her large body overflowing, melting, and oozing into it. He felt no motivation from the patient other than a wish to blend into the upholstery. Her posture and disposition revived feelings in the therapist that working on the inpatient service was like tending a "slug farm." As he listened, the supervisor had the fantasy of trying to get a slug to move by poking it from the rear with a stick. He told the resident of his own association.

The association to a slug, which was initially presented by the supervisee and then further elaborated upon by the supervisor, had several effects. There was an immediate increase in the energy and animation of the supervisory discussion. The comical image of the slug allowed some mobilization and expression of the therapist's anger toward the patient and relieved some of his tension. The image also helped focus the discussion on several aspects of the patient's feelings and behavior: her passivity, the fear that kept her from being more active, her reluctance to take responsibility for her fate, the formlessness of her requests for help, the lack of clarity about her intentions, as well as the use of her body to express her poor and confused sense of herself. The slug image also captured some of the issues about aggression. The supervisor's fantasy of poking the slug captured the aggression mobilized against her by Dr. Y. and the staff. The supervisor re-created in fantasy the history of the patient's physical and sexual abuse, and this led to the realization by both supervisor and supervisee that some aspects of the patient's earlier experiences were being reenacted on the unit. Her "sluggish" behavior might unconsciously invite being prodded and retraumatized. *Slug* also means "to punch," further echoing the aggression the patient had experienced as a child, which was now being reenacted between therapist and patient.

As Dr. Y. and his supervisor discussed these varied meanings of the slug image, it became clear to both of them that the resident himself had felt prodded. He was struggling with what he felt to be the implicit demand that he be omniscient—able to foresee what the patient's condition would be after ten days of hospitalization—and omnipotent—able to guarantee that her condition would be nonregressed on that day. It also became apparent to the resident that, given the severity of the patient's illness and the constraints on his own therapeutic efforts, her transfer to a locked unit had been appropriate. The staff could not control her condition on a given day, but there were actions they could take.

Dr. Y. then had another association, a thought of how another supervisor had suggested saying to a distraught patient, "How awful it must be not to feel that your needs are being met." This last association, to a more empathic position, was a sign to the supervisor that the trainee had worked through his initially irritated, frustrated, and self-doubting position to a sufficient degree that he was allowing himself greater flexibility of response toward the patient and himself.

The use of associative thinking in this instance was facilitated by the supervisor's simple question, which initially directed the trainee's attention to a visual image (the patient's appearance) rather than a cognitive explanation. The supervisor's question opened the door to freer associations by the therapist. His visual response and the supervisor's subsequent nonjudgmental discussion of it enabled Dr. Y. to gain greater psychological distance from the frustrating immediacy of his situation and to begin to develop increased empathy for the patient and for himself. It may have also taught him to value his associations and showed him how he could work with them for his own and his patient's benefit. All this might have been lost if the supervisor had chosen to answer directly Dr. Y.'s question about whether or not he should have transferred the patient.

Associative thinking is, of course, the fabric of all thought. Supervisees and supervisors associate one thought to another or are reminded by a comment of some forgotten but important detail of a therapy session. The supervisor can encourage attention to what seem like marginal or irrelevant thoughts and fantasies in order to develop fresh responses to a clinical situation. Associations often lead to recall of details about the patient that have been overlooked or in other ways unintegrated by the therapist into his growing understanding of his patient. Associations, furthermore, may reveal to a therapist his own countertransferences, fantasies, affects, and memories, which can be important sources of information about the current therapeutic encounter. The supervisor can help the trainee understand that one's own fantasies are often responses to subliminal cues, such as preconscious and unconscious communications from the patient. As such they provide valuable information that may be missed if the therapist's responses to the patient are limited to logical, secondary-process thinking.

Supervisory Interventions

If the student seems limited in the capacity to use associations, the supervisor may employ direct questioning, modeling, positive reinforcement, and didactic explanation to demonstrate the utility of this kind of thinking and encourage the supervisee to begin to use it. Asking questions to stimulate associations or images is an obvious place to begin. The supervisor could simply ask, "What did that bring to mind?" or "When the patient was describing her suicidal ideas, did any visual image come to mind?" Or: "Does that session remind you of any other session you had with this or another patient?"

The supervisor may model the associative approach by demonstrating her own use of associations to the material presented. "Let me tell you what this makes me think of . . ." (including images, fantasies, and incomplete fragments of thought) conveys the supervisor's willingness and capacity to be creative, spontaneous, and associative. It demonstrates for the supervisee how such associations can lead to new information and new hypotheses about the patient and the therapeutic dialogue. It sets the tone for what is permissible yet it does not suggest that the supervisor is there to produce perfectly synthesized and illuminating insights, nor that she expects the same from the supervisee. Instead, she invites the trainee to join her in the use of associative thinking to probe and deepen understanding of the therapeutic situation they are discussing.

In some instances, the supervisor may use a more cognitive approach, explaining the value of associations directly to the therapist: how marginal thoughts that seem irrelevant, silly, incongruous, or even irreverent may be invaluable clues to some level of understanding of the patient-therapist relationship not captured in more organized descriptions. The value of associations—the patient's and the therapist's—can be explained. In a situation where the trainee seems rigidly literal, the supervisor may bring this cognitive style to his attention, helping him to evaluate what this style helps him understand and what, including associative thinking, it may leave out.

Channeling Associative Thinking

Although the supervisor can encourage the therapist's associative thinking in the ways described, she must also be aware of the boundaries that supervision imposes. Supervision is not psycho-therapy, and the privacy of the therapist's thoughts, feelings, and fantasies must be respected. Therapists, beginning therapists in particular, often feel embarrassment, guilt, or shame over their angry, rejecting, erotic, or loving responses to patients. They are often relieved by the supervisor's nonjudgmental acceptance of such feelings. Yet the supervisor needs to limit her exploration of the therapist's fantasies and feelings to what is pedagogically (rather than therapeutically) useful. Many times during supervision, the supervisee needs something quite different from the supervisor than an open-ended invitation to associate. Both supervisor and supervisee need to understand, furthermore, that the use of associative thinking in supervision differs in important ways from the free association encouraged in psychoanalysis and psychotherapy. Respect for privacy and a clear pedagogical goal create significant constraints on the types of association that are helpful and appropriate in supervision, as in the situation described below.

A bright, charming, and loquacious trainee entered his supervisor's office located in a teaching hospital, stating that it was hard for him to come because his analyst (a woman) was away. Because the supervisor's office was in the same building, attending supervisory sessions only increased his feelings about his analyst's absence. He was tempted, he said, to use the hour for therapy but felt it unwise to do so. The boundaries would be blurred even more than he felt they already were, given the fact that he usually saw his supervisor right before his analytic hour. The supervisor said nothing. The supervisee then stated, with some anxiety, that he had "kind of fallen in love" with a female patient, someone who had recently come to him and whom he was considering taking on in treatment. He was distressed by his feelings, claiming that there was no sexual attraction, merely that they had a lot of interests in common. Hardly stopping to take a breath, he reported that the coat rack in the supervisor's waiting room reminded him of a penis and the white coat hanging on it, of semen. He then went on to tell of some childhood sexual experiences that might be related to these perceptions.

These associations and the memories that followed initially raised some anxiety in the supervisor. It seemed that the distinction between free association on the couch and its use in supervision was becoming less and less clear to the student. The supervisor was also aware that some supervisees are tempted to convert the unknown of supervision into the known of psychotherapy in order to reduce their sense of ignorance and incompetence in a new learning situation. The supervisor also wondered if the trainee had transferred to her, and to the patient, certain sexual and loving feelings that had been aroused in his relationship with his analyst. The supervisee went on to say that he liked coming to supervision, liked the supervisor, but was afraid that when he liked someone things could get out of control. He wondered whether he was cut out to work with patients and whether it might be too intense for him.

At this point, the supervisor, who had been silent, felt a need to help the trainee more actively to structure the supervision experience. She chose not to explore how matters might get further out of control in supervision, fearing that deeper exploration of the supervisee's fantasies might further blur the distinction between a therapeutic and a supervisory task. Instead, the supervisor told the student that his feelings and the associations that accompanied them in the supervisory hour were important and could be examined in his own analysis in terms of what further he might learn about himself, his capacities to be a therapist, and his own dynamics, but they could also be useful in supervision. They might help him better understand what was going on in his patient and how he chose, as a therapist, to address them. The supervisor then asked him, quite deliberately, to describe the sessions with the patient to whom he was attracted in an attempt to direct the trainee's attention toward his feelings and associations in the context of his training to become a therapist. She did this without inquiring further about his own history or personal experiences outside his work.

As the supervisory hour proceeded, it became clear that the female patient had acted in a manner that appeared very seductive to the trainee, her behavior stemming from the deepest need for attention and love, a feeling with which the student admitted he was acquainted. The challenge for the supervisor in this situation was not to judge or suppress the student's expression of his associations, feelings, and attempts at self-inquiry but, instead, to show him how they could be used to further develop his therapeutic skills. For instance, his feelings could be used to study what the patient was doing to elicit his responses and why. The supervisee began to learn, during this supervisory hour, that the availability to him of strong and surprising affects and associated memories and fantasies could cause him to feel confused and without sufficient boundaries, yet they could serve him well in his development as a therapist if he could learn to use them professionally as part of his analyzing capacity. He might, through his feelings of having fallen in love, his associations to a penis, and his own childhood memories, begin to study the origins of his patient's intense need for love and admiration, how it became entwined in her fantasy life and object relations, and where it impeded her further development. Help for this supervisee in containing and using his affects and associations to further his therapeutic capacities would have to come from his own analysis as well as his ongoing work with supervisors.

The supervisor also had to explore what in her own responses to the supervisee might be stimulating his associations. Was she in some way being subtly seductive, or overstimulating, or too silent and not structuring enough? Had her silence at the beginning of the supervisory hour, for instance, added to the confusion in the student's mind between supervision and his personal analysis? As Casement (1993) points out, supervisors need to bear in mind what their own contribution may be to the difficulties experienced by the student.

This situation illustrates how associative thinking can begin to go awry in supervision. When this happens, the primary danger is unwarranted intrusion into the private life of the supervisee, confusing therapeutic and supervisory functions. This could have been the case, for instance, if the fantasies of how things might get out of control when the trainee liked someone were explored or if the supervisor asked the student to elaborate on his own childhood sexual experiences. Following these avenues would breach the boundaries of supervision and violate the therapist's privacy. Although supervision may shed some light on the supervisee's unconscious conflicts, it is not the instrument through which they can be resolved. The use of associative thinking in supervision should not lead to excessive self-exposure on the part of the student. Within the limits determined by the supervisee's comfort level and the potential utility for further understanding the patient, the use of associative thinking can be helpful as long as it is always within the framework of the educational goal to understand the patient and to teach the therapist.

Another danger is too exclusive a focus on the therapist's subjective experience, to the neglect of careful observation of, and attention to, the patient. The trainee, in the situation described above, needs to distinguish over time what in his associations is revelatory about the patient, and what is revelatory about himself or about his relations with others (including transference to his analyst) that may be displaced onto his patient or his supervisor. These distinctions may be pursued in his own thoughts or in personal therapy or analysis, but supervision provides an appropriate setting for some therapists to express and work with associations. Whatever thoughts, associations, fantasies, and affective reactions one has in response to a patient may lead to important insights and speculations. These responses, however, must be tested against other forms of data derived from careful observations of the patient's appearance, body movements, behaviors in the office, and tone, content, and patterns of speech, among other aspects. The therapist who focuses exclusively on his own associations and impressions, as this trainee seemed to be doing, will need help in developing a better eye and ear for what the patient is doing and saying, so that he can construct a more complex picture of his patient. The supervisor in this case, aware of the supervisee's associative propensity, deliberately asked him to describe what had transpired in his therapy hour with his patient. In addition, the supervisor could have encouraged the trainee to bring in detailed process notes as a way of helping him to focus more on therapeutic process and less on his own associations, which seemed at times not tied to keen observation and careful description of the patient.

In allowing some loosening from secondary-process, linear, and purely descriptive modes of thinking, associative thinking expands the breadth and depth of available data: preconscious threads of memory are expressed, the potential for metaphor is enhanced, and more primary-process connections—nonverbal and nonlinear forms of experience—are made available to the therapist. The availability of these associations, in turn, helps increase the capacity for inductive thinking by expanding the source pool for analogies and producing images and ideas that contribute to hypothesis formation. The therapist's associations to his own thoughts, feelings, memories, and associated affects become an integral component of both self-reflective and creative thinking. From these associations, the therapist, with the help of his supervisor, faces the task of constructing new images, ideas, and formulations about himself and his patient. He is called upon to synthesize his associations and observations in new and creative ways. It is these tasks of creative and self-reflective thinking, and the supervisor's role in their development, to which we now turn our attention.

4

Creative and Self-Reflective Modes of Thought

In chapter 3 we suggested that four modes of thinking are particularly relevant to psychotherapy and supervision, and we explored two of these—inductive and associative thought. We now turn to a consideration of the other two—creative and self-reflective thinking.

Creative Thinking

Supervision involves a curious kind of co-construction. One participant is regularly seeing the patient and forming an image of him and his ways of thinking, feeling, and behaving. The other, the supervisor, largely hears about the patient, yet participates in constructing a portrait of the patient and his interaction with the therapist. The accuracy of the picture that is slowly built up during supervision is always open to question, for the experience of the therapeutic hour under discussion has been described through the highly selective filter of the therapist's narrative and then refiltered through the supervisor's sensibilities and the subsequent supervisory discourse. In this process what has "happened" is recorded and re-created.

What "reality" is addressed during supervision: that of the patient, the therapist, or the supervisor? The patient, were he present, would surely tell the story differently than the therapist. Truth is being told by the supervisee with facts to back it up, but the teller constructs that truth and chooses the facts. Supervision inevitably is, at heart, a creative, imaginative activity. With what freshness, flexibility, clear-sightedness, humility, and relevance it proceeds will have a profound effect on the educational experience of the student.

Winnicott (1951), describing transitional objects and transitional phenomena, writes: "This intermediate area of experience, unchallenged in respect of its belonging to inner or external (shared) reality, constitutes the greater part of the infant's experience and throughout life is retained in the intense experiencing that belongs to the arts and to religion and to imaginative living, and to creative scientific work" (p. 242). Pruyser (1979) applies Winnicott's ideas to a study of creativity, using the terms *third world* and *illusionistic world* to designate this area between "the inner, subjective, private world . . . [and] the outer, objective commonsensically verified world" (p. 318). This area is comprised of "tutored fantasy . . . orderly imagination . . . verbalizable images . . . cultural needs . . . symbols . . . playing . . . [and] creativeness" (p. 318).

Fleming (1987), a pioneer in the study of psychoanalytic supervision, referred to Pruyser's third world in discussing the supervisory dialogue in order to capture the space in which illusion, metaphor, symbolism, and construction lie. Fleming believed that in learning to be a psychoanalyst it is essential to inhabit the third world and become comfortable with ambiguity, uncertainty, and transitional phenomena. The third world floats between the relativism of subjective knowledge and objective knowledge. Patients' communications, furthermore, are a blend of history and fantasy (as are those of the supervisee). The therapist's formulations, as well as the supervisor's, are constructed meaning that refer to, but are not the same as, the reality to which they point. In Fleming's view, teaching involves bringing the student into this transitional world. Inhabiting the world of illusion, construction, and imagination is a component of creativity in any field.

Suspension of reality and the use of metaphor and illusion apply to the process of exploration of problems in any domain, no matter how concrete and tangible they appear. In psychotherapy, the patient's words and the therapist's responses are inseparable from the third world. The stuff of the human psyche (meaning, affect, self-representations, identity, self, beliefs, values, and personal narrative truth) and its symbolic expression in language are constructed of transitional, illusory, and imagined, as well as real elements.

In Fleming's view teaching involves helping the student understand and appreciate the transitional third world in which much of psychodynamic therapy and supervision is focused. The therapist faces the inescapable necessity of learning how to immerse himself in this transitional space where—as Winnicott (1951) noted in writing about the transitional object—one will not ask "Did you conceive of this or was it presented to you from without?" (pp. 239–240). The therapist slowly learns that he cannot listen only with an objective ear, trying to capture some empirical "truth" about the patient. Nor can he listen only subjectively, as therein lie the perils of projection, overidentification, and imposition of one's own meaning on the patient's experience. He must learn to oscillate between these states. At times, he is predominantly the observer, at other times, through empathy and imagination, a participant in his patient's emotional experience. Sometimes it is his own memories and affects that demand the most attention. This flexible and shifting endeavor can lead to new understanding of the psychic life of the patient and of the therapist, as well as fresh and creative interpretations of what is going on between the two. The same holds true for the supervisor, who oscillates among identifications with, and feelings about, both the patient and the supervisee, to which are added her own memories and experiences. From this shifting space, she tries to extract some understanding of what is going on, not only between the patient and the therapist, but also between herself and the therapist.

What are the qualities of mind needed for such a combination of oscillatory and synthesizing work, and how can they be enhanced in supervision? Seeing with a "new eye" requires both supervisee and supervisor to shift frames of reference and points of view, to overcome the constraints of a particular mind-set, and to step out of a conventional paradigm. It includes originality, putting things together in different ways, experimenting with new configurations and patterns, and shifting figure and ground. One is called upon to be flexible in one's thinking, to deconstruct the patient's material and the therapeutic dialogue, to sift among a large and wide variety of possibilities, and to suspend premature criticism, judgment, or censorship. Creativity also involves the capacity to reassemble possibilities in a new configuration that establishes choices and closures and is recognizable within a context of meaning. Having stepped out of the bounds of established patterns and meanings, a creative response ultimately reasserts itself within a framework of meaning and tradition so that it is recognizable and meaningful in a context that existed before the creative act. Creativity, as Perkins (1988) suggests, is characterized by originality and appropriateness. If a production, thought, or work of art is not original, it cannot be considered creative. Yet being original but not appropriate to some relevant context can render it bizarre or idiosyncratic. Supervisors might ask themselves if they look for creative thinking in supervisees. How can they recognize it and assess it? Do they value it if it conflicts with their own existing point of view or paradigm? Is creative thought something that can be developed and encouraged by providing the supervisee with a space to think curiously and imaginatively?

There are elements of creative thinking that can be assessed and encouraged in supervision. A therapist creates a picture of the patient by synthesizing fragments of data, affects, impressions, theoretical considerations, and supervisory input. Supervisors need to take note of the freshness, flexibility of thought, and originality of students. Curiosity involves a willingness to look at things from new and multiple points of view and, most important, the capacity to suspend closure yet work toward synthesis. Effective therapists employ these capacities in their work and supervisors can foster them in their students.

Consider the following vignette: A second-year psychiatric resident was treating a man in his twenties for whom he had great affection. Deeply invested in the outcome of the therapy, Dr. T. presented him in supervision with interest, passion, and intensity. After a year of treatment, the patient, Mr. O., made plans to move to another part of the country to pursue certain interests and to see if he could "make it" without the help of his family or this therapist. He was a man who struggled with intense fluctuations in self-esteem, had experienced several humiliating defeats in prior attempts to separate from his family, and, at times, set himself formidable tasks in an attempt to prove his true worth. Mr. O. felt that this move was one of these important challenges, which would put to the test his ability to survive on his own and function independently.

Dr. T. was also aware that his patient's wish to move arose at a point in therapy during which Mr. O. was angry with him over limits set in regard to unpaid bills. The patient needed to begin paying off a large balance in the outpatient clinic where he was being seen or risk the termination of his treatment. He was openly uncomfortable in dealing with this problem. The resident clearly recognized that the patient might be trying to effect a "geographic cure" for some of the difficulties he was experiencing with his family, the clinic, and with his transference feelings. He was also in strong sympathy with the progressive striving and wishes for autonomy expressed in Mr. O.'s plan. But Dr. T. did not want to lose the patient. His uncertainty about how best to understand the situation, and how to talk with the patient about his plans, left him anxious.

The supervisor felt that Dr. T. was under considerable pressure to establish closure: to know what Mr. O. would ultimately decide, to know how to regard his wish to move. Was this a healthy step toward autonomy or an unhealthy flight from his anger at his family and the therapist? The pressure to find a "right" way of thinking about the situation was, the supervisor felt, constricting Dr. T.'s ability to associate to the issue and preventing him from thinking more freely and fully about the situation.

In an attempt to help the supervisee associate more freely to the situation, the supervisor initially made a direct suggestion: that he and Dr. T. brainstorm together about what the patient's decision might mean. Dr. T. quickly and capably rattled off a series of ways to understand the material, including: the wish for autonomy; a test of the therapist to see how he would react; a transference reaction in which Mr. O. was experiencing Dr. T. as his judgmental and controlling father; a desperate need to establish self-respect by controlling the situation and taking on a great challenge, one in which the patient might well be setting himself up for failure; and, finally, a flight from his conflicts and anger in treatment and at home. But this impressive list of possibilities seemed to the supervisor a perfunctory recitation of prior thoughts, as though the therapist was playing piano scales skillfully but without interest. The continuing need for an answer was preventing him from thinking freely and flexibly about the issue at hand.

The supervisor might have asked about Dr. T.'s feelings about the patient's threat to leave treatment after the resident had invested so much time and interest in trying to help him. He chose not to focus on the therapist's reactions but rather on the patient, and he hoped to enliven the quality of the discourse and make it more affectively flexible. First, he observed that Mr. O. often presented his dilemmas in a heroic framework, as though he were going on a kind of adventure from which he would return "either with his shield or on it." Such a portrait told them something important about how the patient posed problems for himself and paved the way for his own subsequent misery. Two images came to the supervisor's mind, and he shared them with the resident. One was Huck Finn setting off on his raft to discover a wider world and with it his own coming of age. The second was a particular scene in the film version of Thurber's "Secret Life of Walter Mitty." Danny Kaye, playing the protagonist, is about to set off bravely in pursuit of villains but alternates between motions to leave and running back to peer nervously between doors to make sure his mother is still there. These associations led to a discussion of the Winnicottian concept of being alone in the presence of the other and of the rapprochement phase of development: the toddler's thrust for autonomy and the anxious need to check on the availability of safe return, seen also in adolescents and in many young adults. Mr. O.'s concern about where he was in his life led him to seek a solution in a bold action which, like Walter Mitty's, also made him anxious about separation. The supervisor pointed out that the patient's plans were multidetermined, representing ongoing conflicts as well as adaptive attempts. He suggested to Dr. T. that establishing closure over whether the planned move was "healthy" or "unhealthy" would oversimplify the complexity and ambivalence in the patient's communication.

By taking this approach, the supervisor provided a model for how one's associations and the ability to let the mind wander to more remote and seemingly unrelated images (Huck Finn and

Danny Kaye) might prove helpful. His own associations to creative efforts (a novel and a film) also introduced humor into the situation, suggesting one creative way of stepping back from a problem, turning it around, and looking at it from a new angle. He also demonstrated how remote associations and fantasies can lead back to psychodynamic theory and understanding and how disparate images (Danny Kaye portraying Walter Mitty and a seriously troubled patient) can be held simultaneously while new understanding is forged. Dr. T., whose anxiety had temporarily limited his flexibility, was reminded by the supervisor of ways in which he could use associative and creative thinking in his work— the music in a therapist's mind rather than just the scales. He then began to relax in his determination to establish closure and to look for "the truth" in his patient's plans. As Dr. T. was better able to tolerate the ambiguity and hold seemingly contradictory views simultaneously, he also felt more inclined to explore the patient's avoidance and ambivalence, while supporting his autonomous strivings.

Subsequently, Dr. T. noted that when he was anxious about doing the right thing, his patient may have experienced him as rushed and not attuned to the patient's feelings. When the therapist recognized that there was not a single way to understand the material, nor one correct way to proceed, he was able to calm down and thereby listen more effectively to the patient.

Perkins (1988) has written about components of creativity that have relevance for the supervisory situation. He suggests that intelligence coupled with ideational fluency (the ability to come up with a variety of ideas on a topic) and ideational flexibility (the ability to produce varied ideas) appear to lay the groundwork for creative thought. Dr. T., who recited a list of formulations about a patient's behavior but with little interest in the list, was demonstrating fluency but no great flexibility at that moment. Still another capacity involved in creative thinking is the ability to associate to remote areas—not being bound too concretely to the here and now of the task, but allowing one's mind to wander for a while unfettered.

Perkins considers the strategies and schemas used in mental effort that are important to creativity. He discusses "problem finding," the exploration of multiple ways of framing a problem before deciding how best to define it, and emphasizes the importance of this approach. In supervision this occurs when the spirit of inquiry implies: "That bit of behavior is really interesting. Let's try to understand how to think about that. Let's look at it from a few different angles and see how we can frame the problem it presents for the patient and for you." This differs in an important way from the supervisor's delivering the "right" meaning about a patient's thoughts or behavior. Perkins suggests that analogic thinking and brainstorming, as well as the capacity to think in negations, contraries, and opposites also aid in creative thinking. In supervision, the effort to hover among hypotheses, personal impressions, observations, and doubt involves a willingness to bear uncertainty and be skeptical about theory. The tendency to think in negations, contraries, and opposites, which in supervision could be seen as oppositionalism or resistance by the supervisee, may, in fact, facilitate creative thinking.

Perkins also refers to values that influence the form, direction, and extent of the creative process. An artist's creative effort is shaped by certain values: a love of beauty or expression, revelation, or irony, for example. One therapist may most value helping and easing pain, another understanding the patient's experience or self-inquiry, yet another the "objective" description of the patient's mental functioning. In each endeavor values and motivation give shape to one's efforts.

Perkins discusses some values that appear to be more general to creativity rather than domain-specific. He includes originality, appropriateness, elegance, a concern for fundamental problems, and a tolerance for ambiguity and complexity coupled with some effort to resolve ambiguity. In psychotherapy and in supervision, values that silently shape the work vary among individuals. A supervisee who values the relief of suffering above all else and a supervisor who most values understanding meaning and tolerating ambiguity are challenged to establish a mutually beneficial, creative way of proceeding. Where the values of supervisor and supervisee diverge and appear to be in conflict with one another, they need to be identified and openly discussed. In clinical work there are values (such as the alleviation of suffering), pressures (such as the need to make treatment decisions), and psychodynamic factors (such as the disorganizing effect of anxiety on patients and therapists) that directly press for some closure and certainty. Creativity is both constrained (appropriately) and constricted (unfortunately) by these pressures.

Assessing Creative Thinking

In assessing creative thinking and its potential development in the therapist, the supervisor tries to measure the student's capacity to bring ideas, associations, references, and hunches that relate to the material into the supervisory hour. Does the supervisee draw analogies? Or, if analogies are suggested by the supervisor, does the student show a willingness to try to use them, to shift mind-sets and try to work with the metaphors and analogies offered? Better yet, does he build on the supervisor's suggestions and create his own? How flexible, in other words, is the student in considering new points of view and new ways of framing a problem? How open is he to theories with which he is unfamiliar? Is the therapist able to construct a picture of the patient that is imaginative, vivid, three-dimensional, and "alive," yet that seems relevant and sheds light on his patient's conflicts and difficulties? Can the student construct a formulation that is original (not a rote or textbook understanding) while relevant (not "wild" or idiosyncratic)? To what extent can the supervisee tolerate ambiguity and uncertainty rather than press for certainty and closure on a problem? And to what degree can the supervisee enter into a transitional space and play with the material, containing anxiety, suspending closure, and wondering with the supervisor?

Conversely, there are aspects of a student's cognitive style that might be expected to limit creative thinking: a low tolerance for ambiguity, discomfort with complexity, reductionistic thinking, inhibited imagination, constricted associations, and discomfort with one's own affects. We can also consider elements that might interfere with creative thinking, even in a person who has talent. Adherence to "received wisdom," the need for a strong idealized authority, conflicts over autonomy, excessive self-consciousness, and fear of criticism or suppressed criticism of the supervisor each may interfere with creative thinking. Conflicts with a supervisor may result in uncritical submission to the supervisor's views or automatic rejection of her ideas.

The supervisor may also have constrictions including a variety of cognitive, affective, dynamic, and countertransference limitations. What if the student's attempts to express creative viewpoints lead to portraits of the patient, genetic reconstructions, and formulations that contradict the supervisor's own conclusions or theoretical bases of operation? What if the student's views challenge the supervisor's authority, prestige, or self-esteem in uncomfortable ways, as was the case with the resident who announced at the commencement of a supervision that he had already fired several supervisors? The supervisor's own need to demonstrate her creative capacities may get in the way of the student's ability to express himself. In order to assess the student's creative ability, the supervisor should allow sufficient room for the therapist to work with the material presented to him by his patient and to learn from it in his own way. This may seem obvious, but there is a type of supervision that proceeds roughly like this: The supervisee presents the "material," often the un-metabolized notes, process material, descriptions and stories of interactions from therapy, and then remains relatively passive and receptive while the supervisor explains what it means. The therapist provides the grist and the supervisor is the mill, providing the meanings and answers while inadvertently stifling creative learning opportunities for the student. Of course, some students may benefit from this form of instruction for a while, but too often this method of teaching is a way in which the supervisor protects herself from the uncomfortable feelings that may arise out of the student's attempts at autonomous, creative thinking. Student and supervisor may collude to inhibit creative learning, as in the following vignette.

A postdoctoral student entered supervision with a well-known supervisor. She admitted to him that she had some trepidation about the enterprise, as she had been told he could be "very direct." She was afraid he would find her too inexperienced and would be impatient with her. She handled her concern by immediately taking on the role of an eager and somewhat reverential student. It worked for a while; she used the supervisor's comments to great advantage and was very appreciative. Once or twice when she brought coffee for herself to an early morning supervisory hour, she also brought a cup for her supervisor. The supervisor was enjoying the supervision, as was his student, until one day he noted just how much he looked forward to her visits. His attention was focused on this matter when the supervisee canceled an hour unexpectedly and the supervisor found himself unduly disappointed, slightly anxious, and unable to make good use of the free time.

In this state, he began to reflect on how the supervisory hours hardly seemed like work. But why did he enjoy them so much? True, the supervisee was a bright, receptive clinician, but what more? The supervisor's associations led to memories of cozy late night chats with his mother. They would sit at the kitchen table where she provided him with a snack while listening to all his ideas and his adolescent theories about life. The supervisor realized that he had allowed the student's sweet submission to gratify him as his mother's had in the past, at the price of limiting the student's creative input.

On resuming supervision, the supervisor began to notice how his student in fact stifled a good deal of independent and creative thought by minimizing theoretical and technical disagreements between them and quickly accepting his point of view. He realized that he had been telling her his ideas without inquiring as fully as he should about her own. He also noted that she avoided making any interpretation she felt might cause discomfort to her patient, often preferring a sugary solution to one that had any vinegar in it. He observed, furthermore, how frequently she offered him a LifeSaver before slipping one into her own mouth at the beginning of supervision. With these observations about himself and the student, he began to point out how she sidestepped her patient's feelings of anger toward her and, at times, hers toward the patient, rather than finding a way to comment on them. This led to talking about how in supervision she sometimes seemed to take in what the supervisor offered without chewing it over. All this was done without reference to the supervisor's associations to his adolescence or to the supervisee's offer of coffee and candy. But the supervisor's associations to his own experiences as well as his observations about his student were used in an attempt to understand and overcome an impediment to the supervisee's use of her own creative abilities. The supervisor first had to recognize the difficulty and analyze his own contribution to it.

Fostering Creative Thinking

The supervisor can assist in enlarging the student's capacity for creative thinking in a variety of ways. These include consciously immersing herself in the material in an imaginative way (modeling, as in the examples of Huck Finn and Danny Kaye); instructing the student on the uncertain, speculative, and often-changing nature of formulation and informing him of her belief that understanding patients involves an ongoing act of creation (didactic approach); framing questions so as to engage the therapist in wondering, imagining, or exploring symbolic meaning (Socratic method); and supporting the supervisee's tentative and at times awkward attempts to inhabit the transitional world and create a meaningful picture of his patient (permission and encouragement). The supervisor, through the use of clarification, may point out when the therapist is being too literal, subjective, or (as in the situation just described) compliant at the expense of a more fluid, imaginative, and "transitional" appreciation of the material.

In the following example, the supervisor invited the therapist to wonder about a patient's communication rather than take it at face value. Thus they entered the transitional world of encoded meaning. Dr. R. was a second-year resident when she took on the treatment of Ms. V., a woman in her twenties with a history of depression, multiple suicide attempts, many hospitalizations, and a failure to respond to somatic therapies for depression. She frequently reported feeling hopeless with persistent feelings of wanting to kill herself. She was raised in a family in which her mother often fled the house to protect herself from her physically abusive husband, leaving the children alone with an enraged and frightening father. The patient could not recall being physically or sexually abused, but this possibility had been suspected by therapists. In therapy, she presented herself as helpless, urgently in need of answers, and full of wishes that the therapist help her find a boyfriend, an apartment, and a job. Despite a certain lack of insight, the patient was described by Dr. R. as warmhearted and sweet, with a good sense of humor, a nice smile, good eye contact, and admiration for the therapist. Ms. V. felt isolated, alone, and as if she did not "belong in this world."

One day Dr. R. appeared for supervision looking worried. Ms. V. had been calling her and would start conversations with "I'm hopeless" followed by a long silence. Dr. R. reported feeling anxious and not knowing how to respond. Her exchange with the supervisor went as follows:

> **Supervisor:** Why do you imagine the patient might start that way?
>
> **Dr. R.:** Maybe she's trying to make me worry. [Here the resident presents a hypothesis.]
>
> **Supervisor:** And why do you imagine she might want you to worry? [The supervisor encourages her to expand upon her hypothesis.]
>
> **Dr. R.:** Maybe it's a way to be connected.
>
> **Supervisor:** What do you think she fears if you weren't worried?
>
> **Dr. R.:** Abandonment?
>
> **Supervisor:** That was my thought, too. . . . Let's say there's something to that.

The supervisor keeps the idea in the area of play; his "Let's say . . ." keeps the patient's worry about abandonment still hypothetical.

Supervisor: Perhaps when she says, "I'm hopeless," she means "Stay!" If you translate it like that, when she says "I'm hopeless" you might say, "I'm here" and see what happens.

The supervisor suggests that the validity of the hypothesis, and the suggestion that arises from it, will have to be confirmed or denied, in part, by how the patient responds to it. At this point Dr. R. begins to look brighter and less worried.

This is a simple example of therapist and supervisor working together to understand a patient's communication. While the understanding arrived at may be commonplace for an experienced therapist, for a new therapist it is an act of creation that involves inhabiting a symbolic transitional world, in which words do not always mean what they signify. The supervisor took a Socratic approach, asking a series of questions designed to help engage the therapist in this decoding process. This led to a shift in point of view: instead of taking the statement "I'm hopeless" at face value (suggesting despair, depression, suicide, and failed treatment), he reinterpreted it as a plea for the therapist to stay. This involved a shift from a one-person description of an internal state to a two-person interaction that paradoxically involved hope (a reversal of "I'm hopeless" to "If you stay, maybe I'm not so hopeless") and linguistically involved a translation from a declarative to an imperative form of communication. This reinterpretation permitted a lessening of anxiety for Dr. R., which was a precondition for greater flexibility of thought. While worried, Dr. R. was preoccupied with "Is Ms. V. safe? What should I do?" The supervisor helped the supervisee reframe the questions in terms of what the patient means and how she might respond. This reframing allowed for the construction of new meaning with increased flexibility, engagement, and curiosity on the therapist's part. Once the question and the emphasis were on understanding and responding rather than the narrower problem of trying to guarantee safety in a telephone conversation, a greater range of possibility opened for both patient and therapist. Once having found words to use with her patient, the resident could then talk with greater self-revelation about her feelings of exasperation and irritation with Ms. V. While some of this exasperation was stimulated by the patient's persistent demands for help, much of it was due to the resident's frustration in not knowing how to understand and make use of what the patient was telling her. That she could now begin to discuss her feelings of exasperation with her supervisor was the first step in being able to use them to understand better the nature of the therapist-patient interaction. It would help her not to repeat, through silence or exasperation, the abandonment the patient had felt with her mother and secretly expected and invited from others.

This supervisory situation is hardly unique. It is commonplace to listen to the communicative intent of patients' comments about themselves. For the therapist-in-training, however, this involves creating a new picture of the patient, a new way of hearing and understanding language. It involves mental and emotional flexibility, the ability to shift points of view, to deconstruct apparent meanings and then reconstruct new ones. It involves entering into a transitional world where comments may mean the reverse of what they seem to mean, where hopelessness may signify hope, anger mean love. The supervisor is in a position to guide the therapist as together they construct new meanings which are then shared, added to, corrected, or refined in the therapist-patient dialogue. That newly created picture of things as understood by the therapist is then tested with the patient and brought back to the supervisor, where the process of deconstruction and co-construction begins again.

Earlier, we referred to Fleming's discussion of the third world and Winnicott's transitional phenomena. Winnicott used the concept of potential space to denote the area that lies between fantasy and reality. Potential space is neither "inside" nor "outside"; it is "between the subjective object and the object objectively perceived" (Winnicott, 1967, p. 100). Potential space is filled by illusion, play, and symbol. It includes "play space, the area of the transitional object and phenomena, the analytic space, the area of cultural experience, and the area of creativity" (Ogden, 1985, p. 129). In the supervisory situation, the supervisor tries to enlarge the potential space, in which an evolving picture of the reality of the patient-therapist interaction is re-created, first by the supervisee in the recall of the therapeutic hours reported and then resymbolized and re-construed by the therapist and supervisor together. It is not an external reality they agree upon but a conception and an image of the therapeutic encounter that they form. Yet reality is not denied. In the previous vignette, the patient's hopelessness is listened to in light of the risk of self-destructive behavior and the possible need for hospitalization.

On the other hand, this created picture of the patient is not merely fantasy: it is not truly *inside* in the sense of being a creation under magical control. Yet fantasy and subjectivity (of therapist and supervisor) are not denied their vitality in shaping the emerging picture, image, and formulation about the patient. The supervisory space, then, at times becomes a potential space, in which therapist and supervisor implicitly agree to suspend closure on the question "are we creating or discovering the patient?"

As this case illustrates, one of the most powerful forces in constricting the mental play space, with a consequent push for closure in the direction of some concrete reality, is when one of the parties—patient, therapist, or supervisor—seems in danger. If the patient's hopelessness leads to a threat of suicide, it becomes harder (appropriately) for the therapist (and sometimes the supervisor) to play with the material. The student's fear of making a mistake that will lead to death makes imaginative play seem dangerous. The tendency may be for the student to want, too quickly, to substitute some form of action (hospitalization, termination of treatment, etc.) for further inquiry. The supervisor must attend to the dangers of the situation and help the therapist in negotiating, as much as possible, for the patient's safety, adding the meanings, metaphors, and symbolism that are inherent in the plans being discussed. She tries to do so without getting caught up exclusively in concrete planning. Of course, the more anxious the supervisor is about the safety of the patient, the more she may lose her own capacity to keep inquiry open. There are, of course, times when one has to act or direct the supervisee to act first and save deeper inquiry for later. Attending to reality and diminishing anxiety may help restore the play space.

An equally powerful force that may push for closure is countertransference. A therapist under the pressure of strong feelings of anger, anxiety, or shared hopelessness may feel a collapse of potential space in the direction of oversubjectivity, perhaps through magical fantasies of having omnipotent control over the patient. As an infant might feel omnipotent control over a transitional object, so a therapist might imagine that the patient could not possibly commit suicide because of his unconscious belief in his omnipotent ability to dissuade or rescue the patient. The need to try to control or be rid of the patient, as the therapist may have wanted to do to someone or some part of himself, can become paramount and, instead of mutual play, there is a deadly struggle for mastery. Again, the supervisor attends sufficiently to this internal experience to help the therapist make use of the fantasies and countertransference, yet, at the same time, resists closure and protects the potential space of uncertainty, symbolism, illusion, and creation. In the following situation countertransference feelings interfere with curiosity about the patient.

A married resident, usually flexible in her responses to patients, became very irritated when an unmarried woman she was treating expressed an interest in artificial insemination. She complained to her supervisor that the woman was being irresponsible in contemplating having a baby alone. It was, after all, just a defense against facing her own loneliness at a time when the resident was planning a vacation. The resident's disgust and impatience with her patient were clearly conveyed to the supervisor and, in less obvious ways, to the patient as well. The resident, usually curious about her patient, did not inquire further into her patient's wishes to have a baby, which would have kept the desires in the realm of imagination and play, but instead concretized them, asking the patient when she would have the insemination and to which doctor she was going. The patient, sensing danger in her therapist's sudden change of approach, did not broach the subject of having a baby on subsequent visits.

The supervisor was aware that the resident, who was considerably younger than her patient, was childless, but knew nothing about what plans for a family the therapist and her husband were making. As the resident, who was usually open about her own experiences, did not relate her patient's wishes for a baby to anything about her own situation, the supervisor chose not to ask, feeling it would be too intrusive. Instead, she tried to promote a spirit of inquiry by gently pointing out that the resident seemed to have a lot of feelings about her patient's plan for a baby. The therapist readily agreed and restated how irresponsible she thought it was. After all, she said, the patient would have to work, and why have the baby if someone else was going to raise it?

The supervisor responded by nodding sympathetically and

then asking how these opinions might have influenced what she had said to her patient. The resident blushed. "I guess I focused on *what* she was going to do, because I didn't want her to do it. I didn't ask her about her fantasies about what having a child would be like. I mean, what she wanted in having a child." The supervisor agreed and underscored that the resident's strong feelings had temporarily closed off avenues of fruitful inquiry that might have kept conception and childbirth in the arena of playful possibility rather than only concrete events. The resident in the following session was then able to inquire about her patient's silence about a baby and explore more fully her fantasies about artificial insemination and having a child. All this was done without the supervisor's inquiring about the resident's personal plans with regard to children.

The effort to sustain curiosity and suspend premature closure is constantly influenced by the realities of patient care, issues of safety, of technique, and so on. More generally, creative thinking in psychotherapy and supervision is constrained by appropriateness of meaning and action, as well as by the usefulness of the interpretations offered. All listening and co-construction is shaped by existing theory and rules, conscious and unconscious, about what sorts of explanations and actions are permissible. While a patient may feel that his depression is due to the alignment of the stars, the therapist, whose theories of causality are different, will try to enlarge and give new and added meaning to the patient's statement, perhaps ultimately trying to incorporate the patient's explanation into a useful metaphor about misalignments in the patient's internal life, as well as with people around him. The therapist's theories influence his discourse just as the patient's do, and these unavoidable constraints provide relevance and appropriateness. The supervisor can, at times, help the supervisee articulate the theory that underlies his discourse. The supervisor is in a position to help strike a balance, leading to constructions of meanings that are flexible and creative, yet appropriately grounded within a recognizable frame of reference. In this regard, necessary constraints on creativity (to remain appropriate to a context of meaning) can become constrictions (rigid adherence to a set of beliefs, limiting flexibility of thought). What supervisor and supervisee consider to be the boundaries of acceptable theories and conclusions can promote appropriateness, or lead to rigidity and dogma. The supervisee's curiosity and healthy skepticism may be inhibited if the supervisor has too strong an interest in preserving a particular point of view. The multiparadigmatic nature of theories about psychotherapy can cut both ways: the multiplicity of points of view can encourage further questioning and imaginative integration, but at the same time, the theoretical uncertainties can promote dogmatism and defensiveness that limit creative exploration. A supervisor committed to a psychoanalytic self-psychological approach may be unable to help her student think openly and creatively about behaviorist concepts or an ego-psychology approach. Perhaps the best she can do is acknowledge to herself and her supervisee the limits of what she can teach.

Supervisors should try to encourage an "evenly hovering attention" in the therapist, so that he is not overly engaged in his own theories (or his supervisor's) and remains receptive to new images and ideas from without and within. It is in this open and receptive "potential space" that creative thinking can be fostered, and this way of being with and tuning into self and other, not only particular theories and techniques, deserves attention. Supervisees are aware of conflicting theories or emphases and are challenged first to try to understand them, then to integrate them into their own thinking as much as possible. This is a formidable task, and students naturally turn to their supervisors for help. The supervisor can help the student develop a creative way of listening, which does not rely too heavily on one particular theory.

As we have explored the supervisor's role in enhancing associative and creative thinking, an aspect of the supervisory dialogue that keeps reappearing and is inevitably part of these ways of thinking is the aspect of self-revelation. If the supervisee freely employs associative thought during supervision, many of his associations will tell him about himself, his feelings, and his experiences. Some of these will be reported to the supervisor. The flexibility in thinking and capacity to enter "play space" that accompany creative thinking will also inevitably include the supervisee's own memories, thoughts, feelings, and fantasies. The role of these reflections about the self in becoming a therapist and their place in supervision is what we will discuss next.

Self-Reflection

Inductive, associative, and creative modes of thinking are characterized by the types of formal thought processes they employ. Self-reflection is largely characterized by the object of thought: the mind itself. Self-reflection may be defined as the use of the mind to observe its own workings—workings that may take the form of thoughts, feelings, fantasies, images, and memories. It may also include reflection upon the activity the mind is engaged in at the moment—trying to understand the patient, feeling bored, daydreaming, feeling anxious, or trying to relax.

Self-reflection is a central part of the therapeutic experience for any patient engaged in a treatment that fosters self-awareness and insight. Self-reflection is an essential activity for the therapist learning to do psychotherapy, one that is best cultivated by the therapist's personal analysis or psychotherapy. But therapists struggle in supervision as well with distressing feelings, memories, personal fantasies, and upsetting impulses aroused by their work with patients. To what extent are these experiences explored and made use of in supervision or left aside in favor of a patient-centered focus? Supervisees vary widely in their natural inclinations and capacities for self-awareness. To some degree, self-reflection is a specific mode of thinking that can be assessed, encouraged, and taught in the supervisory situation. However, encouraging this mode of thought raises questions about the appropriate limits of inquiry by the supervisor more than any of the others discussed. For it is in the attempt to advance self-reflection that the supervisor may intrude upon the trainee's sense of privacy (Betcher and Zinberg, 1988) and distort the educational experience. (The related question of how personal the supervision should be is taken up in chapter 5.)

There are three foci of self-reflection that we wish to discuss: the *activity* of self-reflection, the *application* of what is learned by self-reflection to the work of psychotherapy or psychoanalysis, and the *management* of self-reflection in supervision.

The Activity of Self-Reflection

The extent to which we can attend to and describe our own mental processes—our ongoing affective responses, fantasies, impulses, memories, shifts in level of arousal, and so on—while listening to a patient is influenced by our character, conflicts, background, motivation, experience, and "psychological mindedness." The value we place on self-reflection as psychotherapists is based not solely on natural inclinations and internal dynamic factors, however, but also on a conscious, learned belief about the importance of self-awareness in being a good therapist.

Supervision helps the therapist develop that belief. He learns to be aware of what mental activity he is engaged in at the moment, and how it relates to what he is being told. For example, in doing psychotherapy, one is usually (but not always) engaged in an effort to understand the patient. The therapist may, consciously or inadvertently, be trying to make himself or the patient feel better, even if it temporarily weakens the effort at understanding. At times, the therapist may be trying *not* to understand the patient, if he is too anxious about what he may find out. For example, a therapist threatened by the patient's hostility toward him or murderous rage toward another person may deny the patient's feelings and repress his own affective responses which may make him aware of his patient's anger. He may then attempt to control what is discussed in the therapy hours as a way of distancing himself from his own and his patient's unwelcome feelings. Or he may be open to fantasies or memories of violence that help him better understand and address his patient's affective state.

The therapist-in-training, with the help of the supervisor, can learn through self-reflection to identify the mental activity in which he is engaged and its purpose. A candidate, having begun to analyze a man who had quit several previous attempts at treatment, kept focusing his questions on events in the patient's life that occurred outside the office, never asking him what he experienced during the analytic hours. When the supervisor called attention to this pattern of inquiry, the candidate became aware of how his fear of the patient's leaving him had influenced his conduct of the treatment. He was fearful that the patient would express disappointment in the treatment if he were asked about it.

If the therapist reflects upon the nature of his own therapeutic activity, he or his supervisor will inevitably be led to think about what theory or model is being used to organize (or create) data about his patient, and why this theory is preferred to others. The growing, shifting, and multiparadigmatic nature of psychotherapeutic theory provides an array of models to use in organizing material. One therapist may consistently employ a single theory about human development and its vicissitudes, working to match the clinical data to his particular theoretical framework. Another may work in a more ad hoc way, using various psychological theories as they seem useful in understanding the therapeutic moment. One aspect of self-reflection is the awareness of the models one is using and how and when they are used.

A young man came to therapy one day feeling angry about having to sit in the waiting room. It rubbed in the asymmetry between himself as a patient and his therapist, a doctor, which made him feel bad. Whether the therapist hears the patient's complaint primarily in terms of his struggle with competitive feelings (inferring envy, aggression, and a wish to be powerful) or as an injury involving the loss of self-esteem (emphasizing feelings of shame, inadequacy, and inferiority underlying the anger) will be influenced, in part, by the theoretical model the therapist employs.

Supervisees naturally try out different points of view as a way of learning what seems most helpful to them. Development as a therapist involves identifying with various mentors and their theoretical viewpoints. At times, one is immersed in the "psychic landscape" of the patient and unaware of the lens being used to view it. At other times, one attends to the lens, both the theory being applied and the identifications that support it. Self-reflection means being aware of one's activity: of the interplay of listening, applying theory, identifying with one's teachers, and developing one's own independent clinical impressions.

The supervisor, too, has her own theories, arrived at through identifications, clinical experience, and the unconscious meaning of certain theories to her. If she is to remain flexible and open to her students' experiences and their experiments with theory, ongoing self-reflection about her own attachment to certain the-

ories—what she has ruled in and ruled out as useful and why—
is an important part of her work. In the following vignette, a
supervisor's self-analysis led to insight into his reaction to certain
theories.

For some years, a supervisor had found himself resistant to
some of the theories of Melanie Klein, in particular her insistence
on the infant's early struggle with the death instinct through
paranoid and projective mechanisms. He marshalled for himself
and his supervisees the objections of many who disagree with her
view that the infant develops a paranoid-schizoid position within
the first few months of life. In coming back to Klein's work as part
of his preparation for teaching a course on theory, he noticed that
in reading her theories he experienced a profound sense of discomfort he could not fully explain. He noticed, too, that this
feeling seemed to keep him from deeper involvement in Klein's
theoretical contributions. At first, he attributed it to a strong
identification with his own psychoanalytic teachers, who had
looked with some disdain on her work. He began to wonder why
this identification was still so necessary and from what might it be
protecting him. He had been musing off and on about the matter
when he went for his weekly massage. That day, the masseuse
suddenly put her fingers behind his ears on the spots where, at age
two, part of his mastoid bones had been removed because of a
life-threatening infection. The actual position of being naked under a sheet while the area behind his ears was being vigorously
probed—a physical reminder of the early surgical experience—
awakened long-repressed affects of sadness, anxiety, and helplessness, as well as anger with his mother, whom he blamed as a
toddler for the pain of the surgery, as well as for the separation
from her that was inflicted upon him.

When he went back to reading Klein that evening, it was clearer
to him what his resistance to her theories about the infant's par-

anoid position and projection of the death instinct had been about, in terms of his own early affect and object relations. He had used his identification with admired male teachers (including his training analyst) and their theoretical orientations as protection against overwhelming affects aroused by this life-threatening illness and early separation, which undermined his sense of well-being. His strong identification with the teachers and their theories represented a turning away from the fantasied dangerous mother (represented by Klein and her theories) to a protective father. It served to separate him, he realized, from the more frightening aspects of his mother's care. Klein's theory had come to symbolize the intensely painful aspects of this separation from his mother and his intense anger with her as a result, without his being conscious of it. Klein's general lack of attention to what Winnicott later called "the holding environment" inadvertently awakened in the supervisor echoes of his own early experience, which he had successfully avoided by failing to consider Klein's contribution fully in his own studies and in his supervision. This bit of self-reflection on his relationship to a psychoanalytic theory did not make him into a Kleinian, for many of his objections to her developmental theory remained, but it helped him to be open to a less encumbered appraisal of her contribution in his teaching and supervision (Jacobs, 1993).

Self-reflection also involves being aware of one's characteristic modes of thought. One therapist may work intuitively, relying mainly on associative thinking and a capacity to grasp imaginatively the underlying meaning of the patient's words. Others may work in a more methodical, incremental, data-gathering, inductive mode. Ideally, through supervision the therapist can call upon an array of modes of thinking in listening to his patient. Even with the availability of multiple modalities and a flexible approach, questions still arise: what guides the therapist in understanding this patient? When puzzled, does he tend to listen more closely to the language the patient employs, to attend to his own associations and countertransference, to begin to think of a theory to explain what is happening? There is a level of choice (conscious or instinctive) in selecting among the different modes of thinking. Self-reflection helps make that choice conscious and available for criticism. Awareness of one's typical (and atypical) forms of thinking about a patient and attention to where one looks for further understanding are part of honing what Isakower (1957) referred to as the "analytic instrument." This use of self-reflection can enhance the analyst's understanding of how he gathers knowledge and his appreciation of the strengths and limitations of his approach.

A problem arises when the trainee appears limited in the ability to reflect on his or her own experience. The phrase "having a tin ear" has been used to refer to an incapacity in the therapist to detect nuance, suggestion, or latent meaning in the patient's communications. It suggests a form of literalness that limits creative and imaginative listening. One may have a tin ear to oneself as well and be relatively tone deaf to one's own mind at work. The development of overly literal modes of listening can be the result of conflicts around exhibitionism, performance anxiety, or transference to the supervisor as well as natural limitations in intelligence or imagination. While sitting with a patient a therapist may, in fact, have strong feelings, fantasies, or daydreams that are suppressed or split off from consciousness during supervision. Or a supervisee may have a good deal of conscious awareness of his mental activity during a therapeutic hour but may hesitate to bring his observations of himself to supervision. One trainee reported that, for better or worse, she had clear categories concerning which of her responses to her patients she would bring to supervision and which to her therapist. Such a decision may arise from an appropriate sense of privacy or from some sense of shame that compromises learning. It may be difficult for the supervisor to distinguish between a lack of talent for self-reflection, an inhibition that grows out of conflict, and a conscious and rational decision on the student's part to take his observations to his therapist instead of his supervisor.

A problem of a different kind is the supervisee who is so focused on his own feelings and reactions that his attention to the patient is limited and he fails to describe the patient clearly. One supervisee, for instance, frequently presented patient material primarily in terms of the dilemmas it caused herself. She would describe to the supervisor her own discomfort, confusion, and distress in not knowing what she could do for a particular patient. While the supervisor found himself sympathetic to the therapist's plight and initially tried to help her with her frustration, it dawned on him that he was hearing too little about the patient and too much about the trainee. Self-reflection can become self-absorption, interfering with the therapist's capacity to see and hear the patient. As the supervisor began to ask more about the patient and to help the trainee with how she could help her patient, the supervisee became more focused on describing the patient's difficulties and less involved in her own frustrations.

The Application of Self-Reflection

Once having observed his own mental activity, the therapist tries to understand how what he is feeling and thinking is related to the current clinical situation and how it can be used to further the therapy. His own feelings may provide hints to emerging, but not yet explicit, trends in the patient's material. For example, a therapist reports that he felt very angry during a session with a patient and concluded that these feelings arose from the patient's sadistic wishes to harass and torture him. Whether this statement represents a conviction on the therapist's part, a hypothesis, or a transient impression depends on how he is applying self-reflection and answering the question, "Why do I feel as I do?" In this case the supervisee seems to be proceeding rapidly from a feeling state to a conclusion about its origin in his patient's wishes. While his inference may be right, the supervisor should be aware of the possibility of premature closure about the origins of the therapist's reaction without sufficient evidence. The supervisor can help the supervisee to study the nature of the evidence he relied upon, exploring the relationship of what the therapist felt to the clinical situation. What had the patient said or done that indicated sadistic wishes toward the therapist? Could there be other sources for the therapist's anger in that session—for instance, his agreeing to the patient's request for a change in his appointment time even though it was inconvenient for the therapist?

In the following vignette, a psychoanalytic supervisor helped a candidate reexamine a moment in his analysis of a patient and so helped him to reflect on the meaning of his countertransference. The candidate and his analysand were entering the sixth year of analysis. The patient, an obsessional woman in her thirties, proceeded through the analysis in a slow, plodding, resistant way, avoiding in particular her transference feelings. The candidate felt that the patient had made great strides in many areas but was stuck at this point, seemingly unable to work through a hostile-dependent relationship with her mother, consciously avoiding talking about sexuality, and feeling pessimistic about making her life truly her own. Frustrated about the slow pace and uncertain outcome of the treatment, he saw the patient's passivity as a hostile sit-down strike. In response, he felt annoyed and impatient.

From time to time, the patient cancelled sessions because of conflicts with work. When the candidate inquired about these cancellations, the patient responded with the practical realities of her situation. In one session, when the candidate asked how the patient felt about the recent conflicts between work and the analysis, she noted that it was unavoidable and annoying. The analyst commented that her reply sounded defensive. The patient confirmed that she had heard the analyst as wondering whether the cancellations were legitimate.

The analyst commented, "I'm not trying to judge the legitimacy of the cancellations, but what I notice is a lack of curiosity about the process. You tend to say: 'Here is the reality, I have no choice. Period. Let's talk about something else.' It's the lack of interest in the process or feelings that I am noticing." The patient's response conveyed that her back was up: "Some things I try to change so I can come here, some things I have no choice about. So it's period, end of story." The analyst replied, "It's hard for us to talk about this without you feeling defensive. I feel like your mother is in the room, about to get angry at you for being late. Or as if you experience me as being like your mother." The patient responded, "It's not you. But it's what I bring to it anyway." She associated to snapping at her mother and felt that when the analyst had made the comment about lack of curiosity, it was as if she heard "What is wrong with you? Why haven't you looked at this?" She went on: "I also do it to myself. It's not necessarily what you say. It's my own feeling that I'm not supposed to be late or have conflicts, or . . . get angry."

The analyst presented this material to his supervisor. He felt uneasy and guilty about having spoken to the patient in what he felt was a critical way and believed he had lost control of his countertransference irritation. He felt, however, that this had led to a useful interchange, and wondered whether this countertransference "enactment," as he called it, had somehow been necessary to intensify the transference affect and get beyond the passive-aggressive standoff.

The supervisor commented that she was unclear as to where the candidate's enactment was and asked that they go over the process material again to pinpoint what he thought had been enacted. In doing so, the candidate realized that what he had said to the patient had not been judgmental or overtly irritated in content or delivery. Perhaps, he now thought, his inner feeling of anger at the patient combined with her feeling of being criticized had led him to conclude that he had spoken critically. The supervisor gave her view that she did not see an enactment of a countertransference in this material and that what the candidate had said sounded fine. She went on to say that examining the patient's lack of curiosity was an appropriate aspect of defense analysis. The candidate needed to explore how the patient avoided subjects that she thought might rock the boat. Supervisor and candidate discussed the patient's negative transference, in which she experienced the analyst as a critical mother toward whom she felt angry and rebellious. Resisting change and being passive were ways to fight back with her mother and analyst. Further, using projective identification the patient unconsciously tried to turn the analyst into a frustrated, angry, intolerant figure, as she experienced her mother to be. The candidate felt that the supervisory clarification was helpful in understanding this session and the active transference-countertransference matrix.

In this situation, the candidate was called upon to reflect on his feelings and behavior toward his patient. In trying to sort out his own contribution to this dynamic with the patient—what he had elicited in her—and what the patient brought to this, out of her conflicts and transference, he had to examine whether his overt behavior had in fact been critical and judgmental or merely reflected his unexpressed inner state. The analyst felt angry and impatient while the patient felt judged, pushed, and criticized. The candidate concluded, therefore, that he had acted in an un-empathic way. The further self-reflection facilitated in supervision helped to clarify an assumption that was largely colored by his internal affective state. The candidate was concerned with whether the patient might be reacting to subtle aspects of his inflection or unwitting communication (and this could not be entirely ruled out), but, upon closer examination, it appeared that his actual behavior had not conveyed this. This bit of self-examination also helped him understand what was going on in the treatment. Recognizing the patient's negative maternal transference in this interchange helped him focus on the intensity with which this transference was operative at the time.

The supervisor had to decide how to handle this material and encourage the candidate's self-reflection. The supervisor initially reserved judgment on the candidate's diagnosis of an enactment that she had not heard in the material. In asking to return to the data (the process notes), she questioned the candidate's view and implicitly asked for further self-reflection. This led the candidate to rethink the meaning of the analytic interchange. The supervisor, in giving her opinion about how she heard the material, in essence clarified her view that the candidate was reacting to something other than his technique with the patient. In so doing, she substituted her own kinder assessment for the harsher reaction of the patient. The exploration of the candidate's feelings was undertaken only to understand the analytic process and transference better in an educational setting. There was no attempt to explore any deeper components of the candidate's feelings that might have contributed to his feeling that he had made a mistake. The supervisor could have inquired how the candidate could resolve the doubts he had about his conduct, and what he would consider evidence in judging his therapeutic technique and effectiveness. This could have deepened their examination of the candidate's feelings and his use of self-reflection.

A different problem arises when the therapist does *not* apply his knowledge of his feelings to the clinical situation or use it to further his understanding of the therapeutic dialogue. For example, when a patient becomes provocative or devaluing of the therapist, the therapist may respond inwardly with anger. He may feel guilty about his response and berate himself for having unkind feelings toward his patient. But he does not use his feelings to shed further light upon the therapy in the supervisory dialogue because he regards his feelings as his own problem rather than information about the patient. Each supervisor evaluates how each supervisee uses or fails to use self-reflection to further his work.

What the therapist makes of his own experience involves his beliefs about knowledge and how it is attained. A therapist may believe that intuitively grasping the patient's latent meanings via subliminal communication and the affects they arouse is a reliable way of knowing his patient. Another may find such an approach overly subjective and unreliable, believing that careful analysis of the spoken word is the best basis for understanding the patient. Every supervisor and supervisee implicitly or explicitly establish parameters for what constitutes useful information, how it is to be generated, what is the nature of evidence, and what degree of uncertainty and ambiguity is tolerable in the supervision.

The Management of Self-Reflection

Beyond the activity of self-reflection and its application to clinical work, supervisors encounter challenges concerning the titration of self-reflection in the supervisory situation—that is, how to deal with the therapist's inner experience in a way that is educationally helpful and appropriate to the supervisory setting. This issue will be developed more fully in chapters 5 and 8, but we note it here because in order to be a psychodynamic psychotherapist the trainee needs exposure to self-reflective knowledge and its uses. Supervision is an obvious opportunity to learn to use inner experience in the service of patient care. Yet supervision is not therapy. It has different goals and boundaries. Each supervisor must decide to what degree his student's unusual or upsetting feelings, impulses, and associations can and should be explored in supervision in order to understand a therapeutic encounter better, to what degree they should be left alone, or whether the supervisor should suggest that these feelings be explored through personal therapy or analysis.

A candidate in his second year of supervision of an analytic case was surprised and confused by the sudden experience of deja vu in the supervisory session. When he told his supervisor about the first sexual experience of the very inhibited young man he was analyzing, he suddenly had the uncanny feeling that he had told the supervisor all this before. The candidate tried to understand his reaction but seemed uncomfortable when reflecting upon the experience with his supervisor. He said that he had never read or understood much about deja vu experiences, implying that he was therefore in no position to discuss them.

The supervisor did not comment directly on the student's remark. She did try, however, to engage the candidate's curiosity about his experience, asking him why he thought it had occurred when it did. She met with little success. The candidate's discomfort was evident. The supervisor responded by dropping that line of inquiry and suggesting instead that the therapist might learn something more about himself as well as his relation to his patient if he took it up in his own analysis. She also suggested some reading on the subject, offering to review it with him, feeling that gaining an intellectual grasp of the phenomenon might be a first necessary step toward greater self-understanding. The supervisor never learned what the candidate did with this experience and the opportunity for greater self-knowledge it afforded him; he never mentioned the incident again.

The supervisor, a member of a study group on supervision, asked her colleagues whether they thought she should have inquired about the fate of the deja vu experience in subsequent supervisory sessions. Or should the student be allowed the privacy of his experiences, whether or not discussed with his analyst, without further comment or intrusion? How could an atmosphere of safety be established in which a discussion of the candidate's capacity for associative thought and self-reflection in supervision could be discussed openly and without fear of judgment on the candidate's part?

The supervisee and supervisor had arrived at a critical moment, an opportunity for heightened self-reflection and deeper understanding, not only of the relationship between the candidate and his analysand, but also of the relationship between the candidate and the supervisor. It crystallized the issue of how the goals and limits of supervision were to be arrived at by supervisor and supervisee. The supervisor, uncertain about how to proceed, could have asked whether the candidate felt that further inquiry into his understanding of his deja vu experience fell within the bounds of supervision or he felt that it would be overly intrusive. This could have led to a discussion about the boundaries and goals of supervision. She did not do this in part due to her reluctance to place herself too much in the role of analyst to the candidate. Furthermore, she wondered how much she could help him understand this phenomenon and its meanings for the analysis she was supervising when she knew so little about the candidate's inner psychological workings.

The deja vu experience seemed related to the sexual experiences of the patient and some anxiety they engendered in the analyst. Later, the supervisor recognized that her own intense curiosity about this psychic event and its fate in the candidate's mind had its origins in part in her own voyeuristic wishes. The inhibition she felt in pursuing the deja vu experience further with the candidate arose not only from her sensitivity to her student's embarrassment but from her voyeuristic wishes, which were still conflictual for her and had made further inquiry unacceptable to her. The supervisory group was then able to show her how the conflicts aroused in her about looking and knowing might be used to understand further how her candidate could have similar conflicts and how she could begin to note more clearly when his curiosity and inquiry about the patient's experience could be inhibited. She could then, without inquiring directly about the deja vu experience, begin to point out to him those moments of constriction in his approach to the patient.

While supervisors' conscious and unconscious attitudes vary in how far to proceed in such matters of self-reflection and self-inquiry, so, too, do the views of supervisees. Some seem to feel that any discussion of their feelings, fantasies, and countertransference reactions is unwelcome. They focus exclusively on descriptions of their patients and their theoretical understanding of their problems. At the other extreme is the supervisee who, under pressure to relieve inner distress, treats the supervisory session like therapy, seeking out opportunities for self-disclosure and offering deep interpretations of his work in hopes of therapeutic feedback from the supervisor. The problem with the former is that much can be missed that is crucial to learning, mainly that therapy is a very complicated two-person undertaking, not merely the intellectual study of psychopathology in another. The problem with the latter extreme is that supervision is not therapy. Excessive focus on the therapist's inner experience can misdirect supervision away from the patient and away from learning to listen, and can serve as an avoidance of the patient's experience. Furthermore, excessive self-disclosure in supervision is likely to activate in the student latent feelings of shame, vulnerability, and anxiety.

In the following dialogue, the supervisor addressed the supervisee's feelings to help clarify a conflict he was experiencing with a patient. A first-year psychiatric resident came to supervision one day, upset over the demands of the residency. He reported having felt "burned out" the previous week, with "no energy left." He described how busy and stressful work had been, including great pressure on the inpatient unit where he was working and a demanding night call schedule. Over the prior weekend he had come to the conclusion that he did not have "limitless energy" and could no longer operate on feeling "I can do anything." He felt that he had limits and must become more self-protective, even distant from the work.

These feelings, he went on, arose around three patients currently on the inpatient service. All three were women with histories of childhood sexual abuse, and all now had young children of their own. The resident was finding aspects of this "unbearable." The supervisor initially referred to recent research in the area of sexual abuse and the challenge this research posed to traditional views of character development. Supervisor and therapist discussed the theoretical controversies as well as the emotional stress of working with abuse victims.

The discussion shifted to the resident's feelings, and the supervisor agreed that a therapist cannot—as the resident put it—"do and do and do." Recognizing the limits of one's energy and thera-peutic abilities, the supervisor noted, was good for the therapist and for the patient as well. The supervisor also described this as a common problem in working with more disturbed patients. The resident then went on to describe one of the patients in greater detail, a woman who was trying to work through her feelings about her history of sexual abuse. "She grabbed the unit by the neck, and told them to hold still, while she felt her feelings." Holding still meant not forcing her to attend groups, participate in family work or other aspects of the inpatient routine, and letting her wrestle with her memories and affects in her own way. The unit had decided to go along with this, and the resident, as her inpatient therapist, felt compelled to hold very still while she did her work in a way that felt safe to her.

The supervisor thought of how the patient's immobilizing message to the ward staff might represent an enactment of her feelings about her trauma. She put the staff, including the resi-dent, into the helpless position that she had surely suffered. Even the resident's description of her "neck hold" on the unit evoked the image of an assault, perhaps like the sexual assault of which she had been a victim. The supervisor might at this point have explored this reenactment on the ward and focused primarily on the patient's dynamics. Instead, he was mindful that the resident had begun this discussion by expressing his own fatigue and dis-tress as his principal concerns. With this in mind, the supervisor opted to address the enforced helplessness in a way that included the resident's feelings as well as the patient's dynamics. This in-volved the resident's wish for unlimited energy and perhaps an omnipotent wish to help this patient.

The supervisor said, "That powerful thrust—the patient's neck hold—collides with your wish for unlimited energy, and wish to be able to come to the rescue." The resident's eyes widened and he exclaimed with some excitement, "That's it! It was an irresistible force versus an immovable object. That's what was impossible." He felt that this approach had been a defense against recognizing the limitations of what one could do.

In this hour, the supervisor had several options for how to hear this material and how to respond. He redirected the focus of supervision toward patient material, addressing the patient's pathology, the resident's possible interventions, and so on. He could also try to place the resident's feelings in an educational context, explaining that struggling with issues of therapeutic zeal and limitation is a normative phase of early training in psychotherapy. Or he might explore the resident's remarks further, helping the therapist to understand the nature of his unrealistic expectations for his own performance. Further, the supervisor might listen to this as a communication to the supervisor: asking him for permission to relax, seeking reassurance that he was doing a good job, despite being rendered relatively helpless by the patient.

The supervisor chose to begin with a general, theoretical, impersonal focus (the emergence of a trauma paradigm). The dialogue then moved to a more personal focus, but in a normalizing, educational, supportive way ("What you are struggling with is common in working with such patients"). Eventually the supervisor addressed the resident's feelings more directly and clarified the point of conflict between the therapist's wish to feel more powerful and rescue this patient and the patient's wish to immobilize him as a way of dealing with feelings of being overpowered and helpless. In the process, the resident moved beyond his fatigue and burned-out feeling and reflected upon his experience. He recognized how his therapeutic zeal and omnipotent wishes conflicted with the patient's need to render him motionless. The self-reflection was applied to understanding the patient's need better and to clarifying a distressing dynamic in the therapeutic work.

In addressing the resident's feelings in this way, the supervisor relied on several factors. First was the resident's openness to self-disclosure and his eagerness to understand what he was struggling with. Further, the supervisor and resident shared a respect for an implicit boundary: while the resident's experience was a focus, the discussion was not exploratory or intrusive. Whatever deeper conflicts he might have had over omnipotence and helplessness or what had gotten in the way of his seeing the reenactment of trauma were not examined. Rather, the supervisor allowed the resident to titrate the extent of the discussion and of his self-reflection.

The supervisory dyad faces the ongoing challenge of finding the right balance and defining the boundaries of self-reflection in which the educational work will proceed. There is often no explicit understanding at the beginning of supervision as to what the limits of personal revelation will be. Addressing the supervisee's inner experience may also feel critical or judgmental. Further pressure arises from transferences to the supervisor and the authority relationship. The quality of their dialogue is determined by the degree of familiarity that both supervisor and supervisee have with their inner lives, the degree of comfort in revealing certain aspects to one another, and their motivation for doing so. The personality of each member, his or her trust and safety in the supervision, and the supervisory "fit" also influence this balance. The difficulties that arise in supervision around the uses of self-reflection and the dangers of intrusion can sometimes be surmounted by an explicit discussion between teacher and student as to what each believes the appropriate boundaries for such discourse should be.

Enhancing Self-Reflective Capacities

Six forms of intervention, which will be described further in chapter 7, can help to enhance a student's capacity for self-reflection. They are modeling, questioning, permission and encouragement, didactic explanation, clarification and labeling, and interpretation.

The supervisor's readiness to be self-reflective and to demonstrate the usefulness of self-reflection in clinical work can serve as a model for the therapist. For example: "That reminds me of a patient I once treated as a resident. I was feeling very guilty about not doing enough for this poor woman. She was so troubled, and her life was always in such a mess. I always thought there was more I should be doing to help her. One day it dawned on me that this sad, rather marginal woman was really quite demanding in the therapy. She passively waited for me to take charge of the sessions and her life and make her feel better. And I, for reasons of my own, had gone along with it, feeling somehow that I shouldn't ask too much of her. Once I realized that, I could focus on the issue of who had been assigned responsibility for improving her life and why." Such an approach models the use and boundaries of self-reflection in supervision and shows how self-awareness can be applied to improve the understanding of a therapeutic encounter. It also conveys the supervisor's comfort with revealing less-than-ideal aspects of his or her own responses and technique.

Through questions like "How did you feel when the patient said your tie had a stain on it?" or "How did you arrive at the conclusion that the patient is angry with his mother?" the supervisor brings the therapist's experience and feelings as well as his personal approach to meaning and understanding into the supervisory discourse. Such questions show that the supervisor is interested not just in how the patient is doing but in what kind of mental activity the trainee is engaged in and how it can be used to sharpen his therapeutic skills.

As self-reflection and self-disclosure can lead to shame and anxiety, the trainee may need permission and encouragement to reflect upon and share his inner experiences in supervision. This is not given directly but through modeling, and by the noncritical tone that establishes an atmosphere of safety for the student, and implies that his revelations will not be judged but used to advance his education as a therapist. Students who seem not to employ self-reflection in their work may need to hear more explicitly, in a clearly didactic manner, that their inner experiences are relevant and valued aspects of psychotherapy and can be the source of knowledge about the therapeutic encounter.

If adequate supervisory rapport and a sense of safety are established, the supervisor has greater freedom to address the supervisee's experience directly. The supervisor may observe, for example, "Your reply to the patient suggests that his comments made you angry. Were you aware of such feelings?" Or she may comment: "I think not being able to rescue this patient from his isolation and suffering upsets you. Is that so?" If the supervisor sees a pattern in the therapist's responses, she may offer a clarification. "You've told me you wish this patient weren't so hard on himself. At times, though, this may interfere with your exploring certain subjects in greater depth. When, for instance, you told your patient not to worry about being late, you were telling him, I suppose, to go easier on himself, but you missed a chance to try to understand what he felt about coming late. Perhaps you feel reluctant to make your patient angry by asking such questions."

Interpretive comments that touch upon the motivation of the trainee must be made carefully, after trust and a good learning alliance have been established. "When your patient begins to belittle you, you become silent and seem to withdraw, and when you present these incidents to me, your tone is a bit derisive. Perhaps in your silence with him you are controlling a temptation to counterattack. If so, it might shed some light on this man's difficulties with aggression. We might also consider how your anger could be used to better explore what goes on between the two of you at these moments."

The skill and timing with which the supervisor uses these pedagogical methods will dictate, in part, the depth of the supervisory discourse. A comment on the student's motivation made before a solid learning alliance has been established is likely to retard its development. Likewise, too heavy a reliance on one form of teaching may make the shape of the supervisory dialogue predictable and limited. Expanding a student's ways of knowing requires flexibility and a tacit agreement that neither party knows where the discourse will take them. The supervisor, however, has certain educational tools at her disposal which, when used effectively, can enliven the discourse and expand a student's ways of knowing.

The supervisor and supervisee face issues concerning self-disclosure in supervision—how much revelation is appropriate and educationally useful. The way in which the supervisory dialogue addresses the supervisee's affects, internal experience, and personal revelation is the subject of the next chapter.

5

How Personal Should Supervision Be?

"Because I'm with a group of psychiatrists, I don't want to get too personal," Stephen Sondheim told a group at the 1990 American Psychiatric Association meeting. There was laughter from the audience at Sondheim's making light of an issue that all of us take very seriously: namely, the public exposure of what we regard as private. The topic of his address, "The Creative Process," seemed at first glance impersonal enough. However, he was supposed to illustrate and comment on his internal experience of his own creative process: what it was like for him, what he thought about, what he felt. He was also supposed to take questions from the audience, a group of professionally trained intruders. Sondheim was in a potentially difficult spot.

His situation had interesting parallels to that of the psycho-therapist during supervision. The student therapist is also in the awkward situation of deciding how much exposure will be part of the examination of his creative process. It is true that a main (perhaps the primary) focus of psychotherapy supervision is the patient: the patient's psychological experience of his or her life, the patient's history, the patient's actions. In fact, one orientation to doing psychotherapy supervision is to focus exclusively on the patient (Betcher and Zinberg, 1988). In so doing, one can often detour around the kinds of questions and issues that are dealt with in this chapter. However, if one is not to be so circumscribed, then how personal should supervision be? What should be revealed and discussed beyond the patient's material? Unless both supervisor and therapist are committed to ignoring these arenas of supervision at all costs, they will sooner or later be confronted with how best to discuss the clinician's feelings in relation to his patient and what educational use to make of those feelings.

Emotions can be stirred up and expressed in a variety of educational processes, not just in psychotherapy supervision. Any student may feel anxious or depressed about some new phase of the work or personally moved by an aspect of the material being learned, and strong feelings may then surface. Characteristically, the teacher behaves in a supportive fashion, nonpunitive and compassionate, but usually not focused on elaborating the content of the student's feelings. When the feelings subside, the teacher and student again turn their attention to the material being studied. The emotion that surfaced is dealt with humanely, perhaps in a psychologically informed way, but the feelings themselves are not the educational focus to be explored and elaborated.

Such might be the case, for example, in the supervision of a medical resident learning cardiology. Imagine for a moment that the resident, while reporting on the emergency room evaluation of an older man, mentions to his attending supervisor that the patient made him very angry. The patient had been uncooperative because he was panicked at the prospect of having something wrong with his heart. The resident was worried that the patient might die before the appropriate medications could be administered and was angry at the patient for impeding the medical workup and treatment. In a medical supervisory setting, the resident's overall concern would be acknowledged. However, if any educational mention were made of the angry feelings, it would probably be in the context of how the resident could more effectively calm a patient in such a situation. The medical trainee's emotions would not assume center stage in the educational interaction. The educational role, if any, of the trainee's emotions would be to signal the teacher about what educational content to focus on (in this case, managing recalcitrant patients).

Contrast this situation with the supervision of a psychotherapy trainee who reported feeling angry at a patient who was hindering his own psychological care. In this case, a psychiatric resident described the emergency room evaluation of a patient with panic attacks. The patient, who had an institutionalized relative, was very anxious at the prospect of having a psychiatric diagnosis and even more frightened of needing psychotropic medications and psychotherapy. The resident also talked of feeling angry and frustrated with the patient. The supervisor could concentrate on the patient's dynamics to clarify his psychological concerns as well as their contribution to the therapist's feelings. The supervisor could also focus didactically on different ways of responding to this patient and to others like him. Both of these interventions and the role of the trainee's affect would parallel, in a sense, what might have unfolded in the medical resident's supervision. In both situations, the therapist's affect (anger) signals the teacher as to what material needs to taught, but the affect is not explored in and of itself. However, what if a psychotherapy trainee is having a persistent problem with getting angry with this patient, or several patients? What if the trainee, after mentioning her anger, added that she was about to stop her own therapy and wondered if that had a bearing on how she had responded to her patient? What if the trainee volunteered that this patient reminded her of a close relative or that the issues coming up for the patient felt similar to issues she was dealing with in her own treatment?

This series of "what ifs" from real supervisory situations illustrates issues about affect and the unconscious that were raised by the supervisee and not by the supervisor. These were not situations in which the supervisor initiated an exploration of affect that the clinician wanted to keep personal and private. These examples illustrate that the supervisee's affect and his feelings about discussing them cannot be avoided without significantly limiting the depth of the dialogue. A patient-oriented focus in supervision would not provide the supervisor with any guidance as to how to respond to the above list of hypothetical questions. While it is not our intention here to suggest that the trainee's affect should be the primary focus of his or her education and supervision, the trainee's affect will at times be the central concern of supervision. Our aim is to outline an educationally useful but personally respectful way of dealing with those moments.

The interwoven nature of the educational and therapeutic goals of psychotherapy training has roots in the beginnings of psychoanalysis. From the first, training in psychoanalysis reflected awareness of the clinical importance of both self-examination and psychological understanding in the educational setting. As we have noted, the earliest psychoanalytic seminars incorporated examination of one's own psyche as the first domain in which to look for a demonstration of intrapsychic theory (Fleming and Benedek, 1966). Early training in psychoanalysis was composed of the trainee's personal analysis and a series of accompanying seminars, a process measured in months, not years. However, the therapeutic component—the training analysis—was considerably more didactic than it is today. It was to be both therapeutic and instructional, in the service of experiential education. Through the study of one's own psyche, one would not only learn to treat neurotic issues but also see the forces of the psyche convincingly demonstrated (Fleming and Benedek, 1966). The issues of privacy in psychoanalytic education had not yet been clearly identified (Betcher and Zinberg, 1988; Spiegel and Grunebaum, 1977). The special requirements for talking to someone about his or her own affects and unconscious had not yet been fully understood. It was as if the truth of this new theory alone might be sufficient to permit a successful educational dialogue.

Almost a century later, extensive experience with psychodynamic training and practice has clarified the need for the supervisor and trainee at times to examine collaboratively the therapist's emotional response to the patient and the treatment. A psychotherapist needs to learn from the dialogue with his supervisor how to contain and interpret his own feelings, at least to the degree that these feelings are relevant to the therapy. Supervision must not only accommodate a dialogue about the trainee's affective experiences in doing treatment but also teach the skills that eventually equip therapists to identify, contain, and analyze affective experiences on their own. The educational implication is that students should acquire some facility with self-reflection and self-analysis as part of their psychotherapy curriculum.

Three skills, in particular, are central to the therapist's successful management and use of affect in the treatment setting: to contain, to name or identify, and to analyze a given emotion in oneself and relate it to the unfolding therapeutic process. The objective of these three skills is to enable the therapist to tolerate and integrate his own affective resonances to the treatment.

The therapist must be able to bear and examine the intense emotions that are communicated to him by the patient's telling his story. The therapist must also be able to bear and examine a variety of internally generated emotional resonances that occur in the context of and in response to doing treatment. This process becomes more complicated when the therapist's emotional response turns out to be unfamiliar or upsetting to his view of himself.

For example, a second-year female trainee was treating an attractive man in his early twenties. The patient was in treatment because he was unable to disentangle himself from an overinvolved relationship with his mother and to form appropriate romantic relationships. The therapist talked in supervision about the patient's relationship with a woman he was dating. However, she was reluctant to explore the matter in depth with the patient. Her hesitancy, it turned out, stemmed from her feeling that it was seductive to probe into his romantic attachments. The therapist was also concerned about the nascent attachment the patient was forming to her and felt uneasy about exploring this issue. In the course of the treatment, the therapist had been confronted with an experience that was an affront to her professional view of herself: she feared she may have been seductive to the patient. The therapist had two different affective responses: anxiety about her sexual curiosity about her patient and shame and guilt in relation to her professional identity.

It is essential that the therapist be able to contain these affects consciously if she is to determine what, if any, relevance her emotions have to her patient's difficulties. The therapist must be aware of her feelings if she is to relate to them as a barometer of her patient's anxiety about his relationships. Conceptually, the therapist's containment of her affect enables her to be consciously receptive without being reflexively reactive to what she is feeling. She should be interested and curious about her own emotional pulse while not responding impulsively to what she finds.

The therapist's ability to inhibit reflexive responses must likewise not inhibit her ability to identify and analyze these feelings. This represents an interesting professional paradox. In many professions the containment of responses to emotions is achieved by suppressing one's own affects, and the person is encouraged not to think about how he or she is feeling. For example, an attorney must learn to suppress personal feelings about a client's guilt in the service of preparing that client's legal defense. An actor must direct his attention to bringing his or her character to life in lieu of focusing on opening-night jitters. In these and other settings, self-reflection becomes a distraction and an obstacle to good professional work. Therefore, in many educational and professional settings, containment of affect by conscious suppression is permissable and even pedagogically advisable. However, a psychotherapist must be able to contain feelings without diminishing conscious awareness of them. Relying too heavily on other avenues of repression such as minimization, intellectualization, or humor to tolerate the emotional heat of the work situation risks the therapist's losing contact with her own affective resonances to the patient and with the patient himself. The cardiology resident's repression or minimization of the emotional impact of his work may be educationally encouraged as helping him pay closer attention to medical and management issues with the patient. By contrast, in psychotherapy training, self-awareness is crucial.

What, then, is the training therapist to do with this professionally required self-awareness? The skill that should follow conscious containment of affect is the ability to identify correctly the nature of one's own internal affective state: for example, to determine whether one is feeling angry, helpless, or sad. Being able to identify one's own affective state correctly within the context of doing psychotherapy is a complicated task and too often taken for granted educationally. It is, we believe, a different matter than the identification of one's feelings in most nontherapeutic situations, because it is uncommon to force oneself to remain in an interpersonal intimate situation to which one is having a dysphoric or narcissistically injurious emotional response. People commonly leave such situations, either physically or psychologically, or at least protest to the other person. Yet the professional requirements of the role of psychotherapist cut off social and psychological responses that would customarily be used in a nontherapeutic setting. This is another way in which being an analytically oriented psychotherapist does not have a precedent or analog in customary social interactions. Without the usual social options of withdrawal or protest, the therapist is confronted with the need to identify his own affective resonances to the patient. The most problematic of these affects will be those that are dysphoric or narcissistically injurious to the therapist.

The therapist's identification of the category of his own affect sometimes occurs via association: that is, moving from affectively charged thoughts or memories to the affect itself. At other times the therapist will become directly aware of affect without any contextualizing associations. The following two examples, which were brought to supervision by two different therapists, illustrate this point.

A second-year female trainee, Dr. I., was treating a psychologically brittle young woman who alternately was withdrawn or intensely angry. In supervision, the therapist, after reporting some of the content of the patient's material, added that during the treatment hour she had found herself thinking of a segment of an autobiography she had read. The segment, which concerned a mother's sadistic treatment of her daughter, was a disturbing recollection for the therapist and outwardly seemed unrelated to the patient's narrative.

The supervisor, Dr. B., was aware that the therapist had just made an anxiety-producing disclosure. Dr. I. had found herself recalling an upsetting literary reference without knowing either the precipitant or the meaning of her memory. The supervisor was also ignorant of the determinants that evoked the memory. Dr. B.'s goals in the supervision were to help Dr. I. make sense of— to contain, identify, and analyze—the memory and affect being discussed. The degree to which a therapist might be asked to reveal feelings and memories (for example, was there some personal meaning for the therapist about this autobiography?) would depend on whether it would further the educational and therapeutic aims of the supervision. In this case it was sufficient for the supervisor to be supportive of the therapist's own interest in the relationship between her internal experience and the patient's treatment.

The therapist, initially upset and puzzled by the literary association, began to characterize the nature of the affect it aroused (hate or sadism). This therapist became consciously aware of a derivative (a memory) of her emotion before she became aware of the emotion itself. She had to contain and be curious about the memory in order to identify the category of affects involved, and she subsequently began to associate the affect to the treatment. She began to wonder how her patient felt she had been treated by her mother and how she herself felt she was being treated by the patient. Both relationships contained feelings of aggression that previously had been unarticulated and could now be brought into the treatment.

In another supervisory example, the therapist took a different psychological route to identify affect. A second-year male trainee reported feeling very discouraged about the treatment of a narcissistic man in his early thirties. In contrast to the therapist's view, the supervisor felt the treatment was progressing reasonably well in terms of the patient's willingness to begin to talk more meaningfully about his current life situation. Despite the supervisor's bringing up this more hopeful vision of the treatment, the therapist found himself feeling depressed and discouraged. The therapist had at this point already successfully contained and identified his affective experience (depression and discouragement). He and the supervisor were now collaboratively engaged in trying to analyze and relate the affect to its origin. The therapist had initially attributed his feelings to the treatment's inadequate progress. However, a reexamination of the course of the therapy in supervision had clarified that this was not the cause of the therapist's depression.

The supervisor and therapist again turned to the clinical material the patient was presenting. The therapist talked about the sense of hopelessness the patient felt about himself. This review allowed the supervisor to contrast the patient's fears and hopelessness with the actual progress that had been made in the treatment. In the course of this supervisory discussion, the therapist realized he was resonating to the patient's expressed fear that his life and future were hopeless. This component of the therapist's affect having been clarified, the therapist was better able to understand his identification with the patient's fears. He was able to reframe his own emotion as countertransference and utilize the feeling to deepen his understanding of the patient.

The therapist's curiosity about his own affective responses warrants further explanation. The process involves the therapist's review of hypothetical precipitants until a substantive connection can be found between a precipitant and the affect being experienced. In the current example, precipitants the therapist may have imagined include recent disappointments for the patient, the patient's long-term conflicts and hopes, and current and resonant issues from the therapist's own life.

The trainee in the first example reported having affectively charged thoughts without being clear about the particular emotion involved or the stimulus for it. The second therapist had a more "pure" affective experience, without any cognitive or associational derivatives of the emotion. Having contained his dysphoria, he was able to identify his mood as depression; however, at first he did not understand why he should feel that way. By using associative thinking (in this case, by allowing himself to associate to the therapeutic material), this therapist was able to determine the primary source for his experience: his resonance with the patient's depression. It is as if he thought, "I don't know why I should be feeling this way, but at the moment I find myself feeling depressed." The mood had been consciously contained and then observed and identified.

In contrast to the second therapist's internal processing of emotion, the first therapist, while sitting with her patient, found herself thinking of a character in an autobiography she had read. What she noticed first was a sequence from a literary memory, itself a derivative or by-product of the feeling generated in response to the patient. She then had to martial her ability to contain consciously and be curious about her own associations in order to identify the emotion involved. Having identified that affect but without yet knowing its cause or precipitant, the therapist then needed to review the material of the treatment to determine what had evoked these affective resonances.

Both therapists had a dysphoric emotional resonance to the unfolding treatment and both would eventually have to review the material presented by the patient to appreciate the source of their own affective experience and its relevance to the patient's treatment. However, the initial psychological awareness experienced and the necessary response were clearly quite different for these two therapists. One therapist began by having to contain and identify an emotion that initially did not have a known source. The other began with an associational derivative of emotion, a memory, the affect around which also needed to be contained, identified, and retraced to the treatment. These vignettes also illustrate the three skills or steps utilized by therapists to process their own affective resonances to a treatment. In the two examples, the stimulus for the affective experience was primarily the treatment. This is not invariably so; sometimes the stimulus is from the therapist's own psyche and has less to do with the material the patient is communicating. The affect might also originate in the supervisor or the interpersonal process of the supervision.

Perhaps most common is a mixture of sources. However, a therapist dealing with any of these situations must rely on the same set of intrapsychic processes used to respond to the purely countertransferential emotion: the ability to contain, to identify, and finally to analyze or relate the internal affective experience of the therapist to the current stimulus.

Developing the therapist's abilities with these processes presents an important supervisory challenge. We have seen that during psychotherapy, the therapist is instructed to be aware of his own affective response when there may be an automatic, defensive wish to do just the opposite. During supervision, the therapist is then confronted with making his self-examination public. This is not customarily done in a work or professional arena, and is customarily reserved for the therapeutic domain.

Fostering the development of affective awareness followed by self-examination or self-analysis is a complex goal of supervision, requiring the development of special educational methods. An individual's affective awareness and self-examination are not analogous to the usual factual and theoretical material taught with existing educational techniques but are highly personal subjects. As a result, teachers of psychotherapy once derived much of their educational technique and understanding from the familiar framework for conscious and unconscious affect they used in the settings of psychotherapy and psychoanalysis. The historical precedent for doing this was that a training psychoanalysis was originally and to some degree still is conceptualized as experiential psychological education for the training therapist, as opposed to a solely psychological treatment (Fleming and Benedek, 1966). Not only is the therapist to be treated for his neurotic blind spots, he is also to have the experience of seeing his own psychic forces in action.

In psychoanalytic and psychodynamic training, a therapist's

problems in professional efficacy have tended to be broadly characterized as products of either therapist ignorance and innocence or therapist psychological conflict and deficit (Ekstein and Wallerstein, 1958). In this educational model, ignorance can be dealt with by traditional educational methods, while problems of presumed conflict or deficit were understood as manifestations of psychopathology, to be dealt with by a modified use of the transference, clarification, and interpretation (Ekstein and Wallerstein, 1958; Lawner, 1989).

There are, in fact, many parallels between psychotherapy and psychotherapy supervision, making understandable the appeal of transplantation of psychotherapeutic concepts to an educational framework. Both psychotherapy and supervision are dyadic situations that carefully examine serious life events and different individuals' emotional experience of those events. Both psychotherapy and supervision are revelatory processes; they are self-reflective and self-conscious; both generate and reveal unanticipated affective responses in the context of an unequal power relationship; and each fosters a level of dependency and/or regression. In view of these many parallels, it seems reasonable that concepts from psychotherapy and psychoanalysis were utilized in the hope of shedding light on how to understand and respond educationally to issues of affect and the unconscious.

However, the essential differences between psychotherapy and supervision have been less clearly appreciated. During the course of a psychotherapy or a psychoanalysis, for instance, the patient shares a wide range of information about himself or herself with the therapist. This includes the history of the patient's experience and the history of his or her level of function in a variety of settings, past and present; the patient's fantasies; and information derived from the collaborative examination of the relationship between patient and therapist. In psychotherapy, this relationship itself is, by agreement, a legitimate arena for collaborative exploration.

However, the information available to trainee and supervisor in psychotherapy supervision is very different. No shared history, personal or professional, is comprehensively elaborated in the supervisory dialogue, nor is information about the trainee's function in any settings other than the therapeutic hours being discussed and the supervisory interactions being directly observed. The relationship between supervisor and therapist, unlike in psychotherapy and psychoanalysis, is not customarily available for collaborative examination. As a result of these profound differences, the data available on which a supervisor might make formulations, educational or otherwise, is very constricted compared to the data available to a therapist in psychotherapy or psychoanalysis.

If, for example, a trainee is observed to be having difficulties with a given issue as a therapist, it is very difficult for the supervisor to know with certainty whether the issue extends to other areas of the trainee's life, past or present: that is, whether a problem identified in supervision is primarily an educational issue or a personal issue that extends into professional life. Even if the problem is evident in a variety of professional settings, caution is needed before making psychopathologic generalizations or diagnosis.

Regression and depression are frequently observed early in training as a phenomenon that has been understood as the trainee's psychological response to the new work being undertaken (Shershow and Irwin, 1976). This observation underscores the difficulty in making accurate psychological formulations about a trainee who may be temporarily in psychological flux as a response to his or her professional development. In our experience several trainees who appeared to have serious difficulties with narcissism, anxiety, or depression went on to do well professionally. The change took place in a much shorter time frame than would have been expected if these problems had been primarily characterologic rather than related to a stage of professional development.

We have considered some of the informational issues that make it possible to talk to someone in psychotherapy about his or her affects and unconscious, yet the informational base is much more restricted in supervision. Having less access to information lowers the likelihood of being able to speak knowledgeably about a trainee's affects and unconscious. However, being right or well-informed is only part of the supervisory issue. A therapist or supervisor can be correct about her observations and still lack the interpersonal context that would permit their discussion. What then are the aspects in a relationship that facilitate someone's openly considering psychologically clarifying or interpretive remarks? Alternatively, what in a relationship makes it likely that someone will disregard or feel injured when being told the same information? We compare the relationships that exist in psychotherapy and in supervision from this relational perspective. Our purpose is to contrast the conditions in psychotherapy and supervision that are most relevant to elaborating an educational theory and method for dealing with affect and self-revelation in psychotherapy supervision.

Both psychotherapy and supervision take place in a relationship that is goal-directed, dyadic, consultative, and ongoing. However, in supervision, unlike psychotherapy, more than one individual must be served in the relationship. In psychotherapy, that individual is the patient. In supervision, the trainee, the patient, and not uncommonly the institution also have a stake in the outcome. There are also different levels of freedom of choice in the two relationships. Therapists are customarily chosen; supervisors are usually assigned. Likewise, patients can initiate ending a therapeutic relationship; supervisees usually cannot. Patients can to a great degree choose the material brought for discussion to therapy. Supervisees must select from what the patient has chosen to bring to the treatment (Betcher and Zinberg, 1988). No one of these differences is sufficient to create or destroy a sense of safety in a psychotherapeutic or supervisory relationship. The effects of the characteristic differences of the two relationships are additive. However, the basic structure of the supervisee relationship does not itself provide the same level of security that is inherently provided in the therapeutic relationship.

In both relationships, a feeling of safety or security for the patient and trainee (Maltsberger and Buie, 1969) is central to a successful discussion of the individual's affect and unconscious. There must be the safety of knowing that the dialogue will remain within the stated goals of the relationship and that there will not be an alternate agenda. For example, the individual will not be asked to reveal personal information in the service of the personal needs of the therapist or supervisor; personal information should be asked for only in the service of the therapy and the supervision. Second, there needs to be a sense of security in the predictability of the consultative relationship, the assurance that once having revealed one's foibles, one will still be treated fairly rather than shamed or humiliated. Finally, the belief that the consultant has a basic confidence or favorable impression of the consultee is an extremely important counterweight to the inevitable feelings of shame and guilt that surface in both psychotherapy (Lewis, 1985) and its supervision (Lewis, 1986).

The perception of these relational qualities ultimately resides within the individual's inner experience of the relationship. There is no objective standard of interpersonal relating that can be met or measured; an individual's feeling of security is an internal experiential matter, subject to the inner forces of that individual's psychology. An individual may feel safe in relationships when he should not and conversely may not feel secure even though the relationship is, in fact, safe. The inner experience of the trainee or patient ultimately determines whether the relationship is perceived as sufficiently sustaining to support personal discussions of affect and the unconscious.

In supervision, a considerable level of feeling safe and secure is achievable. An appreciation of the inherent differences between the supervisory and psychotherapy relationships regarding their voluntary nature, the control over the choice of consultant, the content and duration of the relationship, and the number of people who must be served simultaneously helps in understanding the potential problems that can arise in the supervisory relationship.

Relational issues of safety and security have been discussed without further reference to psychological and psychotherapeutic concepts of the working alliance, empathy, and the self to avoid relying on and transplanting metapsychological concepts of psychotherapy into an educational setting. The most relevant experience and understanding about conducting a dialogue concerning affects and the unconscious lie within the fields of psychotherapy and psychoanalysis. However, the direct transfer of psychoanalytic concepts (such as conflict and defense) to the supervisory dialogue has significant limitations. In psychotherapy, these concepts are derived from a metapsychology that itself is based on certain assumptions about the therapeutic relationship and goals of individuals in therapy. The supervisory relationship and goals and the individuals involved (student and teacher) are not similar enough to their therapeutic counterparts to make use of the same assumptions or metapsychology.

Consider the following supervisory material presented midway in the academic year. A capable third-year male resident was discussing the evaluation and treatment of an intermittently psychotic and impulsive woman in her late twenties. The treatment was just beginning and both the patient's diagnosis and underlying dynamics were by no means clear. The therapist was in the process of presenting the information he had about the patient and then abruptly and deliberately shifted to disclose something very personal about himself. He told the supervisor that he had a sister who had been diagnosed with a psychotic illness and had committed suicide several years before. The therapist said that working with the patient who was currently under discussion was reminding him of his own sister.

The supervisor, presented with this information, was confronted with deciding both how to understand and how to respond to the therapist's disclosure about himself. What did the disclosure mean? What would be educationally helpful? What would be helpful to the patient's treatment? What would be personally respectful of the therapist's privacy and the therapist's needs? She had general confidence in this therapist's skills and personal strengths, but this was not the same as knowing why the therapist had brought these personal facts into the supervision at all and why at this point in time.

There is no generalizable answer as to whether this kind of disclosure ought to be encouraged as part of the supervisory dialogue. The decision depends on a variety of factors. Supervisors and supervisees may have differing ideas about what is appropriate to discuss in supervision. When there is a major difference in their respective expectations that is unrecognized, it is unlikely that the supervisor will respond effectively. Alternatively, recognition and tolerance of differences in orientation usually results in a degree of flexibility even in the absence of agreement.

A supervisor must also make a judgment about the capacity of their working relationship to sustain an exploration of personal material. A similar judgment must also be made about the personal and professional strengths of the trainee. What is the likelihood that the therapist will feel invited or even coerced into making personal disclosures which he will then regret? What chance is there that the discussion will foster anxiety instead of relieving it? Will the therapist ultimately feel embarrassed? The supervisor can elect to raise some of these questions directly in the dialogue. She can outline her recognition of the personal nature of the material and openly discuss some of the options and the attendant risks.

Even having made the judgment that it will be possible to discuss this material, a supervisor must decide whether or not such an exploration will be profitable and in what direction the exploration should proceed. The supervisor is frequently without the necessary data from which to formulate an informed decision. The therapist's personal revelation can represent either an important deepening of or a detour from the educational goals of supervision.

In this example of a therapist's disclosure about his sister's suicide, talking about the therapist's memories and feelings may be important to understanding the therapist's emotional and therapeutic reactions to the patient. However, this is not the only possibility. It might also represent the therapist's unacknowledged or unconscious wish for therapy about the death of a sibling brought to the surface by this patient. There are also times when a therapist is more comfortable talking about himself than confronting some issue in his own education. In such situations, self-revelation can be a way *not* to attend to the patient's treatment and the therapist's training. Personal disclosures may also derive from the therapist's feeling that the supervisor is educationally unhelpful and so the therapist begins to talk about material outside the treatment to fill up the supervisory hour. In the present example, this last possibility is unlikely in view of the gravity of the disclosure. It is not so unlikely a possibility when the content of what a therapist brings to supervision seems persistently to be about material outside the treatment (for example, future professional plans, vacations, other supervisors, family developments).

The supervisor's first reaction to this therapist's disclosure was anxiety about being privy to such personal information in the absence of knowing why she had been told it. Her anxiety was also a response to her uncertainty of what to do next. She would acknowledge both the personal and professional dimensions of the disclosure, and then focus their attention primarily on the latter. In this case the supervisor said that treating the patient was probably reviving the therapist's memories and feelings about his sister and that he might well find himself reworking and even regrieving the loss of his sibling. The supervisor went on to say that it would be important for the two of them to be thoughtful about how that might also affect his treatment of his patient.

The supervisor's response invited further disclosure that would be relevant to the mission of the supervision: the training of the therapist and the treatment of the patient. The supervisor neither invited nor foreclosed on the therapist saying more about the personal or private dimensions of what was being evoked by this patient. The legitimate claim of supervision is to that aspect of material pertinent to the treatment. Yet it seems artificial and rigid to suggest there is no place in supervision for personal revelations unrelated to the clinical work. However, these revelations should not be in lieu of supervisory work.

The therapist responded to both aspects of the supervisor's comments. He spoke briefly about how the experience of working with seriously ill patients was reviving feelings of grief and anger and questions of responsibility concerning his sister. He also talked about the anxiety he felt when faced with treating someone whom he realistically knew to be a high-risk patient. In the supervisor's view, there was a professional educational dimension to the therapist's experience. The therapist, as a result of his own life experience, had a heightened awareness of the possibility of a bad therapeutic outcome for the patient.

The supervisor, based on her educational assessment, shifted from an exploration of the therapist's own life experience to the realistic appraisal of the treatment options and risks for this patient. This led to a more focused treatment plan for the patient and the therapist's greater appreciation of the realistic risks and limits of treating patients who are seriously ill. In this supervision, the supervisor and the supervisee remained aware of the educational context within which the dialogue was unfolding as they explored a very personal (and, in our view, appropriate) disclosure about the therapist.

The example demonstrates several principles or themes which we feel are important to keep in mind when dealing with the inner life of the therapist in supervision. The first of these is that the litmus test of self-revelation in supervision is the degree to which it contributes meaningfully to the therapy of the patient and the education of the therapist. Will the self-revelation relate to or interfere with the basic goals of supervision? The discussion of the most private material could have either a proper place or no place at all in a given supervision. Often, supervisors will not have enough information to determine beforehand whether the self-revelation will further or impede the educational goals of supervision. In view of this uncertainty, the questions about the relevance to education and the patient's treatment can be openly raised and collaboratively explored.

Second, whether a personal revelation is educationally relevant or not, supervisors must also assess whether the material is discussible with that supervisor and supervisee, at that particular stage in the supervisory relationship. The answer depends on the nature of the individuals involved and on their working relationship. Within the supervision, have supervisor and therapist both been able to contain, identify, and reflect on their feelings? Has their relationship provided containment and security or has it tended to generate anxiety and embarrassment? Have the uncertainties about these specific questions been collaboratively discussed so that the therapist is also copilot of and not just a passenger in the supervisory process?

Third, having embarked on self-revelation, the therapist and supervisor do not need to continue for longer than seems educationally useful. They can also simultaneously make use of other more typical, less personal educational interventions. In the example above, the supervisor felt that the therapist's principal professional concern was his fear that his own therapeutic skills might have little effect in a serious clinical situation. That having been clarified, the supervisor tried to respond to specific educational issues by helping him sharpen the clinical assessment of the patient, improve the emergency contingencies of the treatment plan, and acknowledge the limits and uncertainties of treating a patient who was seriously ill. They did not make the supervision more personal than it needed to be.

A supervisor can develop her own comfort in moving back and forth between a more affectively charged exploration of a therapist's self-revelation and other more customary, less personal interventions such as modeling, didactic instruction, and clinically focused questioning. After clarifying an educational or clinical issue from a therapist's self-revelation, a supervisor may then make use of interventions that respect the therapist's privacy but still address the identified clinical or educational need. The supervisor can be responsive to the concerns of the trainee who, like Stephen Sondheim at the psychiatric meetings, was concerned with how exposed he would be in a work-related setting. The supervisory discussion of therapist self-revelation contributes to a loss of therapist privacy. Another aspect of supervision that determines how personal supervision becomes is the role of affect in a therapist's training and professional development, to which we now turn our attention.

6

Affect and Professional Development

The interpersonal role requirements of the therapist, which demand the conscious containment of emotion, are new ones for the student, and he needs help from his supervisor to master them. For example, patients' negative transferences that must be endured and analyzed present a significant emotional burden for the therapist. Being the object of intense negative feelings is something usually tolerated only in the most intimate of relationships, but the role of psychotherapist is an exception to this rule. The beginning psychotherapist is exposing himself to a variety of affective experiences for which there can be no prior analogous experience or earlier opportunity for mastery. As a result, the therapist must acquire a new psychological competence in identifying his individual emotional response to a novel social relationship. The therapist's affective responses will be a product not only of the patient he is seeing but of his personal psychic structure and experiences. The therapist's responses therefore will be to some degree unique and, in that sense, impossible to anticipate.

The therapist needs to develop tolerance and understanding of his own affective experiences because of these unique role requirements of the psychotherapist. A model for how to aid this process during training can be derived from the normative, nonprofessional development of affective learning. Individuals evolve their own topology for identifying the category of emotion they are feeling and then connecting the feeling with relevant internal or external events. An individual gradually gains competence in sampling his internal affective state and distinguishing the class and determinants of his emotions. People use a variety of inputs to arrive at a conclusion about what they are feeling and why, including somatic correlates of affect, memory, associative thinking, and deductive thinking. Normally this process of learning to identify and articulate how one is feeling takes place in childhood. Children are not born with the capacity to recognize their own affective states or the language to decipher them. Through a process of developmental learning and in the setting of empathic and informed relationships a child acquires the capacity to know how he or she feels. Ideally, this early portion of psychological development has been completed long before professional training. (Where it has not—for instance, in an individual who has serious and persistent blind spots with respect to his own emotions— there is a need for treatment, not just supervision.) However, even if this normative development has taken place, the professional requirements of learning psychotherapy add another dimension to the process of learning about one's own experience of affect. This part of professional development involves identification, tolerance, and familiarity with one's own affective responsiveness. The supervisor's role in this phase of professional development is not to explore historic roots and transferential derivatives of these affective responses, as she would in psychotherapy. Instead, the supervisor must help the therapist identify his unique affective signals and must promote a state of shame-free tolerance and curiosity about these affective states. In so doing, the supervisor helps the therapist to recognize and modulate affect so that he can incorporate this new affective information about himself without feeling emotionally overwhelmed or injured.

At this juncture several issues relevant to affect and privacy in supervision should be clear. The trainee and the supervisor need to be able to converse about the therapist's affects in response to treating the patient. Within a socially novel relationship, the therapist will need to develop skills in tolerating and understanding his affective resonances. The supervisory challenge of this learning cannot be met by using borrowed psychotherapeutic concepts to frame and organize the issues. Alternatively, we feel that a professional developmental model for psychotherapy supervision encompasses what professionally must be learned without being personally intrusive to the trainee.

A clinical example demonstrates how a therapist must learn to bridge professional developmental skills and affect and how the teaching of those skills can be incorporated into supervision. We begin by focusing on the ways in which the supervisor can orient her comments about the content of the therapy being presented. Particular aspects of the therapeutic interaction strongly influence the degree of affect evoked during the supervisory hour.

A first-year resident early in the academic year introduced a case by saying: "This patient is making me very angry. I don't know what to do about it." The patient was a thirty-year-old male borderline who had been transferred from the medical service following a psychiatric consultant's conclusion that the patient was at risk for suicide. The resident on the inpatient unit did not agree with the conclusions reached by the consultation service. The patient had quickly become the focus of a number of staff conflicts about the amount of monitoring he would need while on the unit and how much cooperation would be expected of him under the unit's treatment plan.

A number of clinical issues could have been the focus for supervision of this patient, including the affect he stirred up in others. However, this particular trainee had framed the clinical problem in terms of her feeling angry, so the therapist's affective experience of the patient was the leading edge of the supervisee's concerns. However the supervisor chooses to respond, the educational focus of the supervision should in some way relate to the issue of affect presented by the trainee as primary in her concerns. The supervisory approach should help the trainee with the professional tasks of containment, identification, and integration of this affective experience as it relates both to this phase of the patient's treatment and to this phase of the trainee's professional development.

There are several potential responses, each with educational advantages and difficulties. We present three approaches representing a progression of the degree to which the trainee's affect is made the explicit topic of the supervisory discussion: patient focus, interpersonal focus (that is, interpersonal situations exclusive of the treatment relationship), and transferential/countertransferential focus.

The educational orientation of a patient-focused approach is to help the trainee see the world from the patient's subjective frame of reference. To illustrate, the supervisor could begin by developing with the trainee a detailed description of the patient, to help the therapist imagine and then conceptualize the patient's subjective experience of himself and his world: what is the patient feeling, what are his concerns, over what kinds of interactions is the patient conflicted? A clear picture of the patient's inner experience would be constructed in supervision from material found within the patient's life without bringing in the treatment relationship. The supervisor would have the opportunity to interrelate the patient's interpersonal difficulties in making people angry, while at the same time keeping the educational focus on the patient's subjective or inner experience of the moment. The supervisor is free to clarify the patient's dynamics and their relationship to his ability to make people angry. The ultimate goal is to help the training therapist step inside her patient's psychological skin for a moment.

This approach minimizes the tendency for the supervisor to

address the therapist's subjective experience of the patient: in the present clinical example, the therapist's anger is not directly discussed. Instead, the patient's internal experience and intrapsychic dynamics are made central to the supervisory dialogue. This is particularly helpful with inexperienced therapists who are unable to make empathic contact with the patient or are defensively avoiding such contact. It offers a way to be psychologically and educationally precise without being too personally stimulating or revealing in the supervisory dialogue. The material stays at a distance from the supervisory dyad, with supervisor and supervisee looking on together. The educational spotlight is turned away from an examination of the interpersonal aspects of the therapeutic process and the therapist's personal experience of the patient.

Rather than heighten the trainee's affective experience of the treatment during the supervisory hour, this approach draws on intellectual and clinical understanding to modulate the therapist's emotion by clarifying the nature of the patient's inner difficulties. In addition, the therapist's increasing ability to imagine the patient's internal experience helps her view the patient's outwardly aggressive behavior as a response to inner turmoil. This insight into the patient, in turn, helps the therapist modulate her own anger at the patient.

This approach to psychotherapy supervision is the least explorative of therapist affect and the least likely to produce an emotionally charged situation that will be embarrassing or anxiety provoking to the trainee. It requires of the trainee the least amount of self-awareness. In addition, it does not rely on an established close alliance between supervisor and supervisee. Finally, in terms of the trainee's educational development and sophistication, the patient-focused approach concentrates on presenting the kind of clinical information that is fundamental to know in order that other dimensions of the therapeutic process can be properly explored and integrated in supervision. A clear concept of the patient's subjective experience at a given moment in time provides intellectual context and foundation for understanding both interpersonal and transferential/countertransferential aspects of treatment as derivatives of the patient's basic pathology. The chief drawback to this approach is that it excludes or minimizes some clinical material from supervisory discussions.

Let us assume for a moment that the supervisor wants to widen the clinical dialogue of the case and still respond to the therapist's stated affective focus: namely, that this patient was making her angry. The supervisory field of view could be enlarged to include the interpersonal processes of the patient's life, while still excluding discussion of the therapeutic relationship. The supervisor could begin by examining vignettes in which the patient angered a friend or family member. This discussion could be extended and generalized to similar types of angry interchanges the patient had with people in the hospital. In analyzing these interchanges with the trainee, the supervisor could explore emotionally and psychologically someone else's angry response to the patient and yet not intrude upon or reveal the trainee's own feelings about the patient because the responses to the patient belong to someone other than the therapist.

The clinical material continues to stay distant, with the supervisor and trainee looking on together, side by side in this educational endeavor. The imagined inner experience of a particular friend of the patient or of a hospital employee could be discussed in depth and then connected with the patient's behavior, to which it was a response. The supervisor would be free to etch out very clearly the intrapsychic dimension of other people's responses to this patient and then make links to the patient's affective issues. At the same time, the trainee is never called upon directly to elaborate or examine his or her own inner experience of the patient. Although the trainee's privacy is respected, the supervisory dialogue is more affectively charged than with a patient-focused approach because the supervision now includes detailed discussions of interpersonal conflict, not just the patient's subjective sense of being failed by others.

In an educational context, clinical information of an increasingly complex nature is being presented within the supervision in a didactic as opposed to an experiential framework. There is added opportunity for the trainee to use the supervisory information personally or experientially, but in private. The trainee can incorporate what she has learned in supervision about the interpersonal realm of the patient's life and extend it to the interpersonal arena of the therapy. In so doing, the trainee could begin to see and analyze the parallels between the patient's interactions with her in therapy and with others. The trainee would be transforming didactic teaching into experiential learning. This educational opportunity is inherently respectful of the trainee's privacy and defenses, placing minimal strain on the alliance between supervisor and supervisee because it does not raise for examination material that is likely to be embarrassing or anxiety provoking. In addition, it leaves open for the trainee the option of whether to verbalize her more personal experience of the patient in supervision or to keep that experience to herself. A trainee's introduction of such material into the supervisory dialogue frequently is an implicit statement of confidence about the supervisory experience and relationship.

In contrast to patient-focused and interpersonally focused supervision, a transferential/countertransferential focus is likely to be the most emotionally evocative for the therapist. If the supervision is focused on the affects and process in the treatment relationship itself, the therapist will no longer be able to analyze a relationship that remains at a distance. It will no longer be happening to some other person, and the therapist will become aware that the processes are now unfolding with her.

Although most therapists come to training with an intellectual awareness of the existence of the transference, the experiential awareness of the transference is another matter. It is a professional developmental milestone when the therapist becomes aware that she herself has become emotionally special (which can be in both a positive and a negative sense) to someone who not long ago was a stranger. At the same time, the therapist is required to be aware of the paradoxically impersonal nature of this attachment (Freud, 1915; Modell, 1991).

A therapist's initial experiential awareness of the transference is an anxiety-provoking professional developmental phase. Trainees have frequently commented on feeling an added burden and sense of responsibility coincident with increasing awareness of the transference in action in a therapy. The therapist must come to terms with this newly experienced element of the therapeutic relationship. Being the object of transference requires the therapist to tolerate having become very important, very quickly, to another person, without the usual consensual or familial bonds that accompany such relational intensity. Even if the initial transference is relatively positive and unconflicted for the patient, for the therapist who is newly aware of being the object of a transference, the therapeutic relationship will acquire additional weight.

A separate professional developmental issue for the therapist concerns the experiential nature of countertransference feelings. Again, the therapist is generally intellectually aware of their existence and even of the permutations of countertransference phenomena. With the experiential awareness of her own countertransference feelings, however, the therapist loses the modulating effects of interpersonal and intellectual distance, effects that are quite helpful in the patient-focused and interpersonally focused approaches to affect in supervision. Now the therapist is no longer just an observer but has become part of the process that must be analyzed. Because of this and the concomitant loss of other educational avenues that modulate affect, the supervisory discussion of transference and countertransference must depend more on the supervisory relationship and the educational tact of the supervisor to help modulate affective intensity.

Several strategies have been helpful to modulate the expressed and experienced level of emotion in supervision; they avoid pathologizing the trainee and are consistent with a professional developmental approach to affect. The general themes of these strategies concern the language of affect used in supervision; an awareness of whether the therapist has difficulty with containment, identification, or integration of the affect involved; how supportive is the clinical perspective and self revelation being provided by the supervisor; and whether clarification of an affective issue will upset the therapist's view of his own psychic function.

In the case we have discussed, the therapist was angry principally because she felt caught between the patient's lack of cooperation and commitment to the treatment plan, on the one hand, and the consultant's recommendation that the patient not be released, on the other. She experienced the clinical situation as being out of her control and therefore felt helpless. She was also angry at the patient (and the department of psychiatry) for making her feel this way. This was an experience to which she was especially vulnerable both because of her lack of experience and because of the level of difficulty represented by the patient. The dynamic that was fueling the patient's behavior involved his own feelings of helplessness. He was fearful that neither the therapist nor the hospital would be committed to his treatment and would thereby leave him feeling abandoned and helpless. Conversely, he was equally fearful that the therapist and hospital *would* be devoted to his treatment and leave him feeling engulfed by the relationship and therefore equally helpless.

Language in the supervisory dialogue draws upon a range of words to convey the intensity of a given emotion: in this example, that emotion is anger. The supervisor's saying that the patient was "outraged" at the therapist is likely to be more emotionally provocative for the trainee than simply saying that the patient was angry at her: the more emotionally intense word is likely to evoke a stronger emotional response. In contrast, the supervisor's emphasizing that the patient was actually feeling helpless would reduce the emotional provocation to the therapist by reframing the patient's anger. It is usually safer to begin talking about small increments of affect. A supervisor's comments about a patient's annoyance will evoke less affect than comments about the patient's primitive rage. Similarly, a supervisor commenting on a therapist's countertransference should begin by saying that the patient is irritating rather than that he has made the student furious.

The emotionally less intense terms leave the therapist's defenses and privacy relatively intact and can also serve as an initial probe into the therapist's sensitivity about the material. The supervisee may intensify the emotion being discussed by responding, for example, "I'm past being annoyed at this patient; I'm furious." Consider the differences in the following supervisory comments: "This patient *could be* annoying to treat"; "This patient *is* annoying to treat"; "This patient *might be* annoying to *a therapist*"; "I believe this patient *is annoying you*." These variations in language clearly differ in how confronting and revealing of affect they are. For the supervisor, stating observations tentatively and impersonally is inherently more respectful of the trainee's emotional privacy and leaves more psychological room for the therapist to digest the observation.

A second avenue of affect modulation in supervision involves the supervisor's being aware if the therapist is having difficulty with containment, identification, or integration of the affect involved. It is important that the supervisor not get ahead of the therapist in the observations offered. In the example we have been discussing, the therapist knew that she was angry at the patient. She had contained and subsequently identified the category of her feeling. She was working on the analysis, integration, and tolerance of what she was experiencing.

Another trainee might have had more of an emotional blind spot concerning the identification of affect. Consequently, she could have introduced the case material by saying that she knew she did not feel comfortable with the patient but was unsure why. This would imply that she had the ability to contain her dysphoric state but had difficulty naming the category of affect. The supervisor would then direct her comments to clarifying the type of emotion the therapist was trying to process.

Another therapist could have begun the supervisory hour by prematurely suggesting that the unit chief needed to take charge of the clinical situation. This would imply that the therapist was having difficulty with containment of the affect and was subsequently displacing and perhaps acting out her concerns. In this situation, the supervisor would direct comments to help the therapist to contain, identify, and explore analytically her experience of her distress. In summary, the supervisor should have in mind what the therapist's next educational step is so that supervisory interventions can be fine-tuned to what is being processed. A supervisory remark that is ahead of what a trainee is digesting may expose the trainee emotionally without being helpful.

A third avenue for supervisory intervention in affect modulation concerns the amount of supportive clinical information and professional self-revelation the supervisor provides. In general, the supervisor's providing clinical information or personal clinical experience will create a collegial and collaborative framework for examining a given therapeutic issue, thereby decreasing the level of anxiety and/or embarrassment for the therapist. The converse is also true: the more alone and uncertain the therapist feels, the higher the therapist's anxiety and the greater the potential for embarrassment. This is particularly true regarding the supervision of transference and countertransference, for the reasons discussed in chapter 5.

The supervisor can then offer the trainee a range of clinical support. "What's your understanding of why you're angry at this patient?" is clearly less supportive than "This patient is making a lot of people angry; we need to understand what it means." The latter comment attempts to normalize clinically the affective response and show that the supervisee is in good company.

More supportive still would be the supervisor's volunteering a clinical association of her own to clarify the dynamics: "Underneath all his refusals, I keep wondering if this patient could be just plain scared." With countertransference problems, supervisors have the additional option of professional self-revelation: "This patient reminds me of someone I treated who could be infuriating." In these two instances, the spotlight is off the trainee's affect for a moment and is instead on the supervisor, who is presenting herself as a colleague. At the same time, she is lowering her profile as an object for fantasy by the supervisee because she is supplying information about her professional self. This kind of revelation is consistent with a professional developmental approach to the affective issues at hand. The educational implication is that processing these affects is a normative part of the professional territory that every therapist needs to master.

Finally, the supervisor should consider whether clarification of a particular affective issue will initially prove disturbing to the therapist's view of her own psychic function. In the example being considered, it was likely that this therapist would not feel ashamed to discover that her anger was secondary to her feeling clinically helpless and that this process paralleled the patient's angry response to his own unarticulated feelings of helplessness. Because this information would probably not disturb her view of her own psychic functioning and professional identity, it was appropriate for the supervisor to take this approach.

However, this might not have been the case. Some therapists may be very alarmed to find that they are angry at a patient. Consider the example of a therapist who reported that a female patient left him a series of angry voice-mail messages in which she threatened to complain to hospital administration that she received inadequate treatment. The therapist then raised his concern that the patient might be at risk of self-harm, but a review of the clinical material did not bear this out. The source of the therapist's concern was probably a reaction to his unconscious murderous fantasy about the patient. A supervisory clarification of this matter would have educational benefit to a therapist but would also pose an emotional obstacle: few beginning therapists would be pleased to learn that they fantasized killing someone for whose care they were responsible. If the supervisor clarified to the therapist this kind of affective response to the treatment, the supervision would benefit from some of the modulating interventions (attention to language and supervisor revelation, for example).

This list is hardly exhaustive. A supervisor's humility, compassion, humor, and intellect are all clearly very important. However, the modulation of affect experienced and expressed within the supervision is central to the therapist's eventual understanding and tolerance of the affective experiences of learning and practicing psychotherapy. The preceding discussion of supervisory interventions illustrates conceptually distinct approaches by which a supervisor can actively address the intensity of therapist affect in supervision.

What is an educationally useful amount of affect? How much is too much or too little? On one level, the answer depends on the particular individuals involved, their customary styles of relating and thinking, and what life issues, personal and professional, are currently exerting force on the supervisory process. There are too many potentially significant independent variables to specify or discuss. Yet looking to the end product of the supervision—the process of learning itself—empirically frames the question of how much affect is educationally useful. The answer must be in monitoring the quality of the therapist's learning.

While the ideal time frame for assessing a student's learning may be at a minimum after several months, a supervisor needs to rely on other educational parameters that give more immediate, short-term information about monitoring affective intensity. One of several indicators that can be helpful is the continuity of the supervisory dialogue. If the material in supervision is being integrated, there should be continuity in educational themes being processed during the meeting and from one meeting to the next (or from one case to the next if more than one case is being considered). In the example of the trainee who was angry at her patient, the supervisor should expect the therapist to return to discussions of negative countertransference affects. Suddenly disregard of the issue would suggest that too much affective heat was being generated. Constantly keeping the negative affects at center stage to the exclusion of other material would also indicate a problem.

Another supervisory indicator of optimal affective intensity is the amount of forgetting or remembering of the psychotherapy session that happens in response to a given supervisory intervention. Usually, if supervision is working well, the therapist will recall additional details about a given vignette or related vignettes from the therapy. The additional clinical information will then deepen the ensuing supervisory discussion. Another supervisory indicator is the openness or constriction of a therapist's associations to the patient's material. More open associative responses could include presenting additional material concerning the patient or drawing on related literature, films, current events, or even personal life experiences. In general, freedom in associative thinking in supervision suggests that the supervisory process is working and that the affective temperature is right. Constriction or avoidance suggests that it is not and that some adjustment of the affective level of the supervision is needed.

Therapist affect in supervision is usually difficult to attend to educationally without the risk of opening up more than either supervisor or therapist are prepared to deal with. The difficulty derives from the paradox and conflict of the therapist's public exploration of his private feelings (even for educational reasons). Therapists need to develop a tolerance and understanding of the affective experiences of doing psychotherapy. A professional developmental approach to this part of the supervisory curriculum orients the supervisor's educational formulations and interventions. The role of the supervisor is to help modulate affect and in turn clarify the therapist's experience of this part of his professional development as it unfolds. The supervisory interventions must incorporate the level of the therapist's professional tolerance of affect into the supervisory exploration of the clinical needs of the patient. As a therapist has characteristic ways of feeling to which a supervisor attends, so a therapist also has characteristic ways of knowing what he knows, an epistemology for his clinical work. It is important that a supervisor understand both aspects of a therapist's characteristic approach to clinical work. We turn now to additional educational interventions that represent additional pedagogical choices by which the supervisor can fine-tune her approach to the cognitive and affective makeup of the therapist.

7

Supervisory Interventions

In chapters 3 and 4, we discussed how paying attention to the student's ways of knowing brings his educational needs into sharper focus. In chapters 5 and 6 we examined issues concerning the supervisee's inner life, in particular the boundaries of supervisory investigation and the handling of affects in supervision. Throughout these discussions, we have concentrated on the supervisor's choices in how to intervene. In the present chapter we focus on supervisory interventions and describe a repertoire of pedagogic approaches available to the supervisor and discuss how she may apply these on the basis of the learning style of the supervisee and the educational goals of the supervision. We define these supervisory interventions, discuss the strengths and limitations of each, and show how they are employed to help therapists-in-training further develop their clinical skills in the context of their individual ways of learning. A supervisor can use these interventions regardless of her theoretical orientation, for we emphasize not the content of what is being taught but the method by which it is transmitted.

Modeling

Modeling involves the supervisor's demonstration through her own activity of how she thinks, seeks meaning in patients' associations, formulates hypotheses, bears affects, uses her imagination, and makes decisions. A supervisor cannot function without at times offering herself as a model for emulation. Sometimes the modeling is done consciously, whereas at other times it is merely a spontaneous demonstration of the supervisor's approach. For the supervisor, modeling is often the easiest approach to teaching and the one that comes most naturally. If, for example, a supervisee is quite guarded in talking about his emotional responses to his patient, the supervisor may choose to express her own feelings about the patient or reflect on a similar patient in her practice and how he made her feel. Through example, the idea is conveyed that an emotional reaction to one's patient is expected, important, and worth discussing. The supervisor may do this intuitively or with the conscious intention of providing the supervisee with a model of openness and self-reflection. Similarly, the supervisor sets an example for thinking associatively (often counterintuitive for inexperienced therapists who have not had experience with personal therapy), creatively, and playfully, and demonstrates the relevance of such thinking to a deeper understanding of the patient. The supervisor listening to a case presentation, who had associations to *Huckleberry Finn* and to Danny Kaye in the film version of Thurber's *Secret Life of Walter Mitty* (see chapter 4), told the supervisee of these associations and what light they could cast on the case under discussion. In so doing, he modeled an interest in marginal thoughts and tangential associations and their potential relevance to the clinical discussion.

Each aspect of the teacher's behavior and thought becomes a potential model for the student, often without the teacher's consciously intending it. A psychoanalytic teacher, leading a case discussion with a group of candidates, demonstrated her approach of listening to process material line by line and tracking the rapid shifts in the patient's content, affect, and relationship to the analyst that revealed subtle defensive activity. She related this approach to the writings of Paul Gray on defense analysis and the work of helping the patient to become more self-observing. The teacher pursued this "microanalysis" with skill, perceptiveness, and accuracy, leaving the students impressed with the value of the approach. One of the candidates subsequently described the importance of this continuing conference in his understanding of this element of analytic activity. The teacher had provided a model for a component of analytic listening, and the student had absorbed the approach, the theoretical point of view, and an identification with the teacher as a unified experience. In his subsequent analytic work, the candidate often thought about this conference and teacher as he strove to apply this approach.

The supervisee also looks to the individual supervisor as a model for how to reason and for what kinds of data are relevant in making inferences and formulations about the patient. Although the nature of evidence in psychotherapy and analysis is a matter of controversy and may be confusing to the clinician, individual supervisors may, by their character, charisma, and the strength of their beliefs exert great influence upon supervisees regarding these unresolved questions. This places a responsibility on the supervisor to consider and try to explain how she thinks, reasons, makes inferences, and arrives at conclusions. An implicit supervisory message like, "Because this way of linking the patient's associations makes sense to me, it's probably right, and I hope you can see it that way, too" does not teach how the supervisor has arrived at her conclusions. It is likely, in fact, to leave the supervisee with no idea how she got there. It may, furthermore, convey the notion that grasping the meaning of a patient's associations is a mysterious and magical process, whose secrets only the initiated know.

An advantage of modeling is that it provides a vivid experiential gestalt for the supervisee of a more experienced therapist in action. It enhances learning by identification. When it is done thoughtfully, modeling demonstrates a way of thinking and behaving that the supervisee can emulate. It can expand the sense of a permissible repertoire—"If you thought, felt, and did this and I trust you, then it's OK for me to try too."As an example, inexperienced clinicians may feel bewildered, frightened, betrayed, or angry when assaulted verbally by a patient. The supervisor can identify an educational goal: acquiring the ability to tolerate such an attack, reflect on it, extract useful information about the patient from it, and respond to the patient in a nonpunitive manner. The supervisor, by listening calmly, taking the patient's material seriously but not personally and by implying that the supervisee can do the same, demonstrates an alternative way of responding. If the supervisee does not learn from this approach and, for example, a countertransference impasse is identified, other supervisory interventions will be needed. For more experienced therapists the supervisor may model her intellectual curiosity or an interest in relating clinical material to the literature and diverse theoretical perspectives.

A pitfall in the use of modeling is that the supervisee may lose perspective and not understand that this is only one supervisor's way of thinking, rather than the correct approach. It was because of such dangers that Eitingon favored the notion of each candidate having several supervisors (see chapter 1). The supervisee's judgment and ability to discriminate, as well as the supervisor's reminding him that this is but one way of putting information together, are safeguards. However, when a supervisor is charismatic or when a strong transference develops, the identificatory or imitative pulls can be strong and may limit the supervisee's freedom to evolve his own style of working with patients. Further, the supervisor who conveys excessive certainty about his approach may encourage a docile form of learning in the supervisee (Ornstein, 1968). Such docility often can be mistaken by the supervisor for an eagerness to learn or as a sign of cooperativeness, allowing the underlying resistances to learning or anxiety about thinking for oneself to be overlooked. As Fleming and Benedek (1966) point out, the encouragement of imitative learning, rather than being the main activity of the supervisor, should be used only because of "a specific learning need and should be only a step in the total learning process" (p. 236).

Didactic Instruction

Didactic instruction includes all forms of direct explanation, including providing knowledge of the field (reviewing the diagnostic criteria for a major depression, giving a description of what is meant by "defense analysis," discussing the uses of hypnosis, etc.). It may include an explanation of one's own formulation about and diagnosis of a patient. Such instruction is clearly an essential ingredient of good teaching, as there is a body of knowledge to be absorbed and applied to patient work. Didactic instruction orients the therapist to theory, to different ways of thinking about the patient, and to how these different theories influence technique. By explaining the psychodynamic rationale for using the patient's associations to understand his unconscious or by explaining why self-reflection is important in learning to do therapy, the supervisor helps the therapist-in-training master the tools of the trade.

Ekstein and Wallerstein (1958) distinguish "dumb spots" (an unfortunate term referring to areas where lack of knowledge, or experience is the problem) from "blind spots" (where therapist conflict may interfere). Didactic instruction helps fill in dumb spots, whereas the failure of didactic teaching to help may reflect problems that go beyond inexperience.

Didactic instruction also includes advice and directives to the supervisee about how to proceed with clinical work. If the supervisor feels that the therapist is not interpreting timely and important material, she must decide how to intervene. The supervisor can suggest what she might have said to the patient (modeling), or ask the therapist a series of questions to explore technical options (Socratic method). At times, however, the supervisor may elect a more directive approach if she feels that clinical action should take priority over a more gradual process of discovery by the therapist. The supervisor may perceive a learning need that suggests this approach. For example, the therapist may be hampered by his mode of thinking, such as excessive concreteness limiting the therapist's appreciation of symbolic meaning. Or the supervisee may be inhibited by personal conflict from confronting a patient's hostile behavior. At times the supervisor's responsibility to the patient necessitates telling the therapist what to do. This may be a directive to interpret certain material, perform a suicide assessment, prescribe a medication, or hospitalize the patient.

Along with transmitting information and guiding clinical activity, didactic instruction often helps to reduce uncertainty in the supervisee—and, at times, in the supervisor as well. Containment of anxiety through mastery of facts is a benefit of a didactic approach. Being able to diagnose a patient often helps the student to deal with his anxiety and orient himself to the therapeutic task.

A didactic approach may reflect dogmatism and defensiveness on the part of the supervisor. Premature certainty about how to understand material or what to do with it may protect the therapist and supervisor from uncertainty. For instance, confronted with the disturbing reality of a patient in pain, supervisor and supervisee may opt to review the cardinal signs of a diagnostic disorder as a mutual avoidance of the immediacy of the patient's experience.

Ornstein (1968) describes the stifling effect of the didactic approach taken too far: "The teacher, in one extreme, may give in to the trainee's demands and to the temptation within himself of becoming too didactic. He thus accepts the position on the pedestal, enjoys the admiration he receives, and encourages identification and imitative learning. He rationalizes this 'teaching attitude' by pointing to the trainee's anxiety and helplessness, which, he says, can best be alleviated by imparting a great deal of information" (p. 301). A preponderance of imitative learning on the part of the supervisee fails to allow for the development of the kinds of educational "crises" that lead to deep and creative understanding (Felman, 1991). If an overly didactic approach is applied when the supervisee has already demonstrated the ability to think through a problem, it can retard learning.

It is part of any supervisor's job to convey her impressions and it can be gratifying for her to be able to shed a new or different light on a case. It is rewarding for the therapist, as well, to have confusing material illuminated. However, if the supervisor repeatedly or exclusively discusses the material presented in terms of the conclusions she has reached about the patient, this can interfere with the therapist's developing initiative and the pleasure of his own discovery. What can be lost in this kind of interchange is the therapist's active struggle with the data, the possibilities of mutual revelation for the supervisory pair, the acknowledgment of ambiguity in the material, and the exploration of different ways of thinking about it. If the supervisor includes in her discussion the steps by which she has arrived at her conclusions (Fleming, 1987), the data she has used, and some sense of how speculative she feels her conclusions are, the process of formulating patients' dynamics can be demystified and the supervisee can develop the tools by which to judge the supervisor's conclusions.

This approach can influence the development of several modes of thinking discussed in chapters 3 and 4. A didactic approach may assist the student in the development of inductive reasoning by providing domain-specific knowledge (the data base of the field) and instruction in a methodology for constructing formulations (what observations are relevant, how these may be connected to the patient's associations and history, how thematic similarities in the history and the transference may be understood, and so on). The use of associative thinking and creative thinking in the supervisee may be indirectly inspired by didactic instruction (as, for example, when a newly learned insight or theory may stimulate new associations and efforts by the student to use the new theoretical "lens"). A didactic approach may have the opposite result and stifle associations and creativity. The potential drawbacks of didactic instruction lead us to a consideration of another form of supervisory activity in which the learner participates more actively.

Socratic Questioning

By the Socratic method we mean the use of questioning to draw the learner into active exploration of a problem or issue. It includes a process of question and response between supervisor and supervisee that leads to discovery rather than delivery of knowledge. When we were residents in psychiatry, many of our supervisors seemed to be able to tell what was going on with our patients in a manner that seemed effortless and left us feeling that they often were in the possession of some secret and magical ability that we hoped, perhaps by osmosis, to attain some day. In a distinct minority were those supervisors whose response was sometimes: "The patient's story is pretty confusing, I wonder what we can make of that?" It was not always clear whether such remarks involved some failure of insight on the supervisor's part or were a deliberate supervisory technique to encourage us to think. Whatever the reason, they had the beneficial effect of engaging the residents in trying to figure out with the supervisor what was going on. Through a series of questions, hypotheses, and tentative "what if" scenarios, this kind of dialectic encouraged the trainees' more active participation in understanding the patient. In the following vignette, a supervisor combined didactic instruction with questioning a supervisee in the hope of involving her in actively learning about her patient.

Dr. P., relatively new to outpatient therapy, presented the case of a female graduate student in her twenties who had a long history of depressive feelings, questions about whether her life had meaning, and pressures to be academically extraordinary. In therapy, Ms. L. appeared to be a very intellectualized woman who kept herself at a distance from her emotions. Despite the patient's bringing a wealth of material to each hour, Dr. P. was often left confused about how to organize her impressions of the patient. Ms. L. often focused on external dangers (her mother's stifling of family members' anger, a "cold, scary core" that she sensed in her fiance, a former therapist who she felt was intrusive and overly interpretive). Yet she also feared her own anger, violent impulses, and harsh self-criticism. In one therapy session, she expressed her fear of driving, having just gone to a memorial service for a close friend who had been killed in a car accident. She asked her therapist whether some accidents might be intentional, and associated to how easy it would be to drive off a bridge. She had the thought that it would be "neat" to float in the air, but realized that she would then land, and she wanted to live. Dr. P. commented that floating would be a relief from the scariness of things in her life. Ms. L. responded, "Yes, it's a scary world," and associated to a girl who had been raped and killed. The therapist commented that Ms. L.'s mother had made her feel scared of men and burglars and told her that increased experience with people might give her greater comfort.

The supervisor felt that the therapist was emphasizing reassurance rather than further exploration in an attempt to help the patient deal with her anxieties. Dr. P.'s approach seemed also to emphasize explaining things to the patient (a didactic and soothing style). The supervisor felt that the patient was experiencing anxiety about her inner world (anger, depression, suicidal impulses, and the potential to lose control of herself) as well as external dangers. He was tempted to explain his clinical impression to Dr. P., but resisted this approach, hoping to foster the resident's further reflection on the material. The supervisor also wished to bring Dr. P.'s attention to her reassuring approach. There was a kind of parallel in which the supervisor might have taken a didactic, explanatory approach akin to the therapist's approach to her patient. Instead, he elected to ask a few simple but critical questions.

The supervisor asked what Dr. P. had been trying to do in this session. The therapist said that Ms. L. had seemed uncharacteristically *present* affectively—mainly scared—and that she was trying to make her feel less fearful. The patient's parents, Dr. P. went on, had made her feel that the world was a frightening place and Dr. P. wanted to help her feel more comfortable. With this, the therapist's tendency toward a supportive, soothing style was articulated as her explicit intent. The supervisor asked Dr. P., "What is your picture of what has gone into her being that scared?" The therapist spoke of her patient's mother's fear of burglars. The mother had also made Ms. L. "tiptoe around the house" so as not to anger her father. Further, Ms. L.'s mother had been sexually abused and made Ms. L. feel that she would be safer as a tomboy. Dr. P. further described how the patient was worried that her friend's death might have been prevented had Ms. L.—in a superstitious way—warded off her doom.

At this point, the supervisor noted that while Ms. L.'s childhood and current fears referred mainly to dangers from others, her fantasies of driving off a bridge and her magical thinking about her responsibility for her friend's death suggested to the supervisor that there were dangers from another direction as well—her own impulses and thoughts. Dr. P. immediately replied that perhaps this resembled paranoia: anger and fear inside being turned into outward dangers. The supervisor agreed and noted that Ms. L. seemed to fear her own feelings and fear losing control of herself.

Dr. P. provided some further material that supported the understanding she and the supervisor were building. In the past her patient had fearful fantasies about whether she was the kind of person who might go into a post office with a shotgun. Dr. P. recognized how very frightened Ms. L was of her own anger. She reported another session in which the patient talked about anger at her mother for marrying her stepfather, but felt that she had no idea what to do with her anger. Dr. P. asked her supervisor, "When she says, 'I don't know where my anger will go?' might I ask her where she thinks it will go?" To ask this of her patient, Dr. P. would invite the patient to elaborate on her feelings and fears, rather than prematurely soothe and reassure her. Dr. P. sought her supervisor's guidance on trying out a different approach. The supervisor noted that Ms. L.'s feelings toward her mother, her associations about the shotgun in the post office, and her fears of driving all suggested a fear of losing control. Dr. P. asked, "Do you mean she feels anger and then sees it outside?" The supervisor answered that this was a woman with many real external dangers throughout her life, but that the projection of her inner feelings seemed to be part of what she feared. Dr. P. wondered whether it would be helpful to her patient if she were to acknowledge that Ms. L. feared loss of control. The supervisor thought so.

In this interchange, the supervisor felt that the patient was focusing on external dangers while her therapist kept wanting to reassure her. To help deepen the therapeutic dialogue the supervisor asked several questions in an effort to draw out the therapist's thinking and help her to look at the material in a new way, rather than immediately explain his thinking to Dr. P. This form of interactive dialogue may lead to inferential thinking and formulation. The supervisor was primed to listen for external danger as a possible reflection of internal danger. He pointed to data in support of the hypothesis that the patient feared losing control over her own feelings and impulses. This led to a discussion of the role of exploration and empathic containment as different from reassurance. The therapist, incidentally, appeared to identify somewhat with the Socratic approach by feeling more inclined to ask her patient where she felt her anger and other strong feelings would lead rather than prematurely trying to reassure her and cut off the exploration.

A Socratic approach, in contrast to direct instruction, employs the supervisee's knowledge, creativity, and potential. It encourages reasoning and imagination, and (if questions are directed at the supervisee's emotional responses) self-reflection. The supervisor can ask a series of paradigmatic questions that address the four types of thinking we have described. For associative thought, the key question is "What does this (patient material) bring to mind?" For inductive reasoning and inference, the question is "How did you arrive at that impression? What perceptions, observations, reactions, and data were you using?" For self-reflection, the pivotal questions are "What were you feeling when that happened (with the patient)?" "What do you really want to say to that patient?" "How would you describe your tone or style in working with this patient?" "What was that like for you?" For creative thinking, the question is "How else might we think about this?"

There are limitations to a Socratic approach. It may tend to increase the supervisee's sense of uncertainty, anxiety, and feelings of narcissistic vulnerability. For those students who appear to be prone to shame and humiliation, such an approach may initially be unwise. It may put such supervisees too much on the spot and may inhibit learning. More important, questions may have different intents underlying them, not all of which are benign and helpful. The unstated semantic sense of any question is the command "Answer this!" Even the question "How are you today?" means "Tell me how you are today." In the flow of daily interaction we are generally not bothered by this aspect of a question. But in a psychotherapeutic or supervisory dialogue, where a power differential is present, the semantic framework becomes more significant. Socratic questioning by the supervisor may seem like an interrogation and can be experienced as both demeaning and demanding. A question can be an invitation to greater autonomy of thought or to thinking together about an issue, but it can carry other messages, including the expression of authority, control, and judgment. The supervisor must listen carefully to how her questions are answered, but also to how they are received.

Encouragement and Permission

The supervisor encourages the learner to be curious, to try new behaviors, and to think in unfamiliar ways. Many supervisees will have particular ideas or insights about their patients that they are reluctant to bring into the therapy. They may be uncertain about technique, timing, or the accuracy of a comment they want to make to the patient. There may be an unspoken concern about offending a patient or a nonspecific anxiety about wanting to do the right thing. The supervisee may feel that certain interpretations the supervisor is suggesting do not seem appropriate.

Countertransference, inhibition, and inexperience can influence the therapist in deciding whether and when to offer a remark to the patient. Of particular interest here is the natural reluctance most therapists feel (especially early in training) to make comments that may make the patient angry, that go beyond the patient's conscious experience, or that confront the patient's behavior in the transference. The trainee may need the supervisor's blessing to forge ahead. "It's okay to tell this patient that he acts like you aren't in the room," for example, could be a useful supervisory statement.

There are many impediments to curiosity in doing psychotherapy—anxiety over what may be found, reluctance to disturb a patient's defensive structure, conflicts about voyeurism, to name but a few. Helping the student overcome these inhibitions is part of the supervisor's task. Sometimes it is necessary to inquire about the student's understanding of his own inhibitions, particularly if encouragement does not have the hoped-for effect. But encouragement and the granting of permission are often a good starting point. Supervisees look to their supervisors for guidance in forming an acceptable repertoire of therapeutic behaviors. Acceptable in this sense refers to professional standards that are also in keeping with one's own personality, ethics, goals, and values. The development of this repertoire is a gradual process that involves professional identity formation over the course of one's career. Supervisors play an important role in this development by modeling professional behavior through their manner, attitudes, and values.

Permission and encouragement allow the learning therapist greater freedom to experiment with new therapeutic behavior and may free him from inhibitions about activity that feels inappropriate or forbidden. This approach is supportive, can foster creativity, and can reduce anxiety. As the therapist can be encouraged to try out new behavior in therapy, so, too, he can be invited to participate in the supervisory dialogue in a freer way. In the following supervisory dialogue the supervisee was invited to associate freely to the patient's material in an attempt to generate fresh ideas about a case.

A psychiatric resident was seeing a middle-aged man for therapy. The patient had presented to the hospital emergency room in a panic, fearing that he had contracted AIDS during a single homosexual encounter. The circumstances of the encounter as well as the medical evaluation suggested that his risk was quite low, but he was in a panic and contemplating suicide. He appeared to the resident to be a histrionic man, prone to somatic preoccupations. His father was an alcoholic who had died eight years previously. His mother was indulgent, nurturant, and ready to step in to help at all times. The patient was married to a woman toward whom he felt intense guilt over two episodes of infidelity with female prostitutes in addition to the homosexual encounter. He was a taxi driver and had recently taken out a loan to purchase the cab medallion that would enable him to own and operate an independent taxi. This amounted to a big responsibility that scared him.

During nine months of therapy, the patient oscillated between poor self-esteem and grandiose gestures. He expressed strong dependent yearnings (that his wife should indulge him as his mother had), yet he also engaged in frenetic flights of activity in a panicky escape from feeling passive, dependent, and devalued. He gambled, frantically sought medical advice, and fantasized committing suicide in Lourdes. In therapy he yearned for a maternal father who would soothe him yet give him strength. When disappointed with his therapist or pessimistic over his prospects for feeling potent, he regressed to a more dependent yearning to be taken care of.

In one supervision session the resident asked the supervisor for assistance in preparing this case for a conference. While the supervisor viewed the resident as bright and very competent, their discussions thus far had been capable and workmanlike, but not notable for their spontaneity and flair. With this in mind, the supervisor decided that it might be productive to brainstorm initially, to invite the resident (and himself) to roam freely over the material before pulling their thoughts together. When the supervisor suggested that they might associate a bit to the patient, the resident offered an outpouring of associations, plays on words, and bilingual puns that opened up an atypically lively, spontaneous, playful, and creative discussion.

In associating to the patient's fantasized trip to Lourdes, the resident thought of a string of words: continents, incontinence, countenance. He reflected on these and noted that continents referred to international travel (Lourdes, flight, flightiness), incontinence might refer to the patient's "incontinence of desires" (his difficulty containing his impulses to gamble, for example), while countenance referred to the patient's concerns about his appearance and body. The resident went on to associate to some of the patient's mispronunciations. One was "agryphobia," and the resident's associations included "agree-phobia," the fear of agreeing (referring to the patient's oppositional character), and "agri-phobia," a fear of farming (referring to a fear of settling down, making commitments; as well, a fear of raising things from seed—linked to his guilt over his wayward sexual encounters). Another of the patient's mispronunciations was "papaya on his tongue" (for *papillae*), and here there was an association to growing fruit in the mouth with an echo of oral issues of being fed, as well as sexual identity issues. In other material it seemed that the patient experienced his mouth as if it were a womb and was preoccupied and worried about periodic sloughing of tissue from it. The resident thought of the fantasy of a suicide in Lourdes and had the association to: "French kiss of death." In considering the patient's plans for flight the resident thought that this patient was indeed a "rare bird" and that this might refer both to his being a male hysteric and to his fear of being near extinction.

While this outpouring of puns, plays on words, and associations was lively, energizing, and fun for both therapist and supervisor, it also helped to consolidate their thinking around several key themes in the material. The discussion focused on the constellation of defenses represented by flight, gambling, locomotion, and histrionics, and contrasted this to the things the patient was avoiding: bodily experience, his own desires, his impaired sense of self, and attachment to others. Supervisor and supervisee talked of the patient's oscillation between utter helplessness (epitomized by memories of trembling by the stove, awaiting the return of his drunken and frightening father) and the grand gesture (including grandiose fantasies of gambling prowess and his histrionic fantasy about Lourdes). The central themes included his desperate need to maintain distance from himself and his objects (via geography or interpersonal distance), and his intense anxiety (including fear of passivity, intrusion, and guilt), which kept him moving. He longed for an idealized, maternal man to provide restitution for his actual father and his feeling of impotence, yet this prospect was terrifying because of his anxiety about homosexual tendencies and fear of passivity.

The playful, associative gush of material in this discussion helped to loosen up the dialogue, allowed access to preconscious images and associations, and energized a consolidation of themes in the material. The resident, who dove into the brainstorming with such relish and delight, had not previously revealed this side of his thinking in supervision. He seemed to require explicit permission to proceed in this way. Perhaps this represented anxiety, perhaps his perception of what he thought appropriate for supervision, perhaps a more specific transference to the supervisor that had led to some inhibition. The supervisor did not know, nor did he choose to inquire, but the simple invitation and permission to approach the supervisory dialogue differently produced a dramatic result.

The use of encouragement and permission to think in fresh ways, and to try out new therapeutic behaviors, must be accompanied by guidance from the supervisor about what attitudes and behaviors are appropriate in the professional context. For example, the supervisor encourages the greatest freedom and flexibility in thinking about the patient, which includes awareness of associations, affects, and countertransferences as the therapist uses all parts of his thinking, imagination, and feeling life to understand the patient. At the same time, the therapist's behavior with the patient is careful, thoughtful, scrupulous, and sensitive. This disjuncture between internal freedom of experience and behavioral constraint is, of course, an element of professionalism. It can, however, lead to confusion in some students over what the supervisor is really encouraging. Case discussions may include a tone of amusement in identifying the patient's dysfunctional patterns. Humor helps us understand, provides an outlet for countertransference feelings, becomes a sublimation for hostility, provides distance and perspective, and breaks the tension. At times, it can edge over into more insidious disrespect for the patient. In such instances, the attitudes and ethics that are being encouraged can be confusing to the trainee. In the vignette above, for example, the resident could have taken this playful discussion to mean that the supervisor felt this patient was worthy of ridicule, and this could influence the resident's attitude toward this or other patients.

The supervisor must also take into account whether what is

being encouraged, in the student's behavior in therapy or in supervision, can be tolerated by the supervisee. In offering an encouraging approach—"That's a useful insight. Go ahead and tell your patient. If he gets mad, you'll try to understand why"—the supervisor may underestimate how difficult it is for the anxious beginning therapist to carry this out. Encouragement can feel like a demand and burden for a conflicted learner. The supervisor needs to allow for therapist readiness, as well as patient readiness. Supervisors know much less about the inner experience of supervisees than therapists know about their patients. As a result, assessing the readiness of a therapist to confront a patient or make an interpretation and distinguishing inexperience from neurotic inhibition in the supervisee can be quite difficult. Nonetheless, supervisors need to be sensitive to what the supervisee can bear, and recognize that their encouragement and permission can be a source of conflict for the learner.

Offering encouragement and permission is not the same as being supportive. If the supervisor supports the supervisee without carefully determining what she is supporting and why, she can miss or avoid a student's problem. For example, supervisors frequently help students contain the anxiety of work with patients. Soothing, comforting, and supportive supervisory interventions may not address why a particular therapist is repeatedly flustered by certain patient situations. In psychotherapy, there is an important difference between nonspecific support and support based on a careful formulation of the patient's dynamics. Similarly, in supervision, even as one supports, permits, and encourages, one does well to consider what in the supervisee's learning or character style seems to require it. Is it a normative educational need, based on inexperience? Does it represent a countertransference dilemma in the treatment? Does the need for continued encouragement represent some unresolved conflict in the therapist?

Does it represent a transference to the supervisor, indicating excessive deference and dependence on the authority and wisdom of the teacher? In providing the supportive aspects of permission and encouragement, then, the supervisor may wonder whether a particular supervisee's need for such interventions represents a specific educational need that needs to be addressed.

The supervisor's use of permission and encouragement promotes, when successful, the student's development of his own style and thinking. It thereby involves a subtle form of modeling in which the therapist learns to foster the patient's development of his own thinking and potential.

Clarification

Clarification refers to interventions in which the supervisor comments directly on aspects of the supervisee's attitude or behavior that the student may or may not be fully aware of. Such comments are based on observations of manifest behavior, affects, and supervisee response patterns which the supervisee can readily recognize when they are pointed out. They do not include reference to the supervisee's unconscious conflicts, defenses, or motivations. A supervisor may comment on an expressed but unnamed affect in the supervisee ("You seem irritated with the patient as you tell that story"). Or there may be an observation about a pattern of therapist behavior in the therapy ("It seems that whenever the patient mentions her hopelessness, you sound anxious and begin to assess her suicidality rather than inquire more about the despair").

These kinds of comments, meant to call the supervisee's attention to his own affects and behaviors, involve a shift from the typical focus of supervision (the patient) to the therapist. The potential value of this intervention is to bring to the trainee's attention patterns, affects, and blind spots that are readily accessible but unacknowledged. At times there is much to be learned from commenting on the student's therapeutic or learning behavior and their associated affects. Countertransference, patient-therapist enactments, technical dilemmas, understanding and containment of therapist affect, and many other areas of learning to do therapy can be examined, and the therapist enriched, by the use of clarification.

At the same time there is the potential for exposure, narcissistic injury, and lowered self-esteem whenever the supervisee becomes the object of attention. The supervisee may feel self-conscious, scrutinized, or ashamed. The use of clarification raises questions about the boundaries of supervision and about the potential risk of intrusions into the supervisee's privacy. There are no clear guidelines for what the boundaries of supervision should be. Some supervisors feel that bringing a supervisee's conflicts and affects to awareness is desirable, whereas others focus more strictly on the patient. This division in supervisory philosophy resonates back to the split between the Viennese and Hungarian approaches to psychoanalytic supervision (see chapter 1) and the controversy over whether, and to what extent, the supervisee's inner life should be the subject of supervisory inquiry. There is no consensus among supervisors or in the literature about appropriate boundaries for supervision. In many supervisions, boundaries are not explicitly agreed upon but evolve in a subtle interpersonal dialectic over time, as each participant in the supervision feels out the relationship and determines for himself or herself what kind of dialogue is acceptable and helpful.

A supervisee presented to his supervisor a patient whose father had become ill. The patient had felt great disappointment in his father's lack of attentiveness to his needs when he was growing up. His father's current illness stirred up these feelings of disappointment and emotional deprivation once again. The therapist reported the situation without much affect or apparent empathy for his patient, and without recognition of the transference aspects of this material (that the patient might be feeling disappointed in or emotionally remote from his therapist). The therapist had previously told his supervisor that his parents had separated when he was a child and that he was very disappointed to have grown up without a father. As the therapist reported his patient's feelings about his father's illness, the supervisor commented: "You know something about this kind of disappointment." The supervisor noted that the supervisee's experience of loss might help him to understand disappointment and loss in his patient.

With these comments, the supervisor chose to bring the therapist's past experience into the dialogue and to suggest that it might help him understand, or empathize with, his patient. What was not said, but was implied, was that the therapist's experience of losing his father must have some effect on his sensitivity to his patients and must influence his work as a therapist. With this implied, the supervisor's comment amounted to an indirect clarification. The supervisor could have stayed exclusively with the patient material and examined further how the father's illness reactivated long-standing feelings in the patient. He could have taken a more Socratic approach, asking the therapist for his own thoughts and associations about his patient's situation, focusing on their relevance to understanding the patient. In this case, the supervisor elected to include the therapist's experience, in part because of its obvious relevance to the patient material, but in part because of the supervisor's sense that the therapist's affective remoteness from the material might represent an unconscious identification with the patient's disconnection from his experience.

Supervisees vary considerably in their openness to personal

revelation in supervision. Some are quite self-revealing and seem to find attention to their inner experience not only permissible but welcome, even necessary, to learning. Others focus more exclusively on the patient's material, making it (implicitly) clear that they are not interested in any discussion of their inner experience or affects. Clarification, as a supervisory intervention, facilitates self-reflective thinking and may stimulate associative thinking when the supervisee recognizes the place for his own experience and affects within the supervisory dialogue. To the extent that clarifications encourage the student to integrate subjective experience and personal history into his growing capacity as a therapist, they contribute to the synthetic and creative thinking involved in doing therapy.

However, the supervisor should be sensitive to the supervisee's reaction to clarifications. Because there are no universal or pre-established boundaries for what is fair game in supervision, because the narcissistic stakes are high, because there is an unequal authority relationship in supervision, and because of the potential misuse of supervisory transference, the supervisee's readiness and motivation for self-revelation should influence the establishment of these boundaries and the degree of personal revelation. At the same time, the scope and limits of inquiry should be kept as fluid and negotiable as possible. The supervisory relationship changes and develops. A comment by a supervisor that at one point feels threatening and intrusive may at a later point in the supervision feel playful, respectful, and acceptable, after greater trust and a deeper supervisory alliance are established.

Interpretation

If clarification by the supervisor raises concern over the potential violation of supervisory boundaries, the use of interpretation by the supervisor intensifies this concern. This more controversial kind of intervention includes interpretation of the supervisee's affects, dynamics, and defenses of which he is unaware. Such comments go beyond the manifestly observable (the domain of clarification) to include unconscious processes and motivations. One much-discussed component of this would be the interpretation of the "parallel process" (Searles, 1955; Ekstein and Wallerstein, 1958; Sachs and Shapiro, 1976) pointing out to the supervisee how he has unwittingly behaved in supervision in a way that is parallel to what has been happening in the therapy. Such an unconscious process of identification or replication becomes both an enactment of the therapy and a source of information about it. As Ekstein and Wallerstein (1958) observe, in these situations "therapist and patient *seem* to be constantly working on the same problems. Only as the student is helped in the resolution of such difficulties in himself, will he be able to see objectively enlarging aspects of the patient's problems. It is as though we work with a constant 'metaphor' in which the patient's problem in psychotherapy may be used to express the therapist's problem in supervision—and vice-versa" (pp. 179–180). Lawner (1989) recommends that the supervisor observe and interpret ways in which the therapist is unconsciously identified with the patient's defenses when therapeutic or supervisory impasses arise. Lester and Robertson (1993) advocate that the supervisor interpret the supervisee's countertransference, and they provide an example in which the analytic supervisor actively interprets a candidate's dream in terms of the candidate's anxiety about—and wishes for—her patient (p. 16). The argument in favor of judicious use of interpretation in supervision is that with the right supervisee, with enough information to be accurate, and with a supervisory alliance that can sustain it, interpretation can add depth to the therapist's understanding of his inner life. He can see how his own conflicts, defenses, and countertransference impact his work as a therapist. Maltsberger and Buie (1969) provide the following example of a supervisory interpretation:

> In spite of the supervisor's efforts to deal with the problem, a resident permitted a young woman patient to continue scathing, deprecatory attacks in interview after interview. One day the supervisor asked the resident to think whether he had any guilt about the patient or possibly about aggressive women, since it was difficult to understand how he could permit such punishment to continue with so little concern. The apprentice thought the matter over, and though he did not report the details of his associations to the supervisor, he confirmed that the interpretive guess had been correct. Subsequently, he was able to help the patient to investigate her anger at him instead of acting it out with her in the psychotherapeutic sessions. (p. 84)

Although this kind of intervention may be possible with a good learning alliance, it is the riskiest form of supervisory intervention. The major dangers are the potential intrusion into the supervisee's privacy, boundary violations, the possibility that the supervisee will feel he has been turned into a patient, but without the protections a patient has (Betcher and Zinberg, 1988). In addition, the data base upon which the supervisor makes an interpretation is very limited compared to that available in therapy, so comments about the supervisee's inner life or defenses that go beyond the observable are much more speculative. Supervisors can still observe a good deal about supervisees' character and defenses (and vice-versa). But without access to a detailed personal history of the supervisee or knowledge of how he conducts his daily life outside the supervisory hours, what one observes and can infer about a supervisee's dynamics is very limited. Certainly, there is no room for genetic interpretations. What can be commented on is how certain behaviors and attitudes of the therapist, as revealed in his treatment or in the supervisory sessions, point to unresolved conflicts or feelings that influence his conduct of psychotherapy. Deeper exploration of such conflicts is not the province of supervision, but their manifestation in the therapist's approach to his patient and his attitude toward learning may become the supervisor's concern. When the therapist's conflicts continue to impinge significantly on learning the supervisor may call this to the trainee's attention and reflect with him on how best to begin to resolve them.

Six forms of supervisory activity can help the therapist in training to expand his ways of knowing the patient: modeling, didactic instruction, Socratic questioning, encouragement and permission, clarification, and interpretation. Each approach has a place in teaching the supervisee, though interpretation must be used only after other forms of supervisory intervention have been tried and have failed. The supervisor begins by observing the supervisee's natural ways of learning and working with patients. She makes note of the trainee's interpersonal style and flexibility, learning style, modes of thinking and imagining, susceptibility to narcissistic injury in learning, affective responsivity, and general knowledge of the field. She hopes to respect and nurture the talents she sees and to help him expand skills that seem underdeveloped or lacking.

In chapters 3 and 4, we described four modes of gaining knowledge that are relevant in psychotherapy supervision: inductive reasoning, associative thought, creative thinking, and self-reflection. Supervision can help the supervisee to expand his competence in these forms of thinking. Modeling, for example, may enhance all these modes of thought, as the supervisor demonstrates through her own activity how to use associations, how she reasons, how to use self-reflection, and how to think creatively. Didactic instruction, on the other hand, is probably most effective in conveying knowledge and less useful in encouraging the supervisee's use of associative thought. To the extent that the supervisee becomes a passive recipient of received truth, didactic instruction does not directly encourage self-reflection or creativity. (An inspiring didactic supervisor may encourage these indirectly by identification and modeling, of course.) Socratic questioning is a robust approach for encouraging and teaching all four forms of thinking. Clarification and interpretation address self-reflection most directly but can backfire if the supervisee is threatened by this approach and becomes defensive or overly anxious. Both clarification and interpretation demonstrate the supervisor's interest in the supervisee as an individual and shed light on his talents, competencies, limitations, and blind spots. These supervisory interventions focus on the supervisee as well as on the patient.

Some writings on supervision have emphasized the role of identification—the supervisee's taking on the capacities, attitudes, values, and techniques of the supervisor. While identification is an important and inevitable aspect of supervision, we do not advocate any deliberate effort to encourage it. We favor a more interactive, mutually responsive model in which the talents and personal style of the supervisee are given center stage and the supervisor helps expand on them, strengthening available talents, identifying weaker areas, and rounding out the supervisee's repertoire with additional approaches.

The supervisor can show the student how certain characteristics of his learning style can help or hinder the development of his capacities to be a therapist. Consider the supervisee whose cognitive style is intuitive, with less interest or facility in inferential reasoning. This style may help the therapist to become attuned to the patient, with a sixth sense for affect, nuance, and meaning and a hair-trigger sensitivity to impending danger. However, this approach may become the therapist's touchstone in conducting therapy, to the neglect of detail and other kinds of data. The supervisor should respect and support this mode while helping the therapist to develop other ways of learning about the patient. The supervisor may try to introduce a greater respect for detail, familiarity with inferential reasoning, or an understanding of the limits of intuitive knowledge. These goals may best be accomplished through the use of didactic instruction and Socratic questioning: "What did you observe about the patient that led to your conclusion?" or "How does your feeling that this patient is unable to love fit with his statements about loving his wife?"

The supervisee's learning style and modes of thinking may represent areas of talent and competence while simultaneously reflecting specific problems in clinical work and in learning. Resolving learning impediments that are linked to neurotic or character problems may require personal therapy or analysis. The ability to address or modify them in supervision may be quite limited. We believe, however, that the supervisor has a role in identifying and working with students' learning problems as they arise in the clinical work.

Although the information supervisors have about supervisees' inner lives is limited compared to the information they may have about their patients, there is still much that one can tell about supervisees' personalities, cognitive styles, ways of handling affect and anxiety, interpersonal styles, narcissistic issues, and talents. These impressions can contribute to the assessment of learning strengths and limitations, potential countertransference pitfalls, and likely difficulties in work with patients. The aim is to help supervisees expand, as well as recognize, their ways of knowing, responding to, and thinking about patients.

8

Self-Esteem Issues for the Supervisee

Self-reflection is an essential ingredient in learning to become a psychotherapist. The psychodynamic supervisor encourages the student to become more aware of his responses to his patients. Yet we know that any deepening of self-awareness in the therapist may be destabilizing to his established sense of self (Robinson, 1936). Mehlman (1974) has described the regression, helplessness, and narcissistic imbalances that are inevitable in learning to be (and being) a psychotherapist, with its multiple challenges to and assaults upon self-esteem, based on the training status, the contact with patients, and the learning situation itself. The supervisor tries to balance the need for deepening exploration with an appreciation of the dangers to the student's self-esteem inherent in new learning. In this chapter, we shall explore these threats to self-esteem, looking at how these problems present in supervision and how supervisees cope with these demands. In chapter 9 we shall discuss the supervisor's role in mitigating these problems or contributing to them as a result of her own unresolved conflicts over self-esteem or the need to retain power over the supervisee.

Threats to Self-Esteem in Psychotherapy Training

Challenges to one's self-esteem and narcissism are characteristic of all learning situations. In doing psychotherapy or analysis, the analyzing instrument one has to learn to use and keep honed is fashioned from one's whole self, which gives these challenges a very personal urgency. A carpenter learning to use a new tool or perform a new task faces issues of success or failure, skill or clumsiness, competence or incompetence. The skill to be mastered involves certain parts of the mental and physical repertoire: understanding of spatial relations, motor skills, eye-hand coordination, strength, and so on. These may be very narcissistically invested areas for the carpenter, but they do not involve the whole personality.

Yet the therapist, in order to do his work, must call upon his whole personality: his intelligence, imagination, affective responses, fantasy life, areas of unresolved conflict, and so on. As a result, what is at stake in the learning situation is inherently more personal and risks exposure of fundamental aspects of oneself. As Ornstein (1967) notes, in supervision the recognition emerges that "hour after hour, day after day," the therapist or analyst is confronted not only with the need to demonstrate and utilize his knowledge and expertise, "but with the fact that all facets of his own personality structure—from the more superficial 'habits' to the ingrained characterological peculiarities to the depth of his instinctual strivings—become part of the process of psychoanalysis" (pp. 454–455).

In addition, a carpenter will quickly know whether he or she has learned to use a power nailer properly, as competence or clumsiness will have tangible results. Standardized measures of skill and easily confirmed evidence of mastery provide mooring points for self-assessment. This is often not the case for a therapist-in-training. Certainly there are some competencies, like conducting a mental status exam, that are learned tasks whose results can be gauged. But for the most part in psychotherapy results may not be so clearly measured, may be delayed, or may have to be inferred. Furthermore, results are not the production of the therapist alone, but depend on the patient as well.

Self-esteem is sustained by actual accomplishment, performance, and talent, as well as by intrapsychic determinants. For the beginning therapist in particular, the unavoidable lack of experience, ignorance, and relative incompetence challenge the self-respect that has been gained and supported in other endeavors. Even the experienced therapist is not immune to these problems, however, for the goals of psychotherapy are often more subtle, ambiguous, or open-ended than those in many other areas, and depend on the patient rather than on a priori goals that the therapist can select. As a result, the self-respect that derives from setting clear goals and accomplishing them is often not forthcoming.

Another aspect of psychotherapy that creates narcissistic injuries and pressures is the pull of the patient's experience. The ongoing attempts to resonate through temporary but necessary identifications with a patient's feelings, distress, conflicts, or primitive pathology may destabilize the therapist's sense of his own well-being for a time. If the patient feels depressed, confused, or overwhelmed, or is psychotic, the therapist shares in some of these states, which then exert enormous pressures on the maintenance of his own self-esteem. "For the resident," Maltsberger and Buie (1969) write, "sitting with [psychotic patients] hour after hour has the effect of a sustained assault on his defenses, to the point that his own sexual and aggressive impulses threaten or actually break through to conscious awareness. . . . Anxiety, rejection of the patient, or guilt are likely to ensue" (p. 70).

Furthermore, the therapist has to endure withering attacks on his competence from certain patients without resorting to the conventional methods of self-defense. The therapist tries to endure, absorb, and transform denunciation and attack into greater understanding rather than use the more usual fight or flight mechanisms. Where the trainee, at times, struggles without full success or gratification to substitute insight and self-reflection for counterattack or withdrawal, he is vulnerable to feeling an undermining of his healthy narcissism.

Self-esteem is upheld throughout life in good part by the validation and admiration of important others. The capacity to form relationships with others who contribute to one's feeling of well-being is part of the maintenance of self-esteem. The risk in relying on the respect of others is the vulnerability to negative regard or the anxiety about being evaluated and judged. In supervision, there may be considerable anxiety over how one's work and one's person are being evaluated. Transference, which is universal, may be particularly intense in the supervisory setting, where the student meets with an experienced teacher on a regular basis in an intense dyadic dialogue. Many beginning supervisees report anxiety over being "analyzed" or "seen through" or "diagnosed" by their supervisors, who spend much of their professional lives probing the psyches of others. Meeting regularly with a specialist in understanding people provides not only the promise of learning but the risk of exposure. Supervision is an intimate situation, but without clear and consensually agreed upon boundaries for the discourse, until the supervisory pair establishes an understanding about these. A supervisor and supervisee may explicitly talk about ground rules for supervision, but these are often left unstated, and the dialogue is left open-ended, its direction and profundity to be discovered in process. This situation may make the supervisee feel vulnerable, for it is not clear whether the supervisor will maintain her interest in the patient or will become interested in the experience of the supervisee. And if she does become interested in his experiences, how and to what degree will this interest be expressed? Will he be able to limit the scope of the supervisor's inquiry should he feel uncomfortable? This risk of exposure provides another pressure that the carpenter is free of. As long as he or she builds competently, a carpenter's feelings and fantasies are his own business. Whether a supervisee will be able to titrate his privacy, however, may be less clear.

Furthermore, those pursuing a career as an exploratory psychotherapist are interested in their inner lives and have some awareness of their own process, conflicts, and limitations. They recognize the relevance of such insight into their work. In this respect, psychotherapists-in-training lack certain professionally supported defenses against self-awareness that are available to others. In business or law, for example, aggression, competitiveness, and power seeking are routinely enacted in the external arena, providing a normative structure for directing attention away from the inner life. While therapists-in-training have the full range of defensive activities available, normative expectations in learning psychotherapy include some measure of self-reflection, further ensuring a confrontation with guilt, anxiety, and shame.

The student's self-esteem is shaped by a variety of internal forces: superego pressures, comparison of one's self-evaluation with one's ego ideal, and internalized self- and object-representations. It is beyond the proper scope of supervision to explore these aspects of the supervisee's psychic functioning in depth, yet the supervisor becomes aware of these forces as they come up in clinical work and supervision and is in a position to intervene. For example, a first-year psychiatric resident was struggling with the demands of working on an inpatient unit with psychotic patients. His anxiety about the work and excessive sense of responsibility for patient distress (including that which was clearly outside his or any clinician's control) were, in part, a function of his relationship with a psychotic family member, toward whom the resident felt significant guilt for not being able to help more. The resident's supervisor, in learning of the family situation, noted casually that the resident's feelings about the ill family member were likely to induce an excessive sense of responsibility and guilt in the resident's work with psychotic patients. The supervisor's awareness of the resident's overly conscientious approach led to an intervention in an effort to relieve an overly strict sense of duty. The details of the resident's conflicts were not explored further. The resident experienced the supervisor's comment as welcome and nonintrusive, in part because he sensed that the supervisor was not probing or judgmental in making this observation. The intent was to help him relax some of his excessive expectations of himself.

Ego ideals inspire growth, learning, and the wish for mastery. The gap between one's ego ideals and the perception of one's actual self and actual performance tests self-esteem. As William James pointed out, self-esteem equals success divided by pretensions (Modell, 1993, p. 34). Modell emphasizes Freud's notion that "one loves oneself to the extent that one successfully approaches one's ego ideal. Since the utter perfectibility of oneself to meet the ego ideal can never be achieved, some will seek to maintain their self esteem by identifying with an idealized other" (p. 112). It is not uncommon for a supervisee to feel inspired by a teacher, become identified with aspects of the teacher's thinking or behavior, and try them out clinically, only to have some intervention fall flat, precipitating a crisis of self-respect. The painful realization emerges that one may emulate a valued teacher but one cannot bypass the slow, painstaking process of developing one's own competence. How flexible the therapist is in bearing this inevitable disappointment will ultimately affect self-esteem.

Modell (1993) points out: "Both in loving and learning, one may surrender the self to the other. But if one learns by surrendering the self to the other, one is not truly assimilating knowledge into the self but merely imitating the other. Aspects of one's private self must penetrate the knowledge acquired from the other, so that knowledge is translated into one's private language. It is only in this fashion that knowledge can become one's own" (p. 118). To allow one's private self to engage with knowledge and with the teacher risks exposure that might be avoided by imitative surrender. Narcissistic balance and the capacity for self-regard are intertwined with self-representations (Jacobson, 1964). Coupled with self-loving and self-critical feelings are object-representations of loving and valuing or hostile and critical objects. The degree of integration the trainee has achieved over loving and hostile representations will influence his ability to withstand external criticism or antagonism from patients, colleagues, or supervisors while preserving some stability of self-esteem. A supervisee in the second year of a clinical program felt acutely uncomfortable, embarrassed, and inadequate each time she had a supervisory session. She was very fond of the supervisor, a respected older male, and felt that she learned a great deal from him. In reflecting on the nature of their dialogue that evoked these feelings, she recognized that her supervisor, while not overtly critical, had a particularly dry style, with little facial expression, long reflective pauses, and little overt enthusiasm for her work. She realized that a component of her embarrassment was not knowing where she stood in the supervisor's estimation. This had a painfully familiar resonance with a long-standing aspect of her relationship with her father, who was loving to her but whose own conflicts over his aggression inhibited him from being overt in his criticism or anger. The supervisor's dry style had contributed to a transference in which an absence of feedback activated an object-representation of the reserved but potentially critical father.

Still another determinant of self-esteem in the therapist-in-training concerns the fate of impulses and affects evoked in clinical work. Aggressive, hostile, punitive, and rejecting feelings, for example, are unavoidable aspects of learning to do psychotherapy. "The achievement of this capacity to master affective states . . . is accompanied by a particularly strong enhancement of self-esteem and by increased stability of self-esteem regulation" notes Mack (1983, p. 24). In contrast, the feeling that one is not in control of unbidden impulses and feelings may detract from self-esteem. More seasoned therapists understand that being open to all manner of fantasy and impulse can contribute to the work. Self-awareness becomes an aspect of professional competence and self-esteem. For the inexperienced therapist, however, the confrontation with unwanted impulses and affects may have the opposite effect, leaving the trainee feeling ashamed and guilty for sexual feelings, hostility, condescension, boredom, aversion, and the like.

While many pressures upon the trainee's positive self-regard are an inevitable aspect of the work, we do not underestimate the role of the supervisor, who can help with threats to self-esteem or exacerbate them. The supervisor who is excessively judgmental about the trainee's work or who is condescending, voyeuristic, or punitive will make matters worse for the vulnerable trainee. Out of an urge to preserve his or her authority, prestige, or power over the trainee, the supervisor may command compliance or excessive deference, further stirring the trainee's anxiety over preserving his self-respect in supervision. Alternately, through omission, the supervisor may simply neglect the student's needs for approval, leaving him uncertain about his performance and competence.

The final element of self-esteem maintenance in the therapist-in-training is feeling part of a group. "Throughout our lifetimes the experience of belonging to someone, or of being part of something larger than ourselves, remains an important factor in the maintenance of our self-esteem" (Mack, 1983, p. 18). In training, this urge to belong is met, in part, by the potential to become a member of a larger group (the training program, the profession, subspecialty groups, those concerned with a particular disorder, and so forth). Threats to this source of self-esteem are plentiful. The student may fear for his standing in the program, or wonder if he is fit to be a therapist at all. Split loyalties may generate anxiety and threaten his feeling of membership. An analytic candidate, for example, began to wonder whether an antidepressant should be prescribed for his chronically dysphoric analysand. Surely, if this patient appeared in a different setting, he thought, this would be a reasonable consideration. In analysis, however, the depression was being explored and understood in terms of dynamic factors (as a defense against anxiety, and aggression turned on the self). The candidate felt some mild discomfort about raising the possible use of medication with his supervisor. While his discomfort was a subtle and transient response, his concern that his loyalty to an analytic perspective might be questioned inhibited his learning. This, in turn, evoked issues of inclusion in the group of analysts with an attendant challenge to his self-respect as an analyst-in-training. Theoretical differences frequently evoke such feelings about the stability of one's membership in various groups.

Shame and Exposure

It is impossible to talk honestly about one's work as a therapist without revealing one's personal feelings and sensibilities. This may be overt, as in discussing countertransference reactions, or indirect, as in conveying the values, emotions, and conflicts that shape one's listening and responding to patients. Supervisees vary widely in the extent to which they are narcissistically vulnerable and prone to shame, and how they express and defend against feelings of shame. There is also diversity in the degree of personal revelation supervisees feel is appropriate, safe, and helpful. While one student may be self-confident and another shame-ridden, both expose themselves to possible feelings of embarrassment, humiliation, and inadequacy. How these feelings are handled in supervision can have an impact on the supervisee's self-respect and professional development.

At the beginning of her psychiatry residency Dr. A. was excited at the prospect of individual supervision. She had worked in another medical specialty in which her work was largely unsupervised. The prospect of extensive time to talk individually with senior colleagues was a welcome change. Early in the residency she met with a new supervisor, who told her, "Call me anytime if problems come up with your patients." After a night on call, in which she was up the whole night, and facing back-to-back appointments the next day until 7 P.M., Dr. A. told her supervisor that she was exhausted, upset, anxious, and angry about the pressure to perform all this work. The supervisor commented, "Let's look at your anger." Dr. A. felt betrayed, violated, and "turned into a patient." This moment of crossed expectations had a vivid and negative impact on her. She felt that she was being criticized for feeling angry and that her emotional reaction was being treated as something to be looked into, as one would do in therapy. Perhaps the supervisor felt that Dr. A.'s anger could be profitably examined to help her with the strains of residency. But something in the language and timing of this comment felt like an assault.

The following year, Dr. A. rotated through the state hospital. She was treating a man with schizo-affective disorder who had a history of bizarre psychosis and frightening behavior. She found him "compelling." Dr. A. had told a supervisor at the hospital that she had a psychotic family member. In discussing Dr. A.'s work with this patient, the supervisor commented that Dr. A.'s zeal and expectations for the patient were "not just about the patient. This is about *you*. Your having a schizophrenic family member has led to rescue fantasies of this patient. You should tell him that you have a schizophrenic family member and that you have probably done too much." Dr. A. felt guilty, upset, distraught, and unsafe. She subsequently described how she had "shut down completely" and "put walls up" at that time.

In these vignettes, Dr. A. experienced unexpected, unwelcome, and upsetting intrusions into her inner experience. She felt treated as a patient, her feelings subjected to investigation and interpretation. What the supervisors had in mind is not clear. That Dr. A.'s life, background, and feelings were relevant to her clinical work is obvious. Finding a way to introduce some of this into the supervisory dialogue can enrich the learning process. The resident's countertransference feelings that influence attitudes toward and expectations of the patient are potent forces that may be addressed in supervision. At issue here are questions of style, timing, safety, and learning alliance. Dr. A. recalled these incidents as among the most memorable and hurtful in her three years of training. This is a vivid example of how feelings of exposure, loss of privacy, and a sense of being blamed for her responses became an important element in this resident's feeling unsafe in the learning situation.

In contrast, supervision can approach personal material in the supervisee in a manner that does not activate shame. Instead, the supervisor may facilitate self-reflection and revelation that feel safe enough and contribute to learning. Dr. A. continued to feel defensive and "shut down" in various supervisions for some time. She later described how this began to soften with the help of a gentle and respectful supervisor. Dr. A. was treating a patient who was coughing up blood but was withholding knowledge of this symptom from her physicians and her family. Dr. A. felt upset about her patient's behavior and angry at her. Her supervisor, in hearing this material, suggested that perhaps there was more to her reaction. Feeling safe with this supervisor, thanks to a relationship that had developed over time in which she felt that she was not going to be criticized, "analyzed," or asked to reveal more than she cared to, Dr. A. associated to a close family member who had died of cancer. This relative had experienced bleeding in her stool over several years but had withheld this symptom from Dr. A. and others. Recognizing the connection between this personal experience and what was going on with her patient, Dr. A. began to understand her specific countertransference to this patient's avoidance of medical evaluation, including her anger toward the patient. She felt that it was necessary and helpful to look at this connection in supervision. Her feeling of safety depended on not feeling forced by her supervisor to reveal more than she was willing to share. The supervisor, instead, had respectfully raised an open-ended question, leaving Dr. A. free to respond or not.

Supervisee Responses to Threats to Self-Esteem

In attempting to cope with narcissistic threats, the therapist-in-training may employ the full range of defenses available to anyone —repression, intellectualization, externalization, denial, distortion, and avoidance, to name a few. Feelings of shame and inadequacy may be managed by compensatory feelings of grandiosity; the anguish of helplessness may be fended off by fantasies of omnipotent control over one's patients. A resident may assume a posture of premature self-reliance, disdaining his teachers and fantasizing an unrealistic sense of mastery.

A rejection of the value of psychotherapy may reflect underlying feelings of incompetence. A therapist in the second year of training at an academic hospital was beginning outpatient therapy. She talked angrily about a patient who had called to berate her for having discussed an overdue clinic bill. The therapist irritably declared to the supervisor that she did not understand why a patient would even want to talk about her life and feelings to a stranger (the therapist). If patients were going to treat her this way, the therapist continued, perhaps this was the wrong field for her. The supervisor took a didactic approach, explaining that therapists received all manner of verbal abuse and anger from patients, and that this simply went with the territory. Further, it would be part of the training to learn more effective responses to this. The supervisor provided a specific recommendation for how to answer this patient. The therapist then said, "I don't like doing things that I don't know *how* to do," articulating the feeling of incompetence that underlay her disdain for the enterprise.

It is natural, but unfortunate, that therapist self-esteem often becomes so closely related to the patient's progress. How well one does in helping patients must naturally be an aspect of professional self-esteem. The experienced therapist or analyst knows, however, that many factors outside his control have an impact on patient outcome. For the learning therapist, it is a challenge to understand and integrate this clinical reality. Many therapists believe that a patient's inability to get better reflects their own incompetence (and, at times, it may). Curing patients then becomes invested with one's own personal motives. A crisis may be precipitated when a therapist recognizes the personal stakes and narcissistic investment of what he had previously rationalized as compassionate zeal for the patient. It is always important for the therapist to ask, what does this patient mean to me: what attachment, narcissistic investment, displaced working through of my own conflicts, or enactment of my own unresolved issues are at stake in treating this patient?

The therapist should also think about where his narcissistic investment is in clinical work and in supervision. At times the therapist may be involved in defending his self-esteem against the multiple threats we have noted. Perhaps the narcissistic investment is in curing the patient; perhaps it is in learning and intellectual mastery.

At times, for example, the therapist requires the patient to do well in order to preserve the therapist's self-esteem, or he may have a vision for the patient to fulfill that goes beyond what the patient wants or is ready for. An experienced therapist had been treating a professional man who had initially been referred for treatment because of family problems that involved his mother's drinking, over which he was enraged. During two years of psychotherapy, the patient had expressed his feelings and reactions to family conflicts but had shown little interest in a deepening exploration of his inner world. He seemed to the therapist an inhibited, obsessional man, who plodded through his life successfully but joylessly, with low self-esteem and little capacity for pleasure or relaxation. He experienced life as a series of obligations he dutifully performed, in the process suppressing a good deal of resentment. His anger had surfaced in rageful feelings toward his mother, which he experienced as reactive to her noxious behavior. As the patient's rage diminished and he reflected on his relationships with family members, the therapist was interested in trying to help him address deeper intrapsychic issues. While the patient acknowledged these issues, especially his low self-confidence, lack of satisfaction, and anxiety about being a bad parent (as he felt his mother had been), he was skeptical about what could be done about them and was ambivalent about trying to change them. He lost sight of where he was going in therapy and considered stopping. At the same time, he revealed how unimportant he had felt as a child and movingly conveyed how he still felt like an unimportant little boy at times.

The therapist was fond of the patient and hoped that with treatment he could become freer and less inhibited. He was frustrated by the rigidity of the patient's defenses and tried to make his joyless resignation more ego-dystonic. It was in this context, with the patient considering stopping treatment, that the case was brought to a supervisor for consultation.

The question for the supervisor was: can this man be turned into a patient who would stay in treatment and take an interest in a deeper exploration of his character issues? The supervisor felt, after hearing about the treatment, that this man was clearly very frightened of going further and that the stakes for him in doing so seemed too high. The supervisor suggested that tampering with his rigid but well-functioning defenses might lead the patient to reevaluate his marriage as well as his work, and that he seemed too threatened to do so. In addition, the patient was fearful that loss of control over his anger might damage relationships he depended upon. Could he risk all this? The supervisor felt that if this patient had not entered into a more exploratory therapy after two years, the therapist should not try to persuade him to do so.

The therapist felt disappointed and experienced a deflation of therapeutic zeal, yet he recognized the validity of the supervisor's comments. With this came some relief and a shift out of a polarized position with the patient, in which the therapist stood for further insight and the patient stood for avoidance. The relinquishment of zeal for a greater goal was replaced by a greater respect for the patient's defenses against severe anxiety and more modest goals for his therapy.

The therapist's investment in his own vision for the patient compromised his empathic understanding of the patient's fear, defenses, and inertia. The compassionate wish to help the patient was joined by his personal investment in a treatment outcome for the patient, outstripping the patient's readiness for change. The therapist's deflation over accepting a more limited goal felt to him like a partial therapeutic failure. The supervisor was helpful in underlining what in the patient was determining the impasse, providing a contrast to the therapist's feeling that it reflected his own therapeutic ineffectiveness. The therapist's narcissistic investment was partially redirected from his vision of curing the patient to his understanding the patient's dynamics, defenses, and limitations in greater depth.

As an alternative approach, the supervisor could have pursued the therapist's countertransference frustration and impatience with the patient. What could this reveal about the patient's stubbornness and passive-resistant stance toward the therapy? What could this reflect of the therapist's anger toward the patient, perhaps with links to the therapist's feelings about rigid and inhibited people in his personal life, or his own rigidity? Was he overly identified with the patient, and imposing his expectations for his own growth onto the patient? Such an exploration could have deepened the therapist's understanding of what this patient meant to him and the interplay between his self-representations and his view of the patient. This approach could also leave the therapist open to greater exposure and potential embarrassment.

Therapeutic zeal may inspire clinical work and learning. It may also overlap with feelings of omnipotence that compensate, at times, for feelings of helplessness or inadequacy. "A resident's need to fulfill a narcissistically determined ideal image of himself can be a force to be directed toward professional growth or it can be an impediment," state Maltsberger and Buie (1969, p. 69). Feelings of omnipotence may manifest as unrealistic visions of one's capacity to change and cure a patient and underestimation of the tenacity of the patient's structure. Omnipotent wishes can become sources of great frustration and impatience and can collapse into feelings of helplessness, disillusionment, and depletion.

The supervisor is in a position to recognize these shifts of feeling and help the therapist in bearing these painful experiences. In so doing, she helps the supervisee progressively forge a more realistic and flexible sense of finite but real competence as a therapist.

Dr. C. came to supervision one day feeling troubled. He was six months into his first year of residency. He had recently picked up a new patient on the inpatient unit to follow in outpatient therapy. He was excited about the treatment, liked the patient, and felt he could help him. The patient was a man in his twenties from an angry, controlling, rigid family background who, in the context of a major business failure and family conflict, had become depressed and suicidal, requiring three hospitalizations over several months. During the most recent admission, the inpatient team insisted that the patient have a different inpatient therapist and that Dr. C. (who worked on this unit) function as the outside therapist. Dr. C. did not agree with this plan, which conflicted with his wish to cure the patient on his own, but went along with it. The insult was exacerbated near the time of the patient's discharge when the inpatient therapist (a psychiatric social worker) arranged to have several postdischarge appointments with the patient. Dr. C. felt upset and angry that he had not been consulted about these plans.

As the situation was reviewed in supervision, Dr. C. clearly expressed the wish and belief that he could cure the patient. Anything that came into conflict with this goal was threatening to him. That the patient had been rehospitalized after the beginning of outpatient work challenged his sense of being able to cure him through therapy alone. Further, he felt that he should be able to cure the patient largely on his own. Thus, the intensive team approach on the inpatient service challenged this wish, and the inpatient therapist's making follow-up appointments insulted him. Dr. C. felt confused and frustrated that the patient had not yet been able to pull himself together, as Dr. C. himself had done by resolving some personal conflicts in his own therapy.

The supervisor had several choices about how to respond to this material. He could address the patient's transference to Dr. C. and wonder about its impact on these events. Had the patient's desperation and wish for a savior caused Dr. C. to feel that he must come to the rescue? Or the supervisor could address this in a didactic way, focusing on the patient's dynamics and pathology. Or the supervisor could address Dr. C.'s feelings, exploring why it was so important for him to go it alone with the patient and what the follow-up visits with the social worker really meant to him. The supervisor felt that the most pressing problem was Dr. C.'s distress and wished to help him bear the injuries he felt, reduce his hurt, and help him to put the clinical situation in a different perspective. The supervisor recalled his own experience of having had one of his first private patients hospitalized within weeks of opening his practice, on a hospital unit where he had recently trained. He recounted the embarrassment he felt at the time, as if this exposed his inadequacies as a therapist. By reflecting on this with some distance and humor the supervisor hoped to convey to the therapist that his reactions were understandable but that he need not take this matter so hard.

Dr. C.'s wish to cure the patient by himself was also taken up, in a more didactic way. The supervisor explained that disturbed patients frequently require multiple caregivers. While the wish to go it alone was natural, it was often not possible. Allowing that the patient might at times need more help than the resident alone could provide, the supervisor, nevertheless, supported the resident's role as the primary clinician. The supervisor, in effect, tried to put what felt like a series of narcissistic injuries into a perspective that would be more bearable. The resident experienced some relief of his distress, gained support for his importance to the patient, and looked at the situation with enough distance to lessen his anger. He may have also felt some permission from the supervisor to relax his excessive demands upon himself to bear sole responsibility for this difficult patient. He felt less need to struggle with the inpatient staff over these details of the care plan.

Therapeutic zeal can involve a conflict between narcissistic illusions ("I can cure this patient because I've connected with him, I understand him, and I'm motivated") and the reality that much goes into patient outcome beyond the therapist's skill. Feeling threatened by other caregivers ("Who is *really* curing the patient?") involves a narcissistic threat. Overidentification can cloud the limitations of the patient and the therapy. Supervision can address these issues and help the new therapist grapple with the anxiety, frustration, disappointment, and anger of working with ill patients. Self-respect can be preserved when more omnipotent aspirations unravel. The supervisory interventions here were directed to personal reactions in Dr. C.—affects, competitiveness, omnipotent impulses to cure the patient, frustration, and narcissistic injury. Yet the supervisory interventions were supportive and normalizing rather than exploratory. The supervisor made no effort to deepen or elaborate on the personal material. The supervisor could have focused more on anger and frustration, affording Dr. C. an opportunity to deepen his awareness of the affects stirred up by clinical work, what his feelings disclosed of his motivations, and how his reactions were related to the dynamics of his patient. In a personal psychotherapy, the nature of the resident's anger and frustration and the determinants of his narcissistic vulnerability in his own history would be explored. The more clearly limited educational focus of supervision, by contrast, at times helps to soften the narcissistic blows the therapist sustains.

Several other responses to the perils to self-esteem involved in learning bear mention. These include rigid avoidance of self-revelation in supervision; defensive belligerence against patients, supervisors, colleagues, or a program; competitiveness as a compensation for feelings of inadequacy; and depressive resolutions (Pollack, 1982). While some responses and defenses to pressures upon self-esteem can be handled in supervision, others will limit the student's openness to learning.

The inevitable threats to the supervisee's self-regard posed by clinical work and the learning situation, the diverse ways in which trainees handle these pressures, and the acute distress of shame and anxiety that may be aroused in supervision challenge the supervisor to respond. As in the above vignettes, the supervisor is called upon to recognize these themes and respond to the educational and psychological needs of her student. In chapter 9, we further explore the supervisor's role in handling issues of self-esteem as they arise in supervision.

9

Self-Esteem and the Supervisor's Role

Each supervisory pair establishes a dynamic interplay between the pursuit of deeper understanding (which may destabilize the sense of self in patient, therapist, or supervisor) and the maintenance of sufficient self-esteem in each participant. The supervisor's contribution to this process may be beneficial or detrimental to the supervisee, the learning task, and the degree of safety in the supervision.

"First, Do No Harm"

In the supervisory encounter, the supervisor as well as the therapist confronts her own need to maintain self-esteem. If the supervisor has a well-integrated view of herself with relatively stable and mature defenses, her own narcissistic needs will not interfere with the supervisee's development and learning. Yet the supervisor's unresolved narcissistic issues, especially any tendency to maintain her own self-esteem at the expense of the trainee, will obscure the learning needs and potentially exacerbate the problems of self-esteem regulation with which the student is grappling.

As Fleming points out, for the supervisor as well as the trainee, "narcissistic exhibitionistic anxieties and defenses . . . are stirred up by situations of exposure and examination" (cited in Wallerstein, 1981, p. 120). These anxieties and defenses may take a variety of forms. Schlesinger (1981), for instance, notes his "wish to 'give,' which probably has part of its roots in insecurity about whether I really have enough to give to justify being an analytic teacher. 'Giving' also has within it the sense of wanting to be a plentiful provider, to 'stuff' the candidate who has come under my wing as well as to overwhelm the candidate with how much as a supervisor I have to offer, to awe him. . . . Together with the defense against them, these needs to feed, hold down, impress, encourage and discourage, could certainly influence the teaching process and shape the teaching situation and thereby the nature of the learning alliance" (p. 290).

Schlesinger elucidates how a multiply determined wish to give to a student may include a genuine desire to help, but also a wish to inspire awe, an envy of youth, and a need to triumph over it. Dominance may be achieved by having the student overtly submit to the supervisor's opinions. Or it may be attained more subtly, by overtly championing the student's advancement within the organization, thus putting the student in the supervisor's debt.

The maintenance of self-esteem through dominance has many faces. When the supervisor is too narcissistically invested in a particular approach to treatment, she may take on an inappropriately authoritative role. A description of such a supervisory approach is offered by Shevrin (1981) in writing of his experience with supervision:

The supervisory approach was to encourage silence, judicious facilitation but little interpretive work in the opening phase. In this respect, the emphasis was on the old and—in Gill and Muslin's view—erroneous point of view concerning the role of interpretation in the beginning phase of analysis. Seldom in the supervision were different technical approaches discussed, or different options in understanding the material considered, nor was there recognition that the patient's communications might be simply confusing and difficult to understand at this point in the treatment. There was, in fact, one way to approach the data, one way to understand it; any mystery was a failure in understanding. Certainly at no point were *researchable* issues considered—questions that needed further clarification in theory or technique. It was this approach more than any other in supervision that cemented the candidate's belief that he was to discover what the supervisor wanted and try to do it. (p. 267)

A central question asks where is the narcissistic investment for the supervisor? It may be an investment in the intellectual and affective challenge of supervising, feeling fulfilled by a job well done. Or it may be in the relationships with supervisees, wishing to inspire admiration or awe, as Schlesinger suggests. Is there excessive investment in the supervisee's growth, seen as a reflection upon one's own supervisory skill? Or is there investment in the patients' progress, feeling that therapeutic progress confirms the competence of the supervisee and, therefore, of the supervision? Perhaps the supervisor has his or her own unresolved competitive issues and feels threatened by a student who is exceptionally intelligent or confrontational, or who challenges the supervisor's formulations and beliefs about treatment. Is the supervisor patronizing, sexist, punitive, or sadistic? Does the supervisory setting present an arena in which to enact these attitudes and impulses? Is the supervisor able to tolerate the increasing competence and autonomy of the student without feeling threatened and having to assert dominance? Dewald (1987), for example, suggests that the supervisor should actively present a model for emulation and partial identification, but he does not insist or even expect that the student will follow it completely or exclusively. He notes that "the candidate's independence and decision not to accept his suggestions may at times involve narcissistic injury to the supervisor, who must be able to tolerate such a response for the sake of the candidate's ultimate independence" (pp. 477–478). Further, does the supervisor overtly abuse the authority of the supervisory relationship to intimidate the student, coerce favors, or pursue sexual contact? All these aspects of the supervisor's narcissistic investment will affect the educational experience and, in some cases, be destructive to the supervisee.

There is an inescapable power differential in supervision, inherent in the fact that one participant goes to the other for help, that there is a gap between student and teacher in experience or competence, and that the supervisor often must evaluate the therapist for a training institution. The maintenance of self-esteem in the face of a more powerful and knowledgeable other is a real concern in any ongoing supervision. These concerns about power and its use need to be acknowledged if the dialogue it to be honest and open. When there is a power differential and the vulnerability associated with it is denied or overlooked, pretense and defense can deaden the supervisory relationship. It is not the inevitable and legitimate power that causes concern but rather subtle or glaring abuses of this power.

When the supervisee feels subordinated to the supervisor, it may not be clear how much each contributes to the situation. Dick (1987), writing of her supervisory experience with Dewald, reports that early in the supervision she felt she was expected to become a reflection of her supervisor, who required total allegiance. "If I had other allegiances and identifications, for instance, if I considered other views than those of 'classical theory,' it would not be tolerated" (p. 459). Although she blames herself for these feelings, attributing them to a neurotic transference to her supervisor, neither she nor Dewald considers what he might have contributed to such feelings or how he might have helped her with them. The effects of the power differential and gender differences—a relatively inexperienced female candidate coming to a nationally known older male analyst for supervision—and of the complicated feelings that arise in this context are not dealt with in depth in the book. Dick also describes how she protected herself from "feeling too exposed or self-conscious" in response to the prospect of the publication of the supervisory sessions. She fantasized that the project was helping Dewald in his recovery from a serious illness (p. 448). In other words, she imagined that the project was for his benefit mainly and that she, by her compliance, was helping him. In gender terms this may have been seen and experienced as male dominance and a woman's masochistic, rationalized submission, though we do not have enough information to know if this was the case.

The Supervisor's Beneficial Role

While the supervisor's unresolved conflicts, narcissistic needs, and inappropriate use of power in supervision may stifle the learning process and undermine the supervisee's self-respect, the supervisor is also in a position to help her student with issues of self-esteem as they arise in supervision. We began chapter 8 by posing an inescapable conflict between curiosity, exploration, and the search to deepen understanding on the one hand and the narcissistic vulnerability of the supervisee on the other. In this section we suggest how the supervisor may become more attuned to these issues and seek a beneficial balance between the pursuit of honest exploration and the maintenance of self-respect in the supervisee. The supervisor may become aware of her student's vulnerabilities in various ways. One therapist, for example, presented all his process material with a conspicuous show of anxiety, dismay, and self-doubt, conveying through his facial expression, inflection, and verbal style that he invariably doubted his understanding, technique, and ability to help his patients. The supervisor could not have missed this. Another supervisee's outward style was confident, self-assured, and dogmatic, and what this was covering became clear only when the supervisee explained to his supervisor the pervasive self-doubt with which he had struggled for decades. Belligerence toward patients, the supervisor, or the enterprise of psychotherapy may conceal distressing feelings of incompetence. These examples are not intended to suggest that the supervisor should interpret the supervisee's behavior to reveal underlying narcissistic concerns; rather, the supervisor should be attuned to these ubiquitous issues, as they appear in a variety of forms. Observing how students handle the narcissistic challenges of learning, and how their ways of dealing with these pressures help or hinder their openness to learning, becomes an aspect of the educational assessment.

A basic objective for the supervisor is to promote a safe learning atmosphere. Supervision ought to be an enterprise in which the therapist-in-training feels able to think openly, express half-formed ideas, raise questions (no matter how basic), and discuss inner experiences that arise in learning therapy, to the extent that he feels motivated to do so, without undue fear of criticism, humiliation, or intimidation. To learn optimally, the student must have the opportunity to express instinctive reactions to patients, to talk about countertransference, to wonder aloud, and to offer incomplete associations and hunches in a spirit of open inquiry. The supervisor, who spends much of her professional life looking below the surface of manifest content, must maintain a respect for the educational context of supervision, as distinct from a treatment context, and respond to self-revelation with this in mind. When the extent of self-revelation expected of the supervisee is not clear, or when the supervisee does not feel entitled to privacy (for example, confusing the expectations for an exploratory psychotherapy with the context of supervision), the risk of shame is increased. The supervisee can decline any exploration that is attempted. However, owing to transference, anxiety, and the authority of the supervisor, the supervisee may feel pressure to comply with some imagined or actual demand for self-disclosure.

The supervisor is in a position to provide significant support to the trainee in many ways. Maltsberger and Buie (1969) describe sustaining, supporting, and gratification maneuvers in supervision. Sustaining maneuvers help the therapist to keep the therapy going, aided by the supervisor demonstrating and explaining how to proceed, providing a chance for the therapist to ventilate feelings about patients, and allying with the therapist's competence. Supporting maneuvers include confronting the therapist in order to help him work more effectively with patients, sharing the supervisor's own experience, making clarifications, and setting limits on the therapist. Gratification maneuvers involve the supervisor acknowledging and respecting the supervisee's activity and serving as a catalyst for the trainee's own discoveries. Rosenblatt and Mayer (1975), writing of social work supervision, delineate various "objectionable" supervisory styles, including "unsupportive supervision." The self-esteem of the supervisee can be supported by such responses as empathic interest in the student's experience of doing therapy, validation of his competence and talent, realistic praise and admiration for his efforts and accomplishments, and encouragement of his pursuit of mastery of skills, especially during periods of confusion, doubt, and discouragement. Support may also involve supporting the adaptive defenses of the student. The learning context fosters a cognitive/didactic frame of reference, which—in addition to the content being taught—offers an intellectual defense that may, at times, be adaptive in the face of overwhelming affect or anxiety in the supervisee.

Another supportive use of the educational context of supervision is the normalization of the student's experience. Beginning therapists often feel that their reactions to patients (anger, despair, fear, sexual arousal, helplessness, pessimism, aversion, love, and so forth) reflect on them in a personal way, revealing their impulses, values, inadequacies, neuroses, and unattractive qualities. The supervisor's ability to discuss the kinds of reactions such patients evoke, or to recall her own similar reactions in the past, provides a balance to the personalized distress the therapist may be feeling. This approach, if overused, may be superficial, premature, or gratuitous, and can interfere with the therapist's exploration of the meaning of his responses and countertransferences.

Another ingredient in the creation of a safe learning environment is providing assistance to the supervisee in bearing affects, feelings of uncertainty, or feelings of helplessness. A psychiatry resident working in an outpatient program was treating a woman who was struggling with suicidal feelings, as was her husband. The husband, who worked in a research lab, brought home a vial of potassium cyanide for possible use in a suicide attempt. In order to protect himself from this impulse, he turned the vial over to his wife for "safekeeping," with full knowledge of her suicidal tendencies. The woman, in a panic, brought the vial to her therapist, again, for safekeeping. She was in a turmoil over her own suicidal impulses and her husband's. She was concerned as well about what her husband's actions revealed of his wishes toward her. The resident, picking up the momentum of danger and enactment, felt an urgent wish to review the situation with someone else, get advice, and dispose of the lethal chemical. He promptly sought out a supervisor, reviewed the story, assessed what he needed to do to safeguard his patient, and formed a plan for disposal of the cyanide (to the hospital pharmacy). The supervisor helped the resident formulate a clinical plan of action, assisting him in directing his subsequent efforts, and in the process mitigating the resident's anxiety. Furthermore, the supervisor's calm response (the first such response in an urgent sequence that had encompassed the patient, her husband, and the resident) was reassuring to the resident who—having shared his anxiety and made a plan—was able to return his attention to understanding the patient and her current crisis.

The supervisor could have explored with the resident why this situation made him so anxious. The resident's anxiety may have represented an excessive sense of self-doubt, best pursued in a personal therapy or analysis. Or perhaps it reflected an overidentification with the panicky patient, joining her in her sense of urgency, but impeding decisive clinical assessment. Exploring the resident's feelings may have helped him understand his own reactions, but left him feeling criticized for overreacting. Alternatively, the supervisor could have examined the meaning of the woman's enactment, perhaps that she was passing on to the resident not only the cyanide (and her fear), but also the murderous impulse that her husband presumably felt toward her, and which she perhaps felt toward her husband, or her therapist. In this instance, the supervisor sensed the intensity of the resident's anxiety and the need for rapid clinical decision making. He chose a didactic intervention that led to a rapid solution to the immediate situation in order to diminish the resident's anxiety and provide a tangible path of action.

Beyond the supportive, normalizing, and containing interventions the supervisor makes to foster a safe learning environment, she helps her student manage the assaults on his self-respect by providing distance and a new perspective on the clinical material and on his experience. In fact, putting things into perspective is a major function of supervision. When a therapist is threatened by feelings of shame and inadequacy, excited by grandiose expansiveness, paralyzed by helplessness, or resounding with omnipotence, the resolution of problems that arise generally involves putting the situation into a different perspective. The patient's difficulties, the therapist's capacities (inflated or deflated), reasonable expectations for therapeutic effectiveness, or another factor may require reevaluation. Most broadly, the therapist's inwardly constructed representations of the patient, himself, and the process of therapy become colored, exaggerated, and shaped by wishes, fears, fantasies, magic, and unconscious conflicts. Supervision can be understood as a place for supervisee and supervisor together to construct new perspectives and contexts within which to organize the experiences of therapy. This proceeds cognitively (as with the introduction of a theoretical construct to help organize data) and affectively (as with the supervisor's help in modulating and containing affective experience). Shifting perspective to resolve a clinical and narcissistic crisis is illustrated in the following vignette.

Dr. E. was a second-year psychiatric resident on an inpatient unit when he began working with Mr. Z., a 33-year-old man who had been admitted to the unit for increasing depression, suicidal ideation, and homicidal impulses (toward his outpatient therapist and others). While Mr. Z. suffered from meager self-esteem, a painful sense of sinfulness, and long-standing struggles with anger and anxiety, this crisis had developed after a professional success. He was attractive and energetic, but felt isolated, guilt-ridden, and inadequate. He felt that he had been dominated and devalued by his mother and neglected emotionally by his father. On the inpatient unit, Mr. Z. became furious and mistrustful toward staff in a series of confrontations over passes and privileges.

A crisis developed when Mr. Z. was selected as the subject of a teaching conference but refused to participate. The treatment team decided to proceed with the conference in his absence. Mr. Z., however, objected to this, as well, insisting that the conference be canceled and threatening legal action. Dr. E. felt scared and uncertain of what to do. On the one hand, he recognized that Mr. Z. was in distress over the conference and was feeling violated. Dr. E. felt that holding the conference would compromise any alliance with the patient and might precipitate violence or a sudden flight from the unit. He recognized the patient's chronic feeling of powerlessness and current need to feel in control, as well as his desire to avoid exposure and humiliation. On the other hand, Mr. Z.'s rages were terrifying, to himself and others, and needed to be dealt with. Dr. E. feared that canceling the conference would amount to backing down and thus posed two dangers. First, the patient would take this as confirming how frightening and destructive he was. Second, Dr. E. would feel that he was a weak and inadequate therapist. Standing up to his patient might help Mr. Z. feel contained, reassuring him that someone was in charge. Allowing Mr. Z.'s rage to dictate events might bypass a crucial opportunity to address this core issue, failing him therapeutically. Dr. E. did not wish to incite his rage but felt he must be able to withstand it for the sake of the patient's growth and his own self-respect. To compound matters, the treatment team was pushing for the conference.

In this setting, Dr. E. called his supervisor for guidance. The supervisor advised him to cancel the conference because of the patient's distress and concern over being controlled and devalued. He noted that there would be many other opportunities to deal with the issues that had arisen. Dr. E. felt enormously relieved and arranged with the chief resident to cancel the conference. Mr. Z. then brought about further confrontations over passes and privileges, providing opportunities to work on these issues. He also began to grapple with his usual ways of coping with affect, learning about the nature of his rage and longings. He felt proud of learning new options for resolving conflicts and was especially pleased when he was told that staff had canceled the conference in response to his pain, not his threats. Both Mr. Z. and Dr. E. learned something about conflict resolution and put the incident into a new perspective.

This supervisor, who was away from the heat of the action, helped the resident step back, shift perspective, and find a way through the conflict that preserved the patient's privacy and sense of control and the resident's self-esteem. The resident was able to modify his expectation that he should be tough with the patient in a way that preserved self-respect. The supervisor had given him permission to lessen his own superego pressures without sacrificing his self-respect. The supervisor also became an ally and advocate in the resident's conflict with the treatment team. While Dr. E. wrestled with concerns about his professional adequacy, to some extent his experience was probably intensified in response to projected feelings of inadequacy from Mr. Z. Being helped to view this as information about the patient advanced his clinical understanding *and* supported his self-esteem. The affective intensity was transmitted from patient to therapist, as was the content concerning questions of who is adequate, who is in control, and who will be humiliated. For the patient, this was a decisive encounter, for the stakes included his ability to stay in treatment. The resident began to experience the conflict between them as inflated, almost mythic in proportions: everything was riding on the outcome. The supervisor's intervention helped bring the impasse down to earth with the essential message:"It's just another day. Life goes on, the treatment goes on, and the patient's conflicts go on. There will be further opportunities to deal with this."

An aspect of the supervisor's role in preserving the therapist's self-esteem, then, is the ability to help the therapist achieve some distance from the immediate clinical pressures and to sort out what affects and urgency are coming from the patient and what from the therapist. The therapist's expectations for behaviors that demonstrate his effectiveness and competence need to be recalibrated. Supervision may help to foster a bearable sense of the supervisee's limitations and diminish dysfunctional ways of defending against shame.

A crucial element is the model the supervisor presents for managing concerns and feelings that may be raw and unresolved in the therapist. The supervisor offers herself as an object for identification, which can help counterbalance the narcissistic disequilibrium of learning. In the vignette above, for example, the supervisor modeled an accommodation to the patient's demand that did not represent a personal or therapeutic failure. The supervisor models nonhelplessness: no matter how impossible the situation may seem to the therapist, there is always a next step. It may not be the correct or only step, but it nonetheless represents an educated attempt to do what is best.

Modeling and attaining a new perspective often involve a redirection of the narcissistic investment. Dr. E.'s narcissistic balance initially pivoted on whether he could be "strong" and stand up to the patient. The supervisory intervention permitted a rechanneling of this toward the feeling that he could pin his self-respect on his capacity to understand the patient's behavior and work toward a therapeutic result. More generally, then, the question becomes: where is the therapist's narcissistic investment, and where else might it be directed? Rather than feeling that one's personal worth hinges on winning a battle, one derives satisfaction and self-esteem from the ability to understand why the battle is happening. Rather than priding oneself on never behaving in a foolish manner (in therapy or supervision), one acknowledges the limitations of one's technique and takes comfort in the capacity to laugh at oneself. Instead of thinking one should never feel angry at patients, one feels able to face and explore anger—and use it to understand patients. As self-reflection is valued in psychotherapy training, the narcissistic reward may include feeling honest, brave, and self-aware. Such an appraisal may counter-balance the embarrassment and shame of self-exposure. Most important, the narcissistic rewards of good patient outcomes must often be redirected toward the ability to understand the patient and be the best therapist one is able to be, regardless of patient outcome.

While we have been emphasizing supervisory interventions that support self-esteem in the supervisee (providing a safe learning atmosphere, directly supporting and valuing, assisting in bearing affects, putting things into perspective, and redirecting of narcissistic investment), it is clear that supervisees gain personal and professional self-respect through the achievement of competence and mastery, as well as by working through conflicts and limitations in their work. Supervisory interventions that help the supervisee become a better therapist obviously enhance self-esteem, even if that is not the direct intent. In teaching a body of knowledge, providing a structure in which to learn the art of therapy, and giving the student the tools to do the job (including theory and technique), the supervisor helps the trainee grow as a therapist and develop a professional identity. This may also involve helping him work through an area of conflict. If the therapist-in-training is hampered in doing psychotherapy by personal inhibition, unresolved conflicts, or disorganizing affects, greater mastery of these problem areas will enhance his competence and thus self-esteem. While supervision is not the setting for the supervisee to receive therapy, it may nonetheless help the trainee work through an area of conflict as it arises in the clinical work. The supervisor may be in a position to clarify a conflict, inhibition, or countertransference difficulty that affects the therapy and in so doing may facilitate change in the therapist's attitudes or behaviors with patients (Lester and Robertson, 1993).

In a fashion that is quite different from the more directly support-ive interventions a supervisor may make, the supervisee is pushed to do his best work, to confront difficult affects in himself and his patients, to recognize countertransferences, to try out new forms of therapeutic behavior, to take risks, and to brave uncertainty, ambiguity, and suffering. In being thus encouraged, the therapist grows and gains in self-esteem through successful achievement.

A central dilemma in the management of self-esteem in super-vision is the conflict between the learning imperative (to look be-low the surface, pursue a deepened understanding, and to grow) and the narcissistic vulnerability which inevitably accompanies such learning. Certainly, all therapists recognize this inescapable aspect of psychotherapy: the medicine hurts the patient. To un-derstand himself, deepen his appreciation of his conflicts, and grow, the patient must confront areas of comfort and safety in the service of change. While supervision is not psychotherapy, there is an analogous need for the therapist-in-training to confront uncomfortable feelings, confusion, uncertainty, his affective re-sponses and characteristic sensibilities, in the process of develop-ing his therapeutic instrument. Each supervision implicitly works out a balance between the necessary narcissistic imbalance of learning and preserving therapist (and supervisor) self-esteem. What balance is achieved and how this is achieved will have a significant impact on the learning. Many authors (Imber, 1993; Lester and Robertson, 1993) have advocated the use of clarifica-tions and judicious interpretations of the supervisee as a way of calling his attention to aspects of his therapeutic behavior (and, in the case of interpretations, to the unconscious feelings and conflicts behind this behavior). Lawner (1989), for example, has written of the central role of counteridentification by therapists in therapeutic stalemates. By this, he refers to an unconscious dynamic in which the therapist may identify with the patient's defenses, limiting the unfolding of the relational process of therapy. He argues that this identification will often reveal itself in supervision and that clarifying and examining it is a proper focus for the supervisor in order to overcome therapeutic impasses. The value of such an approach may be the immediacy of the therapist's confrontation of his countertransference impediments to treating the patient. However, this approach may increase the therapist's anxiety and challenge his self-respect. Whether the educational gain is worth the narcissistic challenge will depend on the quality of the supervisory alliance and the degree of trust and safety the therapist feels in the particular supervision. If the therapist's sense of exposure, shame, and anxiety is excessive, it may well interfere with his ability to make use of even the most accurate interpretations.

While we have advocated the supportive and self-esteem-enhancing role of supervision, an overly supportive supervision may be superficial, missing the opportunity for the therapist to deepen his understanding of his patients and himself. If the therapist makes a mistake in treatment and the supervisor, out of a wish to protect the therapist's self-esteem, does not address it or discusses it so gently that the therapist does not get the point, an opportunity for learning is lost. If the therapist appears to be involved in countertransference enactments, is disoriented by his affects, and sees the patient less clearly, the supervisor's decision not to address these problems may only superficially support his self-esteem while neglecting his learning. Ornstein (1968) emphasizes the limitations of an overly supportive approach: "The teacher may . . . assume a supportive, wait-and-see attitude, letting the trainee learn from experience. Here the rationalization is that the initial anxiety prevents learning, and therefore little or nothing can be taught until the anxiety subsides" (p. 302). For Ornstein, the supervisor's supportive passivity can undermine the kind of learning that emphasizes "the process of discovery, the process of acquiring the method through which conviction of the validity of his dynamic understanding could be gained" (p. 305).

In a supervision discussed in chapter 7, Ms. L., a graduate student, was filled with fears from without (robbery, rape, her father's wrath) and from within (her anger and potential loss of control over her feelings). Dr. P., the psychiatric resident treating her, had trouble bringing the patient "into focus" owing, in part, to Ms. L.'s intellectualization and affective remoteness. Dr. P.'s supervisor had used a Socratic approach to help Dr. P. move beyond a largely supportive approach to a more exploratory one. We return to this example to examine how a therapist-in-training was challenged by her supervisor to expand her therapeutic approach to her patient, balancing the therapist's educational needs with a respect for her self-esteem.

Ms. L.'s father was a frustrated academic who dominated the household with his papers, his work, and his need for quiet. Her mother was often depressed and spent part of Ms. L.'s childhood housebound, in what Ms. L. called the "year of the blue bathrobe." Ms. L. was left feeling empty, felt pressured to become extraordinary, and had difficulty establishing intimate relationships. She was also frightened of her frequent anger and had many hypochondriacal concerns. Dr. P. often described a "vagueness" in her patient's presentation, leaving her without a focused picture of who her patient was or how therapy might help.

Dr. P. was eager to learn psychodynamically oriented therapy, but felt anxious and inexperienced. Her supervisor saw her as a warm and nurturant resident whose natural inclination was to offer support and reassurance to her patient. For example, if the patient complained about a visit with her family, the therapist might tell her how hard it must have been, without exploring what made it hard, what the patient had expected, or what fantasies and feelings she had about the visit. The supervisor felt that Dr. P., in her wish to be supportive, was hindered in telling her patient anything that might increase her anxiety or anger. Ms. L. gave her therapist fair warning by referring, at times, to a prior therapist whose attempts at interpretation she had hated.

The supervisor began to see that a learning task for Dr. P. was to move beyond reassurance, support, and containment and to deepen her understanding of her patient. On one occasion, for example, Ms. L. said that perhaps she might be the "post office, shotgun type," leading Dr. P. to say that Ms. L. should call her if she felt like hurting herself or another person. The supervisor, who felt that Ms. L. was expressing an affective state and was not at the time in danger of violence or suicide, suggested that Dr. P.'s response, understandable as it was, might shut down further exploration of what Ms. L. was feeling and communicating in this vivid image.

On another occasion, Ms. L. described her anger toward her mother and considered confronting her mother with these feelings. Dr. P., concerned that her patient might thereby lose her parents' support, wanted to warn her patient against doing this. The supervisor told Dr. P. that such a warning would represent siding with one side of Ms. L.'s ambivalence (to be a "good girl" who would tiptoe around, as she had done to avoid her father's temper). The other side was her wish to express her feelings and her fear of losing control. The supervisor suggested that Ms. L. needed a chance to express her feelings in therapy and that Dr. P. might need to be more prepared to hear out her patient's anger and allow her to decide what she would express to her family. Dr. P. replied that she did not feel comfortable with her patient's anger. The supervisor's sense was that Dr. P.'s emphasis on a supportive approach was linked to her discomfort over Ms. L.'s anger and that Dr. P. might emphasize control and containment at the expense of deeper understanding.

As Dr. P.'s supportive approach was the dominant style with this patient, the supervisor elected to clarify this approach directly, telling Dr. P. that her comments to her patient were generally supportive and reassuring but that she missed chances to learn more about the patient. The supervisor's intervention addressed specific process material rather than being given as a global comment. It was also joined with genuinely felt admiration for the therapist's nurturance, kindness, and warmth toward the patient. No deeper exploration of the therapist's feelings —for example, the conflicts or inhibitions that might have contributed to her approach—was pursued.

Dr. P. responded to her supervisor's comments by increased efforts to ask her patient about her feelings and the meaning of her behavior. In one session, Ms. L. announced her engagement, hinted at much ambivalence about her boyfriend, but felt that she did not want to "look at negative things." Dr. P. indicated the importance of "looking at the good and the bad," examining all her feelings about this decision. But Dr. P. subsequently felt guilty about her comment, particularly when it seemed to anger her patient.

Dr. P. and her supervisor had planned a three-way meeting to help both Dr. P. and the supervisor form a clearer picture of Ms. L. Shortly before the meeting, Ms. L. announced that she would probably stop therapy because things were going well and she was not sure she was ready to look at long-term issues. In addition, she would soon have to begin paying out-of-pocket for her therapy, which had been covered to this point. The supervisor then felt that the three-way meeting might be used as a consultation.

In the meeting, he found Ms. L. working hard to control her

feelings and her ambivalence about several dilemmas by using intellectualization and avoidance of her conflicts. For example, after describing a "cold, scary core" to her fiance and a sense that he often "tuned her out," Ms. L. went on to say that the problems with him "weren't important." The supervisor commented that she seemed to compartmentalize some of her feelings and gave some examples, recommending that she consider staying in treatment, as she seemed to have issues she was working on. In so doing, the supervisor modeled an approach to the patient that clarified her defensive style, and invited Ms. L. to be self-reflective, knowing this was anxiety-provoking and ego-dystonic for her.

Following this encounter, Ms. L. came to her next therapy session angry at the supervisor, feeling that he had implied that she "couldn't feel." She then associated to a former therapist whom she hated and who had made interpretations. She also recalled a former boyfriend's father, a psychiatrist, who had advised his son not to marry her because she was too intellectual. Dr. P. described her patient as expressing "more affect than ever" in this meeting. She tried to clarify to Ms. L. that the supervisor had found her a bright and feeling person. Ms. L. acknowledged that her reaction to the supervisor may have had origins in her past and that she still had problems to work on. She now felt that she should continue in treatment. She subsequently complained that she resented the medical profession, including the supervisor, for "coercing her into treatment." She said, however, that "at a deeper level" getting angry at the supervisor had helped redirect her toward therapy.

Subsequently, Dr. P., while still tending toward a supportive approach, became more inquisitive, tried to make links between Ms. L.'s current experience and past difficulties, and encouraged her patient to use treatment to express a range of affects including her anger and sadness. When Ms. L. made plans to move to a neighboring state for several months, Dr. P. felt that this would be the end of the therapy. She was delighted when Ms. L. indicated her wish to continue the treatment during monthly visits and her intention to resume weekly therapy in several months. At the time of this interruption, Dr. P. felt that she had established a good therapeutic alliance with her patient, and she had a greater sense of actually being Ms. L.'s therapist.

In the supervisory dialogue, the supervisor had praised Dr. P. for her nurturant and supportive approach but also pushed her to expand her therapeutic repertoire. In the process, the supervisor *confronted* and *clarified* Dr. P.'s style, *modeled* an approach to talking with the patient (during the consultation meeting, for example), and *encouraged* Dr. P. to try out new therapeutic behavior. The supervisory interventions included *didactic* elements (explaining the difference between supporting a patient's self-esteem or defenses and an effort to deepen the understanding of the difficulties), and *Socratic* questioning. In achieving greater therapeutic competence, Dr. P. developed an enhanced sense of professional self-esteem, feeling gratified over her patient's decision to stay in treatment. She was challenged to approach the therapy in a way that was more anxiety-provoking and intense for both therapist and patient. Dr. P. grew as a therapist, gaining professional self-esteem through greater mastery in the practice of psychotherapy.

Had Dr. P.'s style been more resistant to educational change, the supervisor would need to decide how to proceed. Should there be a deeper exploration of the therapist's discomfort about provoking anxiety or anger in the patient? Should the therapist be asked to account for her feelings when she was doing something other than being kind and supportive? Should her own wishes for nurturance be examined as a possible source of her conviction that this is what her patient needed? Might her style represent a reaction formation against hostility toward her patient, and should this be examined?

While there are no correct answers in this supervision or in general, each supervisory pair negotiates the boundaries of supervisee self-disclosure, finding a balance that is educationally useful and personally safe. A supervision that protects the self-esteem of the patient, therapist, and supervisor at the expense of understanding and learning does a disservice to all parties. On the other hand, a supervision that neglects the narcissistic challenges and potential injuries of the learning situation may create enough anxiety and lack of safety to interfere with learning. If the supervisee is to trust the supervisory dialogue, it must be understood that the supervisor's attempts to understand the therapist's technique, countertransference, and sensibilities in a more than superficial way derives from her integrity as a dedicated teacher, and not from voyeuristic or punitive motives. If the supervisee recognizes that self-exposure in supervision is part of the quest to become the best therapist possible, then even if such self-revelation is temporarily anxiety-provoking and narcissistically destabilizing, it will be worth it.

Striking the right balance is unavoidably influenced by the fact that all supervision involves a power differential as well as an evaluative component. In training settings, the latter is formalized. But even outside training, the supervisee is surely concerned with how his work is being seen and assessed by the supervisor. The supervisor as well feels the pressure of being evaluated by the student. Supervisors attain reputations for the kind of supervision they offer, and no supervisor can be immune to some interest in and concern about these perceptions. In order not to misuse the power gradient, the supervisor must have an awareness of and some mastery over her own narcissism, sadism, voyeurism, and urge to be controlling. If the supervisor has unresolved conflicts with aggression, difficulty yielding autonomy to the student, or competitive feelings, she does well to pay attention to how these feelings may become activated in the supervisory setting, which can be intense, intimate, stimulating, and narcissistically vulnerable for the supervisor as well as for the student. The goals of supervision include increased competence in the therapist, a deepening understanding of himself and the art of psychotherapy, as well as the growth of his professional identity and self-esteem. The supervisor's sensitivity to the student's fluctuating self-regard can assist him in the risky journey toward becoming a psychotherapist.

10

Termination

While much has been written about the termination phase in therapy and analysis, the ending of the supervisory educational process has rarely been noted. Yet the way in which a supervision ends can influence the learning process that has occurred. It is like the period at the end of a sentence, putting into perspective all that has come before it. "The rest is silence," says Fortinbras at the end of *Hamlet*. But that silence is made meaningful by all the hopes, dreams, and fears that have preceded it. Furthermore, Hamlet, Gertrude, Polonius, Ophelia, and the others remain alive within us, speaking to us long after the curtain has descended, just as we may continue lively internal dialogues with absent friends and foes as well as with former teachers, supervisors, and analysts. Separations are part of a process and are never fully complete. Rank in *The Trauma of Birth* (1929) suggested that the analytic situation represented an intrauterine state, and its ending a rebirth. The patient's anxiety about termination, he said, is an expression of birth trauma. Others have felt that the regressive aspects of the treatment situation are akin to sleep and the associative material some kind of dreamlike production from which the patient must eventually wake to his real life. Perhaps these ways of conceptualizing analytic termination can help us understand the termination process in supervision. For, if all goes well in his education, the student awakens to a sense of mastery and to a style that is truly his own. Education itself can be conceptualized as the ongoing process of awakening and rebirth of one's professional and personal identity, accentuated by sometimes painful, sometimes joyful terminations with teachers and supervisors.

The ending of supervision can bring relief and the possibility of new beginnings. The ultimate silence of the supervisor, at times, can be, as Shakespeare put it in *Much Ado About Nothing,* "the perfectest herald of joy," a chance for the student to hear his own unalloyed voice. What Kanzer points out about termination of a satisfactory analysis has relevance to the ending of supervision: "There is also relief, joy and a hunger for new experiences for which money, time, and psychological preparedness are now available" (Robbins, 1975, p. 172). Ideally, this joy in independence should have been increasingly manifest within the supervisory hours prior to termination and provides a buffer against the more painful aspects of separation. While such pleasure in increased independence mitigates against too difficult a separation, it is the result, in good part, of the internalization of self-analytic capacities learned from the supervisor and reworked during the termination phase of supervision. Leowald (1962, p. 484) considers the end of treatment a "long drawn out leave-taking," which is like the process of mourning in which love objects are lost and then reinternalized in new ways that can bring about greater emancipation and mastery. The same is true for the end of an educational process. The supervisor can remain an object for continued positive identification within the area of the student's autonomous ego functions, as well as a potentially available object in case of future need.

But for supervision to be concluded successfully, it must have been conducted properly and with special attention to the termination phase. In our experience, this is often not the case. Supervisions may be reduced in frequency or concluded as the result of the increased mastery and autonomy of the supervisee. Tapering or stopping supervision in a casual or unreflective way, however, may rob the educational experience of possible richness and depth. What Bird (1972) said about the termination of treatments may also apply in some instances to the ending of supervision: "Any attenuation of the ending, such as casual tapering off or stopping, should be expected to stand in the way of effective resolution of the transference. Yet, it seems to me, that is what most commonly happens to an ending, and because of this a great many patients lose the potentially great benefit of a thorough resolution and are forever after left suspended in the net of unresolved transference" (p. 287).

While the objective of supervision is not the resolution of transference, some clear closure in terms of the educational work and the supervisory relationship is important. The first thing a supervisor can do to help in the meaningful termination of a supervision is to set a termination date well in advance. Sometimes the end of supervision is determined by the educational institution. For instance, supervisors change every July in some psychiatric residencies. In psychology and social work, some supervisions end at the same time as a particular clinical placement. In analytic training, the supervision may go on for years, not ending until the patient has terminated. Whatever the situation, when it is clear that the supervision will end, a date for ending should be set. This will give both teacher and student time to say good-bye and for the teacher to note any difficulties in leave-taking and help the student with them.

And problems do arise during termination. The experience of the prolonged unselfish interest of the supervisor, for instance, may engender a reluctance in the student to give up this attention. The continuing fantasy of a protective figure who will grant the student special knowledge and insight and protect him from his own mistakes and poor judgment may compromise the student's realistic view of his own abilities to work alone. Often the separation anxiety encountered in the termination phase of supervision is not the fear of separating from the person of the supervisor but anxiety about having to give up the wish for guidance and protection. Kramer (1986) points out, "If the notion of mourning has any meaning at all in a universal sense . . . it is in the sense of mourning for one's lost infantile wishes—the renunciation and grief following the recognition that we can never have what we have always wanted" (p. 349). This renunciation is part of what the student must tolerate when he leaves a supervision. He may need to bear not having achieved all that he had hoped to gain professionally and personally from the relationship with his supervisor. The resolution of this conflict between what the student may have always wanted in terms of learning and what is reasonable educationally is beyond the capacity of the supervisor. But she can, at times, help the student see how his wishes to rely on the supervisor and to remain protected may interfere with a realistic assessment of what he has mastered and can count on in himself. She can also help the student to see that learning to be a therapist is a lifelong process and not one that ends with the termination of a particular supervisory experience. A bridge to the future can be built by helping the student evaluate what he has learned from the supervision and what he still feels he needs to learn from another supervision or on his own.

In one instance, a postdoctoral fellow reported during the course of supervision that his own mother had died when he was a child. After five years, a few small educational gains were being made here and there, but the supervision seemed to the supervisor without compelling direction or purpose. Feeling that she had taught the student everything she reasonably could, the supervisor raised the possibility of termination. The trainee appeared reluctant. He acknowledged that he might learn more at this point by being on his own or by having a different supervisory experience, but admitted for the first time that the current supervisory relationship provided him with some needed sense of safety and feeling cared for. Only after having spoken openly of these feelings, related them to the loss of his mother, and begun a process of mourning for the lost mother could he consider stopping. He was helped in this process of leave-taking by his supervisor's reassurance that she would continue to be interested in his progress and by her willingness to have him return for consultation whenever he liked. The supervisor also gave the student a large degree of latitude in setting the date for termination.

One could ask why after so long a supervision, the student still needed reassurance of the supervisor's interest in him or an explicit encouragement to return whenever liked. We do not know if it was his own previous loss that rendered him uncertain or if the supervisor somehow failed to convey an abiding interest in his development. But what is clear was the supervisor's need to address the subtle stalemate that she felt had occurred in the supervisory process and prevented termination.

In the following vignette, the therapist's unresolved feelings about terminating with a patient and with his supervisor led to a less-than-satisfactory ending of an educational experience. A supervisor and psychiatric resident had been working together biweekly for a year. During that time, the supervisor had gained respect for the resident's intelligence, dedication to and deep respect for his patients, as well as his openness to learning. Throughout the supervisory hours, however, the resident remained formal, stiff, and interpersonally remote. As the academic year and the supervision were coming to an end, the supervisor suggested that he and the resident take some time to reflect on the work they had done together. He did not specify what time might be set aside for such a discussion, and the resident made no mention of it in the following supervisory hours. At their final meeting, the resident went right to his patient notes and presented an hour in which the patient with whom he was about to terminate was feeling depressed and lost. She had told him, "You're the only one I can talk to." Her mother had recently died, and she was having trouble on her job. She felt alienated and alone and suggested that as she could no longer talk to the resident she would have to write to him. The resident in his discussion emphasized the patient's increasing distress. He had administered a depression self-rating scale that confirmed his clinical impression, and he had prescribed a new anxiolytic medication. The supervisor pointed out that the resident had not commented on the impending termination of the therapy and speculated that the patient's depressed state was, in part, a response to it. The resident responded by talking about the impact on the patient of having lost her mother and the possible impact of losing her therapist. He reported having offered to increase the frequency of his meetings with the patient from once to twice a week but was uncertain about the wisdom of "giving her more" just before ending the therapy.

With fifteen minutes left, the supervisor reminded the resident that this was to be their own last meeting. The resident, surprised, said he had forgotten. They spent the remaining time talking about the supervision. The supervisor commented on the value of the therapy to the patient over the years and, despite her current depression, recounted the ways in which the therapy had helped her. The resident initially disagreed and said that the treatment had not helped the patient, but then admitted that she had, in fact, made some gains. The supervisor suggested that the resident point out to the patient what she had accomplished in therapy and complimented him on his respectful, thoughtful, and serious efforts to understand and work with the patient.

The resident had been noted to have a formal, somewhat remote interpersonal style. As the patient appeared more depressed, he emphasized her clinical condition and underestimated the effect of the loss of her mother and the impending termination of treatment. He was appropriately worried about the patient and concerned with how to best help her, but his solutions tended toward action rather than understanding—administering a depression test, increasing the frequency of her visits. At the same time, he did not fully recognize how important he had become to her. It was safer for him to focus on the symptomotology. In the closing minutes of the supervision the supervisor tried to put the resident in more affective and empathic contact with his patient and himself by noting the termination of the supervision and reviewing the resident's work with his patient. Despite the supervisor's efforts, the resident's distant style constricted the supervisory termination as well as the ending of therapy.

This vignette raises several questions. Could the resident's need to keep a distance have been addressed earlier in the supervision? Did the supervisor, knowing the resident's propensity for emotional reserve, wait too long to address the issues involved in termination? Could he have structured the termination of supervision differently, asking the resident to focus on his feelings about ending both the treatment and the supervision much earlier, giving them time to explore these issues at greater leisure? After it was clear that the supervisee had "forgotten" that this was the last supervisory session, could the supervisor have asked him to reflect on what such forgetting might mean? Did the resident's willingness to offer extra appointments to his patient suggest that the supervisor offer the resident another few sessions to work on the termination of treatment and his supervision? Or might the supervisor have pointed out how the supervisee was identified with the patient, expressing doubts and reservations about his therapeutic work that echoed the patient's regression? In this instance, the supervisor's not pursuing these problems more actively contributed to a termination of therapy and supervision that was less than optimal. This is not uncommon. Analysts who supervise candidates have noted that many of the supervisions became increasingly attenuated after some years and seemed to end in an unsatisfactory way, candidate and supervisor having agreed in an unspoken manner to slowly drift apart. This is rationalized on both sides as a way of recognizing the candidate's growing autonomy, but it may have the effect of watering down the candidate's understanding of what needs to be accomplished in the termination phase of treatment as well as of supervision.

Some students handle the impending supervisory separation by leaving first, planning a vacation near the end of the supervision or canceling appointments because of changing clinical responsibilities. The failure of the supervisor to inquire about such behavior and to link it to possible feelings about termination often ends in an unsatisfactory conclusion, as in the following example.

Dr. F. was about to relocate upon graduation from residency. After discussing the move with his supervisor, he had informed his patient six months in advance of his departure. The treatment was clearly being terminated by Dr. F.'s move, as the patient had no plans to leave treatment. The patient responded to the news by investing his time and energies in a relationship with a new girlfriend. He spent a good deal of the time talking about how much he liked her, but expressed doubts about how well she understood him and whether he could really rely on her. The supervisor noted that while Dr. F. suggested to the patient that his concerns about his girlfriend might be connected to his feelings about his treatment and its impending cessation, he seemed to do so only occasionally and in a half-hearted manner. When this was pointed out to him, Dr. F. responded that he had not pressed the issue because he got nowhere with the patient when he did. The man seemed to want to talk about his girlfriend and made little of the therapist's move. Dr. F. was also reluctant to consistently interpret his patient's sudden and intense involvement with a woman as a response to termination because he felt that the choice was a reasonable one for the patient and that the patient's inability to form a lasting relationship had been one of the foci of the treatment. He felt that he did not want to "throw a monkey wrench" into the patient's attempts at an age-appropriate task that, after three years of therapy, he seemed better able to handle.

Although much of what Dr. F. said seemed reasonable, the supervisor suspected that a collusion was developing between the patient and the therapist in which both were happy that a girlfriend had arrived on the scene. When the supervisor suggested to Dr. F. that it might make him feel better about leaving if his patient had established a meaningful relationship, he readily agreed. His next association was, however, not directly to his relationship with the patient, but to how overwhelmed he felt by the impending move. In the next few months he would have to make several trips to the West Coast to find housing and a new job. His wife was pregnant and not feeling well, and his four-year-old was whining and asking lots of anxious questions about the move. It was clear to the supervisor that the last thing Dr. F. wanted was a patient who would give him a hard time about his going. When she pointed that out to him, he laughed and said, "You're darned right! But I guess he has a right to his sad and angry feelings." The supervisor agreed but was not sure how seriously her comments were being considered by the resident. She had little chance to find out, for Dr. F. began to cancel supervisory appointments: he had to go to the West Coast; his wife was sick and he was needed for child care. When they did meet, Dr. F. reported on his patient's progress and how he had tried to work with the patient on his feelings about the impending termination. But the limitations of his approach were clear. When the patient complained about his therapist's absences, Dr. F. responded defensively that he had informed his patient of the potential interruptions when he originally told him of his impending move. Dr. F.'s report and his response to the supervisor seemed little more than dutiful and his preoccupation was evident. He stated that he had made no recommendation for further treatment to his patient, feeling that the young man should decide for himself whether further therapy was needed. By this choice, Dr. F. had also managed to avoid a careful review of the treatment which a discussion about the necessity for further therapy might have evoked. The treatment ended without a full exploration of the meaning of the leave-taking to the patient, and the supervision ended in a friendly but attenuated form.

After Dr. F. left, the patient again sought treatment through the hospital's outpatient clinic. The supervisor learned from the next therapist just how angry the patient had been with his therapist, how little opportunity he felt he had been given to explore his feelings, and how uncertain he was of why the treatment had ended in the way it had. The patient conceded that he had gotten a lot out of his treatment, but something had been missing, and the termination put it into greater perspective. He had been afraid to argue with or contradict Dr. F., to get angry with him or to express independent ideas. It was unclear how much of that had been his fault and how much Dr. F.'s subtle discouragement of any attempts to do so. The patient wondered whether his involvement with his girlfriend had been a way of dealing with the separation.

The supervisor, looking back on her own work, wondered why she had not insisted on Dr. F.'s keeping to a regular supervisory schedule or, at least, brought the change in schedule up for exploration rather than allow the attenuation of the supervisory process to go without comment. Could she have pointed out that Dr. F.'s reluctance to acknowledge feelings about the ending of supervision paralleled the patient's feelings about separation

from treatment? Both were so involved with events in their lives—
the therapist with his move, the patient with his new girlfriend—
that they had little time to reflect on the separation. The supervisor's going along with Dr. F.'s plan did not allow them to address
the termination of the treatment and the supervision in greater
depth. She realized that her feelings about her own crowded
schedule had allowed her to overidentify with the resident's feeling of being overwhelmed and with his reluctance to experience
more fully the termination with his patient and his supervisor. In
so doing, she realized that she had avoided dealing with her feelings about certain limitations she had felt in the resident's work
all along, limitations which, in fact, had to do with how well he
was able to hear and address his patient's complaints about him.
She wondered, too, how much freedom of expression she had
allowed Dr. F. What might she not have heard? Had the supervision not been attenuated, she might have had to face the resident's
limitations as well as her own. In her own way, she had colluded
with the patient and her supervisee in allowing all three of them
to avoid a painful evaluation of the work done. She had also
limited their opportunity to see all that had been accomplished
and had not helped Dr. F. (as much as she could have) feel that he
could leave the therapy without having to feel overwhelmed and
guilty. A fuller termination of both treatment and supervision
might have helped all three—patient, therapist, and supervisor—
end on a more forward-looking note with a task having been
worked through, rather than on a note of unarticulated remorse
and regret.

Another source of regret for the student may be some unrea-
sonable notion about what should happen to the patient by the
time the supervision or the treatment ends. The supervisor can
help the student distinguish, as E. Ticho (1972) suggests, between life goals and treatment goals. Treatment goals involve "the

removal of obstacles to the patient's growth and the discovery of what his potentialities are." Life goals are those which the patient would arrive at were he to "put his potentialities to use" (p. 332). The attainment of some life goals requires the exercise over a long period of time of capacities freed by treatment. The therapist should not wait for their attainment before ending treatment. The supervisor can clarify when necessary which goals are the patient's and which are being imposed by the therapist. In so doing, she may also clarify the supervisory goals that have been achieved (better understanding of how transference develops, an increased capacity to recognize and interpret resistances, increased diagnostic skill, among others) and what goals remain for the supervisee to fulfill through other supervision and/or additional clinical experience.

What is at times difficult about the termination phase for both supervisor and supervisee is accepting limitations of time, skill, accomplishment. These blows to one's narcissism are often dealt with by avoidance, lowering of self-esteem, self-blame, or a need to act. All these reactions may occur not only in the student but in the supervisor as well. Fleming and Benedek (1966) point out how termination may reawaken adolescent conflicts (p. 194), in which moves toward separation and independence may be threatening to the parent (supervisor) as well as to the child (student). The recrudescence of symptoms in the patient during the termination of treatment during which the therapist is also terminating with a supervisor may cause complications. The patient's regression during termination, her acts of entreaty and revenge, may, for example, have effects on the therapist, leading him to feel angry with the patient or discouraged with his own efforts. These feelings may, in turn, be brought to supervision in a variety of ways. Through a parallel process, the student may make his patient's regression and complaints his own, leading him to become inattentive to his own feelings concerning separation and doubt-ful of his own accomplishments in supervision. The supervisor may find herself subtly blamed for this state of affairs, the im-plication being if she had been a better teacher and therapist in her own right it would have been avoided. The student may come late or cancel supervisory appointments. He may pointedly talk about his wish for another kind of supervisory experience or his wish not to be supervised at all for a while. While such wishes may be reasonable, they may also reflect a disappointment that the supervision is ending. These feelings may be accompanied by the presentation of crises in the caseload or by the resurgence of learning problems that had been previously addressed in the supervision. The supervisor, too, may show similar symptoms of distress—canceling appointments, being skeptical about the progress made by the patient or supervisee, beginning to think about whom she wants to supervise next. When the supervisor is aware of a negative response to termination by the supervisee, she can be most helpful by describing some of the phenomena that are likely to occur, such as return of symptoms, their general psychological causes, and their particular manifestation in the patient. She can then help the student turn his attention to the way in which his patient handles her disappointment in wishes unfulfilled and what he can help her understand in these wishes. The supervisor can help the student see once again the customary ways in which the patient deals with the disappointment and anger that accompany the frustration termination signifies. At the same time she can gently point out how a similar process may be occurring in the supervision. She can explore with her supervisee his hopes for the treatment and supervision and the ways in which these hopes were realized or thwarted.

Sometimes a termination of supervision is dictated by external factors that are painful to face, as in illness. In one such instance, a supervisor began to cancel appointments without stating a reason. Then she interrupted their work, having her secretary inform the candidate that she was ill and would contact him when she was ready to resume supervisory work. The candidate, in the meantime, learned from a colleague that his supervisor had a probably incurable cancer but was trying to keep her condition a secret. When the supervisee returned a few months later, no mention was made of the supervisor's illness by either of them. The obvious liking supervisor and supervisee had for one another and their distress about the illness found no expression; but it lay across their work like a shadow. The candidate found himself studying his teacher's face for signs of illness or distress. At times, he wondered if her flashes of impatience with him or his patient were the result of some private anguish or physical pain.

One day, the supervisor began the hour by berating him for arriving a few minutes late. "You always come late," she remarked. The candidate was confused, as the statement seemed untrue. "Well, no matter. We can't meet after today. I'm sick and can't work for a while." She then asked him about his case. The candidate's feelings were mixed. He felt unjustly attacked and was angry. But he also felt upset, recognizing his supervisor's need to distance herself from him with an angry statement rather than allow them both the sadness of parting. He felt caught between his wish to give expression to his feelings of affection and sorrow for his supervisor and a wish to respect her defenses. He found himself again playing the role of the submissive and obedient student she had in so many ways helped him overcome. She had helped him over the years to be more straightforward in confronting both his own and his patients' problems. Now it was she who was avoiding what was most on their minds. Yet he admired her wish to stay at her post, to remain supervising until the end.

When the supervisory hour was up, he shook her hand saying he hoped to see her again. She looked at him dubiously and then shut the consulting room door.

The impasse had a lasting impact on the candidate and revised his view of teaching. When he became a supervisor of candidates, he went out of his way to acknowledge and discuss with them the personal events in their life and its influence on their clinical work. He found himself less loath to acknowledge to his supervisees when a mood or personal event seemed to be clearly interfering with the teaching situation, constricting his own ability to listen and respond. He felt, too, that should he become seriously ill, he would leave room for his supervisees to express their curiosity, to share their feelings, and to reflect on how the altered supervisory situation might affect their treatment of patients. In reflecting on his sad supervisory experience, he thought that even when it was unclear to the supervisor how long she could continue her teaching activities, it would have been better for her to have set a date at which the supervision would end—even if it had to be revised. It would have given them room to acknowledge the unusually sad situation they were in as well as provided them with the opportunity to finish their work in the usual way by evaluating their educational experience together.

This evaluation is an important aspect of ending any supervision. It can allow for a full and leisurely discussion of the supervisee's current strengths and weaknesses as a therapist. Reports can be gone over so the student is not left surprised by his evaluation. It can allow both teacher and student to reflect on what is educationally best for this trainee at this time. Does he need to see more patients of a particular kind? Would it be best for him to see a supervisor with a particular theoretical orientation? What reading may best enlarge his understanding at this point? Under the guidance of his supervisor, the supervisee can evaluate his own performance as a therapist and begin to define his further educational needs.

During a termination phase not burdened by such an illness, the supervisor may also ask the student for an evaluation of her own teaching style and skills. In what way has she been effective in conveying information and exploring clinical difficulties? How might she improve? Sometimes suppressed grievances can come to light in this way and finally be resolved. One supervisee, Dr. H., expressed anger at his teacher. His patient dismissed queries about her perpetual lateness with a shrug. When Dr. H. had tried to insist on his patient's looking at her behavior, his supervisor had told him to go easier. He had felt frustrated and silenced by both of them. At one of the sessions near the end of the supervision, Dr. H. reported that he had said to himself, "To hell with this," and had, of his own accord, vigorously pursued his patient's acting out with good results. The patient had expressed her anger at Dr. H., feeling the treatment was cramping her style. Therapist and patient were then able to talk more openly about just how the patient's style was being restricted.

The supervisor was surprised by Dr. H.'s reproaches but recognized that she may have been overly directive. She also understood that Dr. H. had been very compliant in following her advice, unwilling to challenge her or speak of his dissatisfactions until termination. She praised him for doing what he felt was best despite her admonitions. She admitted that it seemed to have worked out well and that she may have been wrong after all. She pointed out that Dr. H., like his patient, was struggling for autonomy, but that each in his or her own way seemed afraid to openly declare the wish for independence. She went on to say that she felt Dr. H. had good therapeutic skills which he could trust and hoped that in the future he would be able to stick up for what he felt was indicated. The trainee, in turn, recognized that some of his fears about standing on his own were unfounded. He felt in a better position to help his patient with these problems and to help himself in the future.

Hoffman (1990) suggests that supervision should end in some form of celebration, perhaps "an informal dialogue about a topic of their choice over a cup of tea or the sharing of a full meal. This celebratory meeting can take place at the location of the supervisory meetings or at a new location, e.g., a coffee shop or restaurant. It can be scheduled at a regular meeting time or at a different time" (pp. 179–180). Her way of terminating is one that many supervisors use. But such a celebration may have its drawbacks. Often, the satisfaction in work accomplished together is celebration enough, particularly if the work has been openly and carefully evaluated and reviewed. Furthermore, not all terminations of supervision are causes for celebration. There are situations in which either supervisor or supervisee is disappointed with the learning experience and may not want to celebrate or where circumstances such as illness do not make celebration appropriate.

The work of supervision, like the work of therapy, goes on until the last minute of meeting time. The supervisor should remain a teacher to the end of the supervision and not change her role to that of more intimate colleague or friend. What is a desirable relationship in the future may be talked about in the present as part of the termination phase of supervision, but it should not be acted upon during the termination phase.

The supervisor needs to be aware that the supervisee's transference feelings toward the supervisor may become more intense during the termination of supervision. There may be an inclination to forsake the educational objectives of supervision and obtain gratification of these feelings in a more direct way. The supervisor too may have feelings of loss and may want in some way to

continue or to alter the educational relationship and its termination phase. As the example below illustrates, termination can
place immense strain on the supervisor who has knowingly or
unconsciously found substitutes for personal difficulties in his
supervising a particular student. There is no more likely time for
an educator to surrender her teaching position and respond to
her own transference, becoming personally involved with her
supervisee, than during the process of ending a long and somewhat self-restrained relationship.

A middle-aged supervisor whose youngest son had left home
for a distant college found himself particularly sad about the
ending of a supervision of a mental health worker who reminded
him of this child. He was aware of his displacement of feelings
and recognized that his fondness for his supervisee was one of the
ways in which he was dealing with the departure of his son.
Nevertheless, he found himself having fantasies of being a mentor
to his supervisee, continuing their relationship through the years,
developing an ongoing father-son relationship with a young man
who was established in the community. As time for termination
grew near, he thought of inviting the supervisee to dinner and
having him meet his wife. It was clear to him that he was developing adoption fantasies as a way of dealing with his own painful
affects around separation. He decided that acting on such feelings
would not be fair to his son or his supervisee, and would not be
respectful of his own grieving process, from which he could learn
more about himself. Perhaps there would be a time when such an
invitation would be appropriate, but not until he had worked out
some things for himself. He continued to supervise the mental
health worker on a regular basis for the few remaining months
and in parting from him expressed the hope that they would
continue to be in contact, but issued no specific invitation.

In another instance, the same supervisor, aware of no particularly strong or troublesome feelings about his supervisee, did accept a dinner invitation from him at the end of their super- visory work. He did so because he felt the resident who was about to graduate wanted to show his teacher his life outside—a life that included a home, a wife and family, and the wish to entertain. The resident's wish to celebrate and make known his accomplish- ments seemed to the supervisor one worthy of response.

Dewald's termination with his candidate Mary Dick ends in his telling her of his plans to publish a book about the supervision and an invitation to her to write a chapter in it. It is clear their relationship will continue around a particular project involving continued evaluation and discussion of the supervision that has been concluded. The publication of the book, like the figures on Keats' Grecian urn, keeps them in a certain way forever joined. In a very different scenario, Schlesinger's failure to tell his supervisee Shevrin, even at termination, that his supervision was being re- ported to a study group and that a book was contemplated about it led to acrimonious lawsuits and to Shevrin's disillusionment about the educational experience (Shevrin, 1981). Whatever diffi- culties Schlesinger and Shevrin had that could not be worked out in supervision or addressed in the termination phase now remain alive in the literature. In psychoanalytic institutes, candidates are likely to develop a collegial relationship with some of their super- visors as they advance in their training, graduate, and serve on committees together. Residents and social workers, however, may be supervised by someone who gives a few hours to the depart- ment or who supervises only in a particular clinic setting. In these instances, the educational institution offers no clear context in which teacher and student may see each other again.

One trainee ended a supervision by giving the supervisor a paper he had written and asking her to comment on it before he submitted it for publication, as he knew the subject was of some interest to his supervisor. The supervisor agreed to do so, stating that she would be glad to meet with him again to go over it or talk with him by telephone. She felt that the trainee was indicating that he wanted further contact with the supervisor, but did not know the extent or intensity of the wish. Offering a meeting or a phone call allowed the supervisee to titrate the amount of contact he felt he needed. He said a phone conversation would be adequate. It was clear he saw himself and wanted to be seen as a colleague with whom papers and ideas could be exchanged. When the supervisor had read the paper and given her comments, she suggested that the trainee might be interested in a grand rounds related to his paper which was being given at a nearby teaching hospital. She said quite honestly that she was sure she would be able to attend, but encouraged him to go in any case, thus reinforcing that they were both common and independent members of a broader psychiatric community.

On some occasions, supervisors give a student a small gift as a way of marking progress. It may be done when a student is graduating from a program or leaving the city. The gift of a book, for instance, may convey the supervisor's respect for the student's intellect and interest in continuing to learn. This kind of gift is less burdensome than a personal invitation to a drink or dinner since the student can do with it as he likes, keep or discard it, read it or leave it unread. The supervisor may never know the fate of her gift, any more than she may know the fate of all she has tried to teach. She is lucky if her students keep in touch with her and inform her of their progress. But she knows that such contact cannot be a requirement and that she must find her satisfactions in the job already done.

One therapist gave his supervisor a gift upon his departure. The gift was an exotic and expensive plant which would obviously require both continued nourishment and ongoing attention. The supervisor graciously accepted it, wondering aloud how the supervisee had decided on so unusual and beautiful a gift. The therapist replied that he thought the supervisor would enjoy it. Then he paused and said, "It is kind of delicate. I hope not too much to manage. But you're such a good supervisor, I figured you could handle it." He laughed. "Rather like the case I presented, I suppose. He was difficult and required rather gentle handling." "So in some way, you are giving him to me?" the supervisor asked. "No, he's still my case. But I suppose it is a way of saying I could still use your help. That I'm sorry we're ending," he concluded. The supervisor said, "I suspect you'll manage quite well on your own, although I'll be here should you feel in need of a consultation. And you've given me something lovely by which to remember you and him and our work together. Good luck."

References

Alonso, A. 1985. *The Quiet Profession: Supervisors of Psychotherapy.* New York: Macmillan.

Arlow, J. 1963. The supervisory situation. *Journal of the American Psychoanalytic Association* 11:576–594.

Bakanowski, T. (1989). La chasse au snark du supervisé. *Etudes Freudiennes* 31:75–80.

Balint, M. 1948. On the psychoanalytic training system. *International Journal of Psycho-analysis* 29:163–173.

Baudry, F. 1993. The personal dimension and management of the supervisory situation with a special note on the parallel process. *Psychoanalytic Quarterly* 62:588–614.

Betcher, R. W., and Zinberg, N. E. 1988. Supervision and privacy in psychotherapy training. *American Journal of Psychiatry* 145:796–803.

Bird, B. 1972. Notes on transference: Universal phenomenon and hardest part of analysis. *Journal of the American Psychoanalytic Association* 20:267–301.

Blitzsten, N., and Fleming, J. 1953. What is supervisory analysis? *Bulletin of the Menninger Clinic* 17:117–129.

Breuer, J., and Freud, S. 1893–1895. *Studies on Hysteria.* In *Standard Edition of the complete psychological works of Sigmund Freud.* Vol. II. London: Hogarth, 1955.

Casement, P. J. 1993. Toward autonomy: Some thoughts on psychoanalytic supervision. *Journal of Clinical Psychoanalysis* 2:389–403.

Crick, P. 1991. Good supervision: On the experience of being supervised. *Psychoanalytic Psychotherapy* 5:235–245.

DeBell, D. 1963. A critical digest on the literature of psychoanalytic supervision. *Journal of the American Psychoanalytic Association* 11:546–575.

Deutsch, H. 1935. On supervised analysis. *Contemporary Psychoanalysis (1983).* 19:53–67.

Dewald, P. 1987. *Learning Process in Psychoanalytic Supervision: Complexities and Challenges.* Madison, Conn.: International Universities Press.

Dick, M. 1987. Contribution. In P. Dewald, *Learning Process in Psychoanalytic Supervision: Complexities and Challenges.* Madison, Conn.: International Universities Press.

Ekstein, R., and Wallerstein, R. S. 1958. *The Teaching and Learning of Psychotherapy.* New York: International Universities Press, 1972.

Eitingon, M. 1926. An address to the International Training Commission. *International Journal of Psycho-analysis* 7:130–134.

Felman, S. 1991. Education and crisis, Or the vicissitudes of teaching. *American Imago.* 48:13–74.

Ferenczi, S., and Rank, O. 1924. Die Entwicklungsziele Der Psychoanalyse. Vienna, Leipzig, Zurich: Internationaler Psychoanalytischer Verlag.

Fleming, J. 1987. The education of a supervisor. In *The Teaching and Learning of Psychoanalysis (Selected Papers of Joan Fleming, M.D.),* edited by S. Weiss. New York: Guilford Press.

Fleming, J., and Benedek, T. F. 1966. *Psychoanalytic Supervision: A Method of Clinical Teaching.* New York: International Universities Press, 1983.

Freud, S. 1905. *Three Essays on the Theory of Sexuality.* In *Standard Edition of the complete psychological works.* Vol. VII. London: Hogarth, 1973.

———. 1909. *Analysis of a Phobia in a Five-Year-Old Boy.* In *Standard Edition of the complete psychological works.* Vol. X. London: Hogarth, 1973.

———. 1910. *The Future Prospects of Psycho-Analytic Therapy.* In *Standard Edition of the complete psychological works.* Vol. XI. London: Hogarth, 1973.

———. 1914. *On the History of the Psycho-Analytic Movement.* In *Collected Papers.* Vol. I. New York: Basic Books, 1959.

———. 1915. *Observations on transference love.* In *Standard Edition of the complete psychological works.* Vol. XII. London: Hogarth Press, 1958.

Gardner, H. 1985. *Frames of Mind: The Theory of Multiple Intelligences.* New York: Basic Books.

Gardner, R. 1993. Reflections on the study group experience and on supervising. In *News from COPE.* New York: The American Psychoanalytic Association, pp. 6–7.

Gay, P. 1988. *Freud: A Life for Our Time.* New York and London: W. W. Norton.

Gifford, S. 1981. The history of psychoanalytic training: Berlin and Vienna, 1920–1938. Paper presented at the Oral History Workshop, Fall Meetings of the American Psychoanalytic Association, New York, December 17.

Gray, P. 1993. Reflections on supervision. In *News from COPE.* New York: American Psychoanalytic Association, pp. 8–10.

Grotjahn, M. 1955. Problems and techniques in supervision. *Psychiatry* 18:9–15.

Harris, A., and Ragen, T. 1993. Mutual Supervision, Countertransference and Self-Analysis. In *Self-Analysis: Critical Inquiries, Personal Visions,* edited by J. W. Barron. Hillsdale, N.J.: Analytic Press.

Hess, A. K. 1987. Advances in psychotherapy supervision: Introduction. *Professional Psychology* 18:251–259.

Hoffman, H. 1990. *Old Scapes, New Maps: A Training Program for Psychotherapy Supervisors.* Cambridge, Mass.: Milusik Press.

Hoffman, I. 1992. Some practical implications of a social-constructivist view of the psychoanalytic situation. *Psychoanalytic Dialogues* 2:287–304.

Horney, K. 1930. Die Einriichtungen der Lehranstalt. A) Zur Organization Zehn Jahre Berliner Psychoanalytisches Institut. Vienna: Internationaler Psychoanalytischer Verlag.

Imber, R. 1993. Notes on the pregnant analyst. Paper presented at the Fall Meetings, American Psychoanalytic Association, New York, December 18.

Isakower, O. 1957. The analyzing instrument in the teaching and conduct of the analytic process, edited by H. M. Wyman and S. M. Rittenberg. *Journal of Clinical Psychoanalysis* (1992) 1:181–194.

Istvan, S. 1990. Letter to Daniel Jacobs, M.D., September 23, 1990.

Jacob, P. 1981. Application: The San Francisco Project—The supervisor at work. In *Becoming a Psychoanalyst: A Study of Psychoanalytic Supervision,* edited by R. S. Wallerstein. New York: International Universities Press.

Jacobs, D. 1993. Theory and its relation to early affective experience. In *Human Feelings: Explorations in Affect Development and Meaning,* edited by S. L. Ablon, D. Brown, E. J. Khantzian, and J. E. Mack. Hillsdale, N.J.: Analytic Press.

Jacobs, T. 1991. *The Uses of the Self.* Madison, Conn.: International Universities Press.

Jacobson, E. 1964. *The Self and the Object World.* New York: International Universities Press.

Johnson-Laird, P. N. 1988. A taxonomy of thinking. In *The Psychology of Human Thought,* edited by R. J. Sternberg and E. E. Smith. Cambridge: Cambridge University Press.

Jones, E. 1953–1957. *The Life and Work of Sigmund Freud.* New York: Basic Books.

Kadushin, A. 1992. *Supervision in Social Work.* 3d ed. New York: Columbia University Press.

Keiser, S. 1956. Panel report. The technique of supervised analysis. *Journal of the American Psychoanalytic Association* 4:539–549.

Kohut, H. 1971. *The Analysis of the Self.* New York: International Universities Press.

———. 1977. *The Restoration of the Self.* New York: International Universities Press.

Kovacs, W. 1936. Training and control-analysis. *International Journal of Psycho-analysis* 17:346–354.

Kramer, Y. 1986. Aspects of termination: Theory and practice. In *Psychoanalysis: The Science of Mental Conflict,* edited by A. Richards and M. Willick, pp. 321–352. Hillsdale, N.J.: Analytic Press.

Kris, A. O. 1982. *Free Association: Method and Process.* New Haven: Yale University Press.

Lawner, P. 1989. Counteridentification, therapeutic impasse, and supervisory process. *Contemporary Psychoanalysis* 25:592–607.

Lester, E., and Robertson, B. 1993. Multiple interactive processes in psychoanalytic supervision. Paper presented at the Fall Meetings, American Psychoanalytic Association, New York, December 18.

Leowald, H. 1962. Internalization, separation, mourning, and the superego. *Psychoanalytic Quarterly* 31:483–504.

Lewis, H. B. 1985. Analyzing sequences from unresolved shame and guilt into symptom formation. In *Analysts at Work,* edited by J. Reppen. Hillsdale, N.J.: Analytic Press.

——. 1986. Shame, the supervisory process and patients' needs. Paper presented at Cambridge Hospital Department of Psychiatry Conference on "Dilemmas and Challenges of Supervision: Case Material." Cambridge, Mass.

Mack, J. E. 1983. Self-esteem and its development: An overview. In *The Development and Sustaining of Self-Esteem in Childhood,* edited by J. E. Mack and S. L. Ablon. New York: International Universities Press.

Maltsberger, J. T., and Buie, D. H. 1969. The work of supervision. In *Teaching Psychotherapy of Psychotic Patients,* by E. V. Semrad and edited by D. Van Buskirk. New York: Grune and Stratton.

Mclaughlin, J. 1981. Transference, psychic reality and countertransference. *Psychoanalytic Quarterly* 50:639–664.

Mehlman, R. D. 1974. Becoming and being a psychotherapist: The problem of narcissism. *International Journal of Psychoanalytic Psychotherapy* 3:125–141.

Modell, A. 1991. The therapeutic relationship as a paradoxical experience. *Psychoanalytic Dialogues* 1:13–28.

——. 1993. *The Private Self.* Cambridge and London: Harvard University Press.

Moreau, M. 1970. Analyse quatrième, control, formation. *Topique Revue Freudienne* 18:63–85.

Morrison, A. 1989. *Shame: The Underside of Narcissism.* Hillsdale, N.J.: Analytic Press.

Nason, F. 1994. Private communication.

Nathanson, D., editor. 1987. *The Many Faces of Shame.* New York: Guilford Press.

Ogden, T. 1985. On potential space. *International Journal of Psycho-analysis* 66:129–141.

Ornstein, P. 1967. Selected problems in learning how to analyze. *International Journal of Psycho-analysis* 48:448–461.

———. 1968. Sorcerer apprentice: The initial phase of training and education in psychiatry. *Comprehensive Psychiatry* 9:293–315.

Perkins, D. N. 1988. Creativity and the quest for mechanism. In *The Psychology of Human Thought,* edited by R. J. Sternberg and E. E. Smith. Cambridge: Cambridge University Press.

Pollack, A. 1982. The depressive position in psychiatric training. *Maclean Hospital Journal* 7:28–48.

Pruyser, P. W. 1979. An essay on creativity. *Bulletin of the Menninger Clinic* 43:294–353.

Rank, O. 1929. *The Trauma of Birth.* New York: Harcourt Brace.

Roazen, P. 1969. *Brother Animal.* New York: Knopf.

Robbins, W. 1975. Termination: Problems and techniques. *Journal of the American Psychoanalytic Association* 23:166–176.

Robinson, V. 1936. *Supervision in Social Casework.* Chapel Hill: University of North Carolina Press.

———. 1949. *The Dynamics of Supervision under Functional Controls.* Philadelphia: University of Pennsylvania Press.

Rosenblatt, A., and Meyer, J. 1975. Objectionable supervisory styles: Students' views. *Social Work* 20:184–189.

Sachs, D. M., and Shapiro, S. H. 1976. On parallel processes in therapy and teaching. *Psychoanalytic Quarterly* 45:394–415.

Schafer, R. 1992. Reading Freud's legacies. In *Telling Facts: History and Narration in Psychoanalysis,* edited by J. H. Smith and H. Morris. Baltimore and London: Johns Hopkins University Press.

Schlesinger, H. 1981. On being the supervisor studied: Observations and confessions. In *Becoming an Analyst: A Study of Psychoanalytic Supervision,* edited by R. S. Wallerstein. New York: International Universities Press.

Schwaber, E. A. 1983. Psychoanalytic listening and psychic reality. *International Review of Psychoanalysis* 10:379–392.

———. 1992. Countertransference: The analyst's retreat from the patient's vantage point. *International Journal of Psycho-analysis* 73:349–362.

Searles, H. 1955. The informational value of the supervisor's emotional experiences. *Psychiatry* 18:135–146.

Shershow, J., and Shershow, Irwin S. 1976. Regression in the service of residency education. *Archives of General Psychiatry* 33:1266–1270.

Shevrin, H. 1981. On being the analyst supervised: Return to a troubled beginning. In *Becoming an Analyst: A Study of Psychoanalytic Supervision,* edited by R. S. Wallerstein. New York: International Universities Press.

Skolnikoff, A. In press. The supervisory situation: Intrinsic and extrinsic factors influencing transference and countertransference themes. *Psychoanalytic Inquiry.*

Smith, H. 1993. Discussion of a paper, "The uniqueness of the patient-analyst pair: Approaches for illucidating the analyst's role presented," presented by J. Kantrowitz at the Scientific meeting of the Boston Psychoanalytic Society and Institute, October 27.

Smith, J. 1990. Unpublished comments. Faculty meeting, Cambridge Hospital Department of Psychiatry, Cambridge, Mass. October 30.

Spiegel, D., and Grunebaum, H. 1977. Training versus treating the psychiatric resident. *American Journal of Psychiatry* 31:618–625.

Styczynski, L. 1980. The transition from supervisee to supervisor. In *Psychotherapy Supervision: Theory, Research and Practice,* edited by A. K. Hess, 29–40. New York: Wiley.

Ticho, E. 1972. Termination of psychoanalysis: Treatment goals, life goals. *Psychoanalytic Quarterly* 4:315–333.

Wallerstein, R., editor. 1981. *Becoming a Psychoanalyst: A Study of Psychoanalytic Supervision.* New York: International Universities Press.

Winnicott, D. 1951. Transitional objects and transitional phenomena. In *Through Paediatrics to Psycho-Analysis.* New York: Basic Books, 1975.

——. 1967. The location of cultural experience. *International Journal of Psycho-analysis* 48:95–103.

Zinberg, N. 1986. Levels of personal interaction in supervision. Presented at Cambridge Hospital Department of Psychiatry conference, The Challenges of Supervision: Teaching the Therapist—Treating the Patient, December 6.

Index